INTRODUCING

CATHOLIC
SOCIAL THOUGHT

INTRODUCING

CATHOLIC SOCIAL THOUGHT

J. Milburn Thompson

ORBIS BOOKS
Maryknoll, New York 10545

Founded in 1970, Orbis Books endeavors to publish works that enlighten the mind, nourish the spirit, and challenge the conscience. The publishing arm of the Maryknoll Fathers and Brothers, Orbis seeks to explore the global dimensions of the Christian faith and mission, to invite dialogue with diverse cultures and religious traditions, and to serve the cause of reconciliation and peace. The books published reflect the views of their authors and do not represent the official position of the Maryknoll Society. To learn more about Maryknoll and Orbis Books, please visit our website at www.maryknollsociety.org.

Manufactured in the United States of America.

Library of Congress Cataloging-in-Publication Data

Thompson, Joseph Milburn, 1947–
    Introducing Catholic social thought / J. Milburn Thompson.
      p. cm.
    Includes bibliographical references (p.   ) and index.
    ISBN 978-1-57075-862-1 (pbk.)
    1. Christian sociology – Catholic Church. 2. Catholic Church – Doctrines.
I. Title.
BX1753.T56 2010
261 – dc22
                                        2009052023

For Mary Ann, the love of my life

Contents

Acknowledgments

I am grateful to Bellarmine University — its President, Dr. Joseph J. Mc-Gowan; Vice President for Academic Affairs, Dr. Doris Tegart; and Dean of the College of Arts and Sciences, Dr. Rob Kingsolver — for granting me a sabbatical leave during the academic year 2007–8 to work on this book. My colleague Rev. Dr. Elizabeth Hinson-Hasty graciously agreed to chair the Theology Department in my absence. Elizabeth also chaired a search committee, which included another departmental colleague, Rev. Dr. George Kilcourse, to replace Rev. Dr. Clyde Crews, who had retired. This committee wisely hired Dr. Gregory K. Hillis, a wonderful addition to the department. Rev. Dr. Martha Gilliss served a one-year appointment during my sabbatical and directed the Master of Arts in Spirituality program. Bellarmine offers this program in collaboration with Louisville Presbyterian Theological Seminary (LPTS), and I want to single out Rev. Dr. Dianne Reistroffer from LPTS, who has twice partnered with me in taking students to study liberation spirituality in Cuernavaca, Mexico. All of these colleagues have supported me in this project.

I spent the Lent term (January through March) of my sabbatical year at the Margaret Beaufort Institute of Theology (MBIT) in Cambridge, England, as the 2008 Cardinal Hume Visiting Scholar. The MBIT was founded in 1993 as a Catholic higher education institute for women specializing in theology for lay ministry. It is the only Catholic member of the Cambridge Theological Federation, a consortium of graduate schools of theology that have close links with the Faculty of Divinity at Cambridge University. The Institute is international in outlook with people from Ireland, Denmark, Kenya, South Africa, Germany, Japan, Poland, the United States, and, of course, England. The faculty, staff, students, and residents form a community of study and prayer through weekly Mass and dinner and through informal interaction.

I want to thank the faculty at the MBIT — Dr. Susan O'Brien, Principal; Dr. Oonagh O'Brien, Director of Pastoral Studies; and Dr. Fainche Ryan, Director of Studies — for their warm hospitality and wonderful conversations. Dr. Charlotte Hansen, the 2007 Cardinal Hume Visiting Scholar, re-joined the MBIT community in February as a research associate. The administrator, Ela Wolbek, was tremendously helpful to me, especially in getting me set up with a computer. Also helpful were the house manager, Lynda

Turner, and the domestic assistants, Anna Rurarz and Michal Wierzejewski. Among the students, I had especially good theological conversations with Debbie Murphy, Ged McHale, Karen Shurety, and my fellow American, Elizabeth Paulhus, and I enjoyed the company of my floormates Richard Fryer and Nicolai Dienerowitz, and the other students and residents — Marie Keane, Seraphine Oweggi, Bernadette Daries, Eloisa Carr-Jones, Sarah Roberts, and Shoko Sacki. I am grateful to Susanne Jennings for including me in the MBIT Newslettter. I often encountered Dr. Janet Soskice, who is associated with MBIT and on the Divinity Faculty at Cambridge, and I was impressed and inspired each time.

I was happy to get reading privileges at Cambridge University Library, but then disappointed that "one of the greatest research libraries of the world" (CUL brochure) did not have a strong collection on Catholic social thought. I found the MBIT library, where I benefited from an orientation by Magda Fletcher, and the Divinity Faculty Library, where I received friendly assistance from Jillian Wilkinson and Jane Thorpe, much more helpful.

During my ten weeks in Cambridge I attended over two dozen lectures and presentations, including four MBIT lectures under the theme of "Theology: School of Mysticism," given by well-known theologians such as the Rev. Dr. Rowan Williams, the archbishop of Canterbury, Prof. Kari Elisabeth Borresen of the University of Oslo, Prof. Bernard McGinn of the University of Chicago, and Prof. John Milbank of the University of Nottingham. It was a theological retreat as well as an opportunity for research and writing. It was an unforgettable experience.

Some of us at Bellarmine University have formed an informal writing group where we read and critique each other's work. I want to thank Dr. Elizabeth Hinson-Hasty, Dr. Greg Hillis, and Dr. David Mosley for their input on chapter 5, and Dr. Charles Hatten who has been helpful on other aspects of the text as well. A former student, David Porter, gave me perceptive feedback on the first chapter.

Finally, I want to thank Susan Perry, senior editor at Orbis Books, for her patience, for her confidence in me in asking me to take this project on, and for her comments, suggestions, and questions. Her expertise has made this a much better text. She has served as the midwife for this book.

Introduction

The idea of the Orbis Books *Introducing...* series is to produce books that can introduce college students and interested general readers to a significant area of contemporary theology. The books are meant to represent sound scholarship and to present it in an accessible manner. It is an honor to join the other authors of this series, including, among others, Leonardo Boff and Clodovis Boff (*Introducing Liberation Theology*, 1987), Dwight Hopkins (*Introducing Black Liberation Theology*, 1999), Anne Clifford (*Introducing Feminist Theology*, 2001), and Paul Knitter (*Introducing Theologies of Religion*, 2002).

This book joins a steady stream of good introductions to Catholic social teaching written by respected Catholic social ethicists — for example, Marvin L. Krier Mich, *Catholic Social Teaching and Movements* (Twenty-Third Publications, 1998), Kenneth R. Himes, *Responses to 101 Questions on Catholic Social Teaching* (Paulist Press, 2001), the fourth revised and expanded edition of Edward DeBerri and James Hug, *Catholic Social Teaching: Our Best Kept Secret* (Orbis Books, 2003), Judith A. Merkle, *From the Heart of the Church: The Catholic Social Tradition* (Liturgical Press, 2004), Marvin L. Krier Mich, *The Challenge and Spirituality of Catholic Social Teaching* (JustFaith, Inc., 2005), Michael Hornsby-Smith, *An Introduction to Catholic Social Thought* (Cambridge University Press, 2006), and Thomas Massaro, *Living Justice: Catholic Social Teaching in Action* (Rowman & Littlefield, revised, 2008). What, then, distinguishes this book from these other fine introductions? Four things.

There have been important new sources of Catholic social teaching published since many of these books were written. In 2004 the Pontifical Council for Justice and Peace at the Vatican produced its *Compendium of the Social Doctrine of the Church,* and Pope Benedict's first encyclical, *On Christian Love (Deus Caritas Est,* 2005), touches on Catholic social teaching. Then on July 7, 2009, Pope Benedict XVI released *Charity in Truth (Caritas in Veritate)*, the first new social encyclical since 1991.

The title of this book, *Introducing Catholic Social Thought*, begins to indicate a second distinguishing characteristic of this text. Most introductions to Catholic social *teaching* focus on explaining the major documents produced by the popes and bishops of the Roman Catholic Church. This introduction to Catholic social *thought* will take into consideration the

1

broader theological and social context of that teaching. (See chapter 1 for a fuller explanation of these terms.) This will allow the book to be more analytical and critical than some of the above. While the Catholic social tradition, which brings Christian faith to bear on social issues, is important, even precious, it is also imperfect. It has developed and changed, and it needs to continue developing.[1] Only a critical conversation about its method and content, mistakes and strengths, lacunae, and future challenges can facilitate that development.

It is a challenge to teach Catholic social teaching. The list of papal documents with Latin titles beginning in the nineteenth century is enough to make eyes glaze over. With some exceptions, such as the two pastoral letters of the U.S. Catholic bishops, the documents are dry as dust. The idea of Catholic social teaching — that Christian faith is relevant to social issues — can be engaging for today's college student or person in the pew, but generally the way the church has addressed these issues is not. Thus this book will focus on the *spirit* of Catholic social teaching rather than the letter. It will of necessity attend to the history and the content of Catholic social teaching, but it will also focus on the "social questions" themselves and the response of Christian faith.

One way to communicate Catholic social thought more effectively is through the lives of people who have incarnated it. When I integrate the biographies of justice seekers and peacemakers into my courses, I have been surprised again and again by the power of story to transform lives. Marvin Mich effectively incorporates such stories into his latest book on Catholic social teaching, and I will as well.

Introducing Catholic Social Thought will include the latest sources of Catholic social teaching. It will approach the topic critically, by adopting a broader theological and social perspective. It will focus on the spirit of Catholic social teaching, and it will weave stories throughout the text to illustrate the themes and engage the reader. The primary audience for the text is college students, but I hope the book will be useful for the interested general reader as well.

Overview of the Text

The first chapter, "The Development of Catholic Social Thought," will describe Catholic social teaching in the context of the history of Catholic social thought — its biblical roots, historical development and modern manifestations. Although the documents are related to one another, Catholic social teaching is not systematic. The stories of some churchmen and saints, such as Gregory the Great, Francis of Assisi, Thomas Aquinas, Erasmus, Bartolomé de Las Casas, and John XXIII illustrate this chapter.

The second chapter, "Faithful Citizenship: The Church and Politics," will explore the basic spirit of Catholic social teaching — the idea that Christian faith is relevant to social issues and that converted Christians should be socially subversive by working to transform sinful social structures toward the kingdom of God. The chapter will examine the biblical basis of this idea, and it will tell the story of the Second Vatican Council's affirmation of the American Jesuit John Courtney Murray's argument for religious freedom and the separation of church and state. It will trace the social mission of the church in the thought of John XXIII and Paul VI and critique the response of Benedict XVI. The chapter will outline seven key principles of Catholic social thought and investigate two test cases related to human rights — torture and immigration. It will conclude with an overview of some Christian organizations dedicated to political advocacy on behalf of justice and peace.

The third chapter focuses on "Economic Justice." It begins with the story of César Chávez and his efforts to organize migrant agricultural workers in the cause of justice. It then focuses on four themes in Catholic social teaching related to economic justice: the dignity of work and the rights of workers, the social purpose of private property, the option for the poor, and authentic development as a response to global poverty. The chapter includes snapshots of people who have opted for the poor and concludes with a portrait of Bono, who has worked for authentic human development and against global poverty.

Vatican II said that the changing nature of modern war made a fresh appraisal of war necessary. The fourth chapter begins with a brief overview of the Christian tradition regarding "War and Peace" and then focuses on the twentieth and twenty-first centuries. The chapter considers the Christian witness of Benedict XV during World War I and of Pius XII in the context of the Second World War. The period of the Cold War in the latter half of the twentieth century gave rise to a Catholic peace movement, to the effective use of nonviolence in movements for social change, and to ethical controversies about nuclear weapons. John Paul II took the church in the direction of peacemaking. The chapter concludes with an examination of the new questions posed by terrorism and preemptive war in the twenty-first century.

The fifth chapter, "A Consistent Ethic of Life and Care for the Earth," examines these two issues. It begins with the story of John Timothy Leary, an exemplar of the "consistent ethic of life" that was articulated by Cardinal Joseph Bernardin of Chicago. The chapter offers a critical analysis of a consistent ethic of life, summarizing Cardinal Bernardin's proposal and exploring the objections of critics on both the left and right. Second, the chapter investigates ecological theology and an environmental ethic, beginning with the life of Sister Dorothy Stang, who was martyred in the Amazon region of Brazil because of her advocacy on behalf of peasant farmers and of the earth. It presents key themes of the church's environmental ethic and then wonders if an ethic of stewardship is adequate for the ecological challenges of our time. The sixth chapter offers a brief conclusion for the book.

I use endnotes to acknowledge my sources, to direct the reader to resources for further information on a topic, and to provide background information that might clutter the text. I have made an effort to keep the endnotes to a minimum. The book also contains a selected bibliography on Catholic social thought. Nearly all the primary sources for Catholic social teaching, that is, Vatican documents and the two social pastorals from the United States Conference of Catholic Bishops (USCCB), except for Benedict XVI's *Charity in Truth* (2009), can be found in *Catholic Social Thought: The Documentary Heritage,* edited by David J. O'Brien and Thomas A. Shannon (Orbis Books, 1992). The Vatican documents can also be found on the website for the Holy See, *www.vatican.va,* and the U.S. documents are also at *www.usccb.com.*

I want to note two other volumes that have been exceptionally useful in researching Catholic social thought: *The New Dictionary of Catholic Social Thought,* edited by Judith A. Dwyer (Liturgical Press, 1994); and *Modern Catholic Social Teaching: Commentaries and Interpretations,* edited by Kenneth R. Himes (Georgetown University Press, 2005).

Chapter 1

The Development of Catholic Social Thought

The doubling of the European population between 1750 and 1850 fueled the Industrial Revolution with a surplus of workers. The development of factories to replace the cottage industry of the eighteenth century resulted in a mass migration from the countryside, with its seasonal agrarian economy, to the cities that offered year-round wages. The surfeit of workers, however, drove down wages and increased the hours a laborer needed to work in order to survive. Miners never saw the sun, as work consumed all the laborers' time and energy. Unhealthy and unsafe working conditions increased the misery associated with textile mills and factories. Women and children also worked under these desolate conditions and received even lower wages. Home was a crowded flat or squalid company row house. This was the world of Oliver Twist and Tiny Tim as described by Charles Dickens. This industrial economy produced astonishing wealth, but poverty continued to be the lot of the workers.[1] In the late nineteenth century, machines, and those who owned them, were transforming human beings into cogs and commodities.

In 1891, forty-three years after Karl Marx and Frederich Engels penned the *Communist Manifesto* (1848), Pope Leo XIII addressed this historical turning point in his encyclical *The Condition of Labor (Rerum Novarum)*. As we shall see, Leo XIII affirmed a limited right to private property and the right of workers to a living wage, to form unions, and to safe working conditions, and he argued against child labor and women working. Most scholars date modern Catholic social teaching from this document because of the importance of the moral principles on the economy enunciated in the encyclical and because of the influence it has had. The successors of Leo XIII have marked the fortieth, seventieth, eightieth, and hundredth anniversaries of *The Condition of Labor* with social encyclicals of their own.

This chapter aims to introduce Catholic social thought by clarifying some terms used in the field, setting parameters for this study, identifying major documents, and examining its history and development.

Definitions and Terms

Since 1740, the popes have been sending encyclical letters to the church, such as Leo's *The Condition of Labor,* on various topics, much like St. Paul and others did in the early years of the Christian community. The official text is usually written in Latin and then translated into other languages, and the titles come from the first Latin words of the document, for example, *Rerum Novarum.*[2] Some encyclicals have directly addressed what has come to be called "the social question," that is, the social, economic, and political issues of the day. The theological basis of this tradition is that the faith of a Christian (one's relationship with God as revealed through Jesus the Christ) affects all of life, including its social, economic, and political dimensions. Since *The Condition of Labor,* significant church documents on the social question have become part of the canon of Catholic social teaching. One book on Catholic social teaching calls this modern tradition the church's "best kept secret," because it seems that so few Catholics are aware of it.[3]

Catholic social *teaching* refers to the documents issued by those who hold an official teaching position in the Roman Catholic Church, that is, by the bishops and especially the bishop of Rome, the pope. This teaching office of the bishop is called the *magisterium* (from the Latin for teacher). While Catholics are called to follow all the teaching of the *magisterium,* the teaching of the bishops has various degrees of authority or weight according to authorship and formality.[4] Encyclicals have significant weight or authority because they are formal statements by the pope. The popes have also produced less formal and less authoritative documents, such as the Christmas messages of Pius XII and the World Day of Peace messages of Paul VI, John Paul II, and Benedict XVI.

The documents produced by a *council* of the church, a meeting of all the bishops in the world, also have great weight or authority. The Second Vatican Council, held from 1962 through 1965, was a turning point in the life of the contemporary Catholic Church, and it produced two important social documents, *The Pastoral Constitution on the Church in the Modern World* (*Gaudium et Spes*) and *The Declaration on Religious Freedom* (*Dignitatis Humanae*).

Since Vatican II, there have been meetings of synods of bishops at the Vatican, meetings of the bishops' conference of Latin America (called CELAM from its Spanish acronym), and of various national conferences of Catholic bishops, such as the United States, Canada, England and Wales, Germany, and the Philippines. All of these have produced documents on social issues, as have groups of regional bishops and individual bishops. All of this Spirit-guided episcopal teaching can be called Catholic social teaching, acknowledging, however, various degrees of significance.

In 2004 the Pontifical Council for Justice and Peace produced its *Compendium of the Social Doctrine of the Church.*[5] Pope John Paul II used the terms social "doctrine" and social "teaching" interchangeably,[6] and Pope

Benedict XVI does as well. Catholic social doctrine is the same as Catholic social teaching, although doctrine seems a more formal, rigid, and authoritative term that is perhaps inappropriate for the ever-changing intersection between the Christian faith and the social question.

Catholic social *thought* refers to the broader theological and social reflection on social issues that takes place in the church. Catholic social thought includes the work of academics and professionals that reflects on social issues from the perspective of Christian faith and that analyzes and interprets Catholic social teaching, as well as the work of activists and social movements that endeavor to put the teaching into practice.[7] For example, Leo XIII was familiar with the "social Catholicism" initiated by Bishop Wilhelm Emmanuel von Ketteler in Mainz, Germany, around 1850 and picked up by other thinkers such as Albert de Mun and René de La Tour du Pin in France, Cardinal H. E. Manning in Britain, and Cardinal James Gibbons of Baltimore. In particular he was aware of the Fribourg Union, which brought together many European lay and clerical thinkers every October from 1885 to 1891 to discuss the social question and in particular the changing economy and its consequences for workers. Some strands of social Catholic thought were critical of the ruthless competition and bleak individualism of early capitalism, yet defended the limited right to private property. This vortex of thought, activism, and experimentation influenced *The Condition of Labor,* which in turn influenced the further development of social Catholicism.[8]

The scope of Catholic social thought, the subject of this book, is broad — encompassing the Hebrew and Christian scriptures, Christian history, and contemporary praxis — and the literature is obviously vast. Catholic social thought includes, but is not limited to, Catholic social teaching. Theologian Judith Merkle uses the term Catholic social "tradition" in the title of her book and throughout her text, and this term is a fitting synonym for Catholic social thought.[9]

Finally, Catholic (or Christian) social *ethics* refers to the academic study of morality as it applies to social issues. Social ethics is the task primarily of theologians and philosophers. Catholic social thought is the work of the whole church and a broader range of academicians. Catholic social teaching is the province of the hierarchy of the church.[10]

The Major Documents of Catholic Social Teaching

There is no canon or accepted list of the documents that comprise Catholic social teaching. This book wishes to be broadly inclusive, seeking wisdom wherever it can be found, yet some parameters need to be set. My list of the major social documents corresponds to those collected in *Catholic Social Thought: The Documentary Heritage,* edited by David J. O'Brien and Thomas A. Shannon, with the following additions: *The Declaration on*

Religious Freedom from Vatican II; the documents from two of the meetings
of the Latin American bishops at Medellín in 1968 and Puebla in 1979; and
two of the encyclicals of Benedict XVI.[11] In the American context, it seems
proper for O'Brien and Shannon to include the two pastoral letters on peace
and economic justice of the United States bishops, and it is also true that
these two documents have received widespread attention.[12] They are major
documents. Likewise, the Medellín and Puebla documents have been widely
influential (see Table 1.1).

Table 1.1. Major Documents on Catholic Social Teaching[13]

Year	Author	Latin Title	English Title
1891	Leo XIII	*Rerum Novarum*	*The Condition of Labor*
1931	Pius XI	*Quadragesimo Anno*	*After Forty Years*
1961	John XXIII	*Mater et Magistra*	*Christianity and Social Progress*
1963	John XXIII	*Pacem in Terris*	*Peace on Earth*
1965	Vatican II	*Gaudium et Spes*	*Pastoral Constitution on the Church in the Modern World*
1965	Vatican II	*Dignitatis Humanae*	*Declaration on Religious Freedom*
1967	Paul VI	*Populorum Progressio*	*On the Development of Peoples*
1968	CELAM		Medellín Conference Documents
1971	Paul VI	*Octogesima Adveniens*	*A Call to Action* on the Eightieth Anniversary
1971	Synod	*Justitia in Mundo*	*Justice in the World*
1975	Paul VI	*Evangelii Nuntiandi*	*Evangelization in the Modern World*
1979	CELAM		Puebla Conference Documents
1981	John Paul II	*Laborem Exercens*	*On Human Work*
1983	USCCB		*The Challenge of Peace*
1986	USCCB		*Economic Justice for All*
1987	John Paul II	*Sollicitudo Rei Socialis*	*On Social Concern*
1991	John Paul II	*Centesimus Annus*	*On the Hundredth Anniversary*
2005	Benedict XVI	*Deus Caritas Est*	*On Christian Love*
2009	Benedict XVI	*Caritas in Veritate*	*Charity in Truth*

If the topics and themes of these major documents set the parameters of
the book, some topics are excluded. Many introductions to Catholic social
teaching include a chapter on the family, often including bioethical issues
related to reproduction and genetics.[14] Although the family, sexual ethics,
and bioethics all have a significant social dimension, official Catholic teaching has not approached these topics from a primarily social perspective.[15]
Thus it seems reasonable to place these topics and the church documents
that address them outside the scope of this text.

Most of the major documents of Catholic social teaching, taking their cue
from *The Condition of Labor*, have focused on issues of economic justice,
but they have also addressed issues of politics, including human rights and
war and peace. There is no major document on environmental issues, but
these are addressed in John Paul II's 1990 World Day of Peace Message,
Peace with All Creation, in two statements by the U.S. bishops, and in a
section (#48–50) of Benedict XVI's *Charity in Truth* (2009). It is an issue of
such magnitude and urgency as to merit some attention here.

Since this book is directed primarily at an American audience, I have also developed a list of many of the contemporary social statements and documents of the U.S. bishops. These will be referred to in the chapters that follow.

Table 1.2. Statements of the U.S. Conference of Catholic Bishops Related to Social Teaching[16]

Brothers and Sisters to Us: A Pastoral Letter on Racism in Our Day (1979)

Statement on Capital Punishment (1980)

The Challenge of Peace: God's Promise and Our Response (1983)

The Hispanic Presence: Challenge and Commitment (1984)

Economic Justice for All: Catholic Social Teaching and the U.S. Economy (1986)

To the Ends of the Earth (1986)

Statement on Central America (1987)

Homelessness and Housing: A Human Tragedy, a Moral Challenge (1988)

Called to Compassion and Responsibility: A Response to the HIV/AIDS Crisis (1989)

Toward Peace in the Middle East (1989)

Renewing the Earth (1991)

A Framework for Comprehensive Welfare Reform (1993)

Follow the Way of Love (1993)

The Harvest of Justice Is Sown in Peace (1993) (tenth anniversary of The Challenge of Peace)

Communities of Salt and Light (1994)

Called and Gifted for the Third Millennium (1995)

Confronting a Culture of Violence (1995)

Moral Principles and Moral Priorities for Welfare Reform (1995)

One Family under God (1995)

Sowing the Weapons of War (1995)

Walk in the Light: A Pastoral Response to Child Sexual Abuse (1995)

A Decade after Economic Justice for All (1996)

Called to Global Solidarity: International Challenges for U.S. Parishes (1997)

Living the Gospel of Life: A Challenge to American Catholics (1998)

Sharing Catholic Social Teaching: Challenges and Directions (1999)

A Commitment to All Generations: Social Security and the Common Good (1999)

A Jubilee Call for Debt Forgiveness (1999)

Everyday Christianity: To Hunger and Thirst for Justice: A Pastoral Reflection on Lay Discipleship for Justice in a New Millennium (1999)

Faithful Citizenship: Civic Responsibility for a New Millennium (1999)

A Fair and Just Workplace: Principles and Practices for Catholic Health Care (1999)

In All Things Charity: A Pastoral Challenge for the New Millennium (1999)

Welcome and Justice for Persons with Disabilities (1999)

Responsibility, Rehabilitation, and Restoration: A Catholic Perspective on Crime and Criminal Justice (2000)

Welcoming the Stranger among Us: Unity in Diversity (2000)

Global Climate Change: A Plea for Dialogue, Prudence, and the Common Ground (2001)

A Call to Solidarity with Africa (2001)

A Pastoral Message: Living with Faith and Hope after September 11, 2001 (2001)

A Matter of Heart: A Statement on the Thirtieth Anniversary of Roe v. Wade (2002)

A Place at the Table: A Catholic Recommitment to Overcome Poverty and to Respect the Dignity of All God's Children (2002)

Statement on Iraq (2002)

When I Call for Help: A Pastoral Response to Domestic Violence against Women (2002)

Strangers No Longer: Together on the Journey of Hope (2003)

Faithful Citizenship: A Catholic Call to Political Responsibility (2003)

"For I Was Hungry and You Gave Me Food": Catholic Reflections on Food, Farmers, and Farmworkers (2003)

Socially Responsible Investment Guidelines (2003)

A Culture of Life and the Death Penalty (2005)

Forming Consciences for Faithful Citizenship: A Call to Political Responsibility from the Catholic Bishops of the United States (2007)

Table 1.3. Some Statements of the United States Bishops' Catholic Campaign for Human Development Committee (CCHD)

Sharing the Tradition, Shaping the Future, series of booklets (1991–96)

The Cries of the Poor Are Still with Us (1995)

Being Neighbor: The Catechism and Social Justice (1997)

Justice Prayer Book (1998)

Principles, Prophecy, and a Pastoral Response: An Overview of Catholic Social Teaching (1991, revised 2001)

These lists of documents make it clear that the official literature regarding Catholic social teaching is extensive.

History and Development

The Christian tradition of bringing faith to bear on social issues did not, of course, begin with Leo XIII's reflections on the condition of labor in the Industrial Revolution. The relevance of faith for life in community is woven throughout the Hebrew and Christian scriptures and the history of the church. The aim of this section is to suggest points of contact between faith and social concerns with an eye toward the themes of modern Catholic social teaching; it is suggestive rather than thorough or thematic.

Hebrew Scriptures (Old Testament)

One of the distinguishing characteristics of Judaism, the religion of Jesus, is its sense of moral and social responsibility. After liberating the Hebrew people from slavery in Egypt in the Exodus, God made explicit God's covenant with this people through Moses at Mount Sinai — "I am your God, and you are my people." The primary conditions for being God's people were to worship God alone (monotheism and the prohibition of idolatry) and to create a just community (righteousness and justice). God insists that

"You shall not wrong or oppress a resident alien, for you were aliens in the land of Egypt. You shall not abuse any widow or orphan. If you do abuse them, when they cry out to me, I will surely heed their cry."
— Exodus 22:21–23

"You shall hallow the fiftieth year and you shall proclaim liberty throughout the land to all its inhabitants. It shall be a jubilee for you; you shall return, every one of you, to your property and every one of you to your family.... When you make a sale to your neighbor or buy from your neighbor, you shall not cheat one another. When you buy from your neighbor, you shall pay only for the number of years since the jubilee; the seller shall charge you only for the remaining crop years.... You shall observe my statutes and faithfully keep my ordinances, so that you may live on the land securely."   — Leviticus 25:10, 14, 18

the Hebrews respect the rights and needs of the alien (or immigrant), the widow, and the orphan — that is, the marginal and vulnerable people — reminding them that they were once slaves in Egypt and that their God is the defender of the oppressed (Deut 24:17–18; 26:12–15; Ex 22:21–24; Jer 22:3).[17] The laws regarding the forgiveness of debts during sabbatical years (Deut 15:1–11 and Lev 25:1–7) and the return to the original equality among the twelve tribes of Israel during the Jubilee year (Lev 25:8–17) symbolize the justice and community required of the Hebrew people.[18] After the Hebrew people settled in the Promised Land, oppression came to characterize Israel. The God who had liberated the people from oppression in Egypt now sent prophets who called them to adhere to the requirements of the covenant or face the fate of the Egyptians — destruction. The Hebrew prophets (eighth century to sixth century B.C.E.), such as Amos, Micah, Hosea, Isaiah, Jeremiah, and Ezekiel, accused the people of infidelity to the covenant because of their idolatry and the social injustice they created.[19] The warnings and the promises of the prophets remind each generation of God's passion for justice and God's faithful love. In Judaism, one's relationship with God (faith) affects one's relationship with others, the community, and the earth (justice).[20] Faith and justice are relational, both personally and communally.

Christian Scriptures (New Testament)

Messianic expectation was at a fever pitch when Jesus began his public ministry. Israel was occupied by the brutal Romans, and the people were expecting God to send a messiah to liberate and restore the nation. They had in mind a warrior, such as King David, riding into Jerusalem on a white horse at the head of a conquering Jewish army. The savior that God sent rode into Jerusalem on a donkey and was crucified by the Romans. Through his cross and resurrection, Jesus ushered in the kingdom, or reign, of God, a notion and a reality that had been central to Jesus' preaching. The messiah sent by God was different from the people's expectations.

The concept of the reign of God is a pivotal theme of the gospels and part of the biblical foundation of Catholic social thought.[21] Clarence Jordan (1912–69), a Southern Baptist scripture scholar, captured the meaning of the reign of God. Jordan had a love affair with the Bible and especially the Greek New Testament.[22] As a student and scholar, Jordan approached scripture critically, but he also approached it practically, as a guide for life. He produced a series of translations of the New Testament into the vernacular of the American south, which he called *The Cotton Patch Version*. Jordan thought of Jesus' incarnation as God's ongoing "invasion" of the earth, and he translated the kingdom of God as "the God movement," God's spiritual organization for accomplishing radical change.

After studying for his doctorate at Southern Baptist Theological Seminary in Louisville, Kentucky, and ministering to the African American community there, Clarence and his wife, Florence, founded Koinonia Farm[23] near Americus, a small town in segregated southwest Georgia, in 1942. Koinonia Farm was a racially integrated Christian community of about sixty people who shared their possessions in common and opposed all forms of violence. Not surprisingly, they were harassed by the Klu Klux Klan, boycotted by the local community, and ejected from the local Southern Baptist Church. The Koinonia community responded with perseverance, courage, and Jordan's plain-spoken wit.

In the year before he died suddenly of a heart attack, Clarence Jordan and Millard Fuller started an organization aimed at building housing for the poor that would become Habitat for Humanity. Another Southern Baptist, former president of the United States and Nobel Peace Prize recipient Jimmy Carter, would do much to garner support for Habitat by swinging a hammer himself for a week each year.

This experiment in Christian communitarianism at Koinonia Farm, still active today, contradicts the individualism, segregation, and greed of American society. It is an example of "the God movement" in action. Clarence Jordan was convinced that if one took Jesus and the gospel seriously, the result would be radical discipleship. Maybe it is Jesus and his message that is the church's "best kept secret."

From a middle-class perspective, Jesus is hard to handle. He identifies with the poor and the marginal. He was born in a stable, and his first visitors are low-class shepherds. He hangs out with the wrong crowd — fishermen, prostitutes, tax collectors. He is a charismatic, itinerant (homeless), God-obsessed preacher and healer. When he is executed, his only possessions are the clothes on his back.

Neither what he teaches nor how he teaches is any more conventional. He often uses parables, which have been described as "blind-side story telling" because the purpose of a parable is to upset our world, to turn our perspective upside down.[24] How could a Samaritan, a Jewish apostate and enemy, be the example of a compassionate neighbor (Lk 10:25–37)? How could a vineyard owner who has hired workers early in the morning and late in the afternoon pay them all a full day's wage (Mt 20:1–16)? What is going on here?

When his teaching is more straightforward, it is no less baffling or challenging. Blessed are the meek (Mt 5:5); to look at a woman with lust is to commit adultery (Mt 5:28); forgive wrongs seventy times seven (Mt 18:22); you can't be my disciple if you do not give up all your possessions (Lk 14:33); no divorce (Mk 10:9); love your enemies and pray for those who persecute you (Mt 5:44). A passage that gives us the keys to the reign, or kingdom, of God is Matthew 25:31–46, the scene of the judgment of the nations:

> Then the king will say to those on his right hand, "Come, you that are blessed by my Father, inherit the kingdom prepared for you from the foundation of the world; for I was hungry and you gave me food, I was thirsty and you gave me something to drink, I was a stranger and you welcomed me, I was naked and you gave me clothing, I was sick and you took care of me, I was in prison and you visited me."

As Mother Teresa put it, we meet Christ in the distressing disguise of the poor.

Jesus' teaching and witness is obviously relevant to social, economic, and political issues. Indeed, the Jewish leaders and the Romans (the powers that be of the time) found his teaching and actions disturbing enough to arrest him and execute him.

A scene from the life of Clarence Jordan drives home the radicalism and relevance of Jesus' message. In the early 1950s Clarence approached his brother, Robert Jordan, a lawyer and future state senator and justice of the Georgia Supreme Court, to legally represent Koinonia Farm.

> Clarence, I can't do that. You know my political aspirations. Why if I represented you, I might lose my job, my house, everything I've got.
>
> *We* might lose everything too, Bob.
>
> It's different for you.
>
> Why is it different? I remember, it seems to me, that you and I joined the church the same Sunday, as boys. I expect when we came forward the preacher asked me about the same question he did you. He asked me, "Do you accept Jesus as your Lord and Savior?" And I said, "Yes." What did you say?
>
> I follow Jesus, Clarence, up to a point.
>
> Could that point by any chance be — the cross?

That's right. I follow him to the cross, but not *on* the cross. I'm not getting myself crucified.

Then I don't believe you're a disciple. You're an admirer of Jesus, but not a disciple of his. I think you ought to go back to the church you belong to, and tell them you're an admirer not a disciple.

Well now, if everyone who felt like I do did that, we wouldn't *have* a church, would we?

The question, Clarence said, is, "Do you have a church?"[25]

The early Christian community tried to live according to the values of the reign of God that Jesus proclaimed, to be disciples. The Jerusalem community was characterized by unlimited liability and total availability for each other, sharing until everyone's needs were met (Acts 2:43–47; 4:32–37).[26] Paul's exhortation to live a new life in Christ in his letter to the Romans, chapters 12 through 15, has remarkable parallels to Jesus' Sermon on the Mount in Matthew, chapters 5 through 7, and Luke 6:20–49.[27] Both Jesus and Paul offer practical steps for conflict resolution and peacemaking. Similarly, the Epistle of James exhorts Christians to "be doers of the word and not merely hearers who deceive themselves" (1:22), and warns against class divisions (2:1–13) and the greed and corruption of the wealthy (5:1–6).

"Now the whole group of those who believed were of one heart and soul, and no one claimed private ownership of any possessions, but everything they owned was held in common.... There was not a needy person among them, for as many as owned lands or houses sold them and brought the proceeds of what was sold. They laid it at the apostles' feet, and it was distributed to each as any had need."

—Acts 4:32, 34–35

The New Testament calls followers of Christ to a kind of community and a way of life that is generous, forgiving, just, and loving, and thus to participate in realizing the reign of God on earth. Christians, like those at Koinonia Farm, have struggled throughout two millennia now to live kingdom values in the changing circumstances of time and culture, to be disciples of Jesus rather than mere admirers.

The First Six Centuries — The Patristic Period

The writings and practices of the "Fathers" of the church from the second through the sixth centuries are given special theological weight because of their proximity to Jesus and the early Christian community. During this period there were several key councils of the church that decided important doctrines about Christ and the Trinity. This was a period of great theologians in the East (who wrote in Greek), such as Clement of Alexandria, Origen, Basil the Great, Gregory of Nyssa, and John Chrysostom; and the West (who wrote in Latin), such as Tertullian, Cyprian of Carthage, Ambrose of Milan, Augustine of Hippo, and Gregory the Great. The voluminous writing of these Fathers of the church, many of whom were bishops, often addressed social, economic, and political issues.

A principal reason for the rapid spread of Christianity was its strong sense of community and its exercise of charity.[28] While the church did not see itself as called to reform social and economic structures,[29] the Fathers of the church condemned, in no uncertain terms, avarice, greed, and economic exploitation, and they required almsgiving and charity as essential to discipleship.[30] Their teaching is based on scripture. The goods of the earth were created by God to meet the basic needs of all human beings, and the rich are obliged to share their surplus with the poor, with whom Christ identifies in a special way. Christians are radically different from "pagans"; they are a new people with transformed values and purified desires who are to renounce wealth and power and, trusting in God, share generously with one another.[31]

The Fathers can be as relevant and challenging as the Hebrew prophets regarding social justice. While I was researching this section of the book, I traveled into Louisville for a lecture. As I was rushing to catch a bus back home, a young African American man approached me, saying "Can I share my situation with you?" I muttered, "Sorry," and hurried toward my bus, which I missed anyway. I thought to myself, "This man is young and able-bodied; he must be a con artist." That night I read a quote from Clement of Alexandria (late second and early third century), "You must not try to distinguish between the deserving and the undeserving. You may easily make a mistake, and, as the matter is in doubt, it is better to benefit the undeserving than, in avoiding this, to miss the good."[32]

And John Chrysostom (347–407) wrote, "So, when you see a poor man and say, 'It really galls me that this fellow, young and healthy as he is, has nothing and yet would like to be fed even though he is idle.' ... If you are prompt in showing mercy, the man who is poor will soon be rid of idleness and you of cruelty."[33] Chrysostom points out that God gives everything in abundance despite our own idleness and corruption, and we should do likewise toward one another. The Fathers are clear that I should have listened to the man's story as I rushed for my bus and offered my help. Later I realized that this brief encounter happened at Fourth Street and Muhammad Ali Boulevard, the location of Thomas Merton's mystical epiphany about the unity and goodness of all humankind.[34] This irony doubled my guilt.

The political thinking of the Patristic period developed after the conversion of Constantine in 312 C.E., when the Christian church was transformed from a persecuted sect to the official religion of the Roman Empire. Most of the church Fathers had a positive view of the state as willed by God and subject to God's will. Ambrose (337–97) defended the freedom of the church in matters religious, declaring that "The Emperor is in the Church, not over the Church."[35] Augustine (354–430) argued that the church and state had distinct spheres and powers, but a concordance of tasks, and thus could collaborate with each other.[36]

Prior to Constantine, the Christian community was basically pacifist, following the example and teaching of Jesus. The early followers of "the Way" were persecuted for their faith, yet they died with love in their hearts and refused to retaliate with violence or to join the army.[37] After Constantine, Augustine, faced with the Barbarian invasions and the collapse of the Roman Empire, baptized the Greek and Roman notion of just war into the Christian tradition. It is interesting, however, that Leo the Great (390–461, pope from 440 to 461), who consolidated the authority of the bishop of Rome in the church, courageously confronted Attila the Hun in 452 and persuaded him to withdraw from Italy. Three years later Leo I negotiated with the Vandal king Gaiseric, successfully persuading him not to torch Rome or massacre its people, although the Vandals did pillage the city.[38] Much of Leo's effort in his remaining years was spent ministering to the broken victims of this event.[39]

The Patristic period comes to a close with Pope Gregory I (540–604, papacy from 590 to 604). He is acclaimed "the Great," a saint, and a Doctor of the church because of his managerial genius, personal holiness, and writings, which were synthetic, practical, and influential, but he referred to himself as the "Servant of the servants of God."[40] Gregory the Great was the first monk to be elected pope. His vision of pastoral care balanced the contemplative and active aspects of ministry, and he practiced what he preached. The term "Gregorian chant" honors his support for the liturgy and liturgical music. He sent Augustine of Canterbury (d. 604) and a band of monks to successfully evangelize Britain. He is also a laudable example of the social witness of the church.

Gregory, who came from a patrician Roman family, received an excellent classical education. When his father died in 575, he gave up his worldly role as prefect of Rome, sold his possessions, gave the proceeds to the poor, and turned his family home into a monastery. In 579, however, he was called to serve the church through a number of sensitive administrative and diplomatic roles. He reluctantly accepted his election by the clergy and people of Rome to be their bishop and the pope. Because of the absence of civil leadership, he in effect administered the local and universal church, the collapsing city, and much of the region, hard hit by a succession of war, famine, and plague. Like many of the other Fathers of the church, he taught that God meant for material goods to serve the basic needs of all and that private property was really a stewardship of God's creation. Generosity toward the poor is a matter of justice rather than charity.

Wrongly, then, do those suppose themselves innocent who claim for their own private use the common gift of God; those who, by not sharing what they have received, are accomplices of the death of their neighbors, since they every day in a certain way kill as many as those who die of hunger whose subsidies they refuse to give. For, when we give necessities of any kind to the poor, we do not bestow our own, we give them back what is theirs; we rather pay a debt of justice than accomplish works of mercy.[41]

The witness and writings of this gifted and holy man are a fitting synthesis of the social thought of the Patristic period.

The Medieval Period (600–1453)

The Hebrew prophets were sent by God not to offer new insights into justice and right living, but to remind God's people of the requirements of the covenant. Although there are important and insightful adaptations of the Christian message to changing historical and cultural circumstances, basically Christian history is a similar story of God's people failing to live according to the gospel. With the ascendancy of Christianity at the time of Constantine, the church became embroiled in the tumultuous politics of empire and the resulting corruptions and injustices. The details of this ambiguous history are beyond the scope of this study. Two representatives, Francis of Assisi (1182–1226) and Thomas Aquinas (1225–74), can remind us of the positive witness and thought of the medieval period.

St. Francis of Assisi (1182–1226)

Perhaps no person in Christian history better illustrates the reversal of values called for by the gospel and encouraged by the Fathers of the church than Francis of Assisi. The son of Pietro di Bernardone, a wealthy textile merchant, Francis was a "bohemian minstrel," the leader of a society of libertine youth who wandered the streets, singing minstrels' songs about knights and romance.[42] He joined a military excursion against Perugia, a neighboring city-state, seeking worldly glory and nobility, and was instead captured and held as a prisoner of war for a year. After being ransomed and recuperating from an illness, Francis began to change. A fastidious youth, especially repulsed by lepers, Francis overcame his revulsion and shared his cloak with a leper and kissed the leper's hand. While his father was away on business, Francis distributed the profits of the family business to the church and the poor. When he was accused before the bishop by his enraged father, Francis stripped off his rich garments and returned them to his father, saying "Hitherto I have called you father on earth; but now I say, 'Our Father, who art in heaven.' " When the bishop covered Francis with a peasant's frock, which Francis marked with a cross, Francis's transformation from a worldly rich kid into *il Poverello,* the little poor one, was symbolically complete. He had left behind the values of his family and the world and embraced the values of the gospel — compassion, humility, and fraternity.

Soon others, many of them from the "Majores" (the upper class), were attracted by Francis's love of God and the poor and by his joy. They joined him in the countryside, becoming the Friars "Minores" (the lowly ones). One of these persons was a young woman, Clare (1193–1253), who was led by Francis's preaching and example to an equally profound commitment to Christ and to poverty.[43] As the community grew, Francis and his brothers made a pilgrimage to Rome and received the approval of Pope Innocent III to form a religious community with a "rule," a collection of precepts to guide the community. The rule Francis wanted for his community was simply the gospel with an emphasis on the Sermon on the Mount and voluntary poverty. The Franciscans, however, eventually overruled their founder, even while he was still alive, and wrote a more typical and practical rule in 1223.

The life of Francis demonstrates three themes that are especially relevant for contemporary Catholic social thought — poverty, ecology, and nonviolence. Francis did not merely accept poverty; he courted "Lady Poverty" like a bride. He wanted to be poor because Jesus was poor and loved the poor. He embraced poverty to become nearer to the marginal and suffering people and closer to God. He began to live for the poor, with the poor, and like the poor. Francis actively pursued downward mobility, a de-class-ification and a dis-appropriation of worldly goods. Thus social poverty (an evil resulting from exploitation and injustice) was cured by voluntary poverty (a simplicity of life and solidarity with the poor). Since all is God's gift, all is available to all. Francis radically grasped what today's Latin American theologians have called the "preferential option for the poor."

A student who researched and presented Francis of Assisi to a senior seminar, a capstone course at Bellarmine University, shared with the class how Francis's love affair with poverty began to affect his own life. The student, Graham, started to pay attention to a homeless man whom he regularly encountered at a local coffee shop. He finally found the courage to begin to have conversations with the man and learned that one thing he needed was a backpack. So Graham bought the man a good backpack and filled it with simple things that he thought his new acquaintance could use. "If I were really caught up in the spirit of Francis, I would have given him the keys to my car," Graham said, "but maybe I am now moving in a different direction."

It is obvious by now that the popular "St. Francis of the birdbath" is a caricature of the radical reversal of values that characterized the man who has been called the first Christian. Francis did have, however, a deep appreciation of the sacramentality of creation, that all of creation reflects the Creator's love and is due reverence and wonder. His reverence for life and for "Brother Sun" and "Sister Moon" is connected to his poverty. "Poverty is a way of being by which the individual lets things be what they are: one refuses to dominate them, subjugate them, and make them objects of the will to power."[44] Thus Francis enlarges solidarity to include not only fraternity and community with all persons, but also fellow creatures — birds and wolves — and nature itself. Since this attitude is essential in order for humankind to constructively address our pressing environmental concerns, Pope John Paul II declared Francis the patron saint of ecology.

Finally, in a time of Crusades, Francis embraced the nonviolence of Christ.[45] "Peace and Good Will" (Pax et Bonum) is the Franciscan motto. How could it be otherwise once one divests oneself of domination and power and embraces poverty and humility, service and solidarity, and genuinely sees God's image in every human being? Francis even traveled to the front lines of the Crusades, where he was appalled by the slaughter he witnessed and where he had an interesting and respectful meeting with the sultan of Egypt. Francis's commitment to a spirituality and practice of nonviolence is also a challenge for our violent age.

While praying before a crucifix in the crumbling chapel of St. Damian in Assisi during the time of his conversion, Francis heard a voice say, "Repair my church which has fallen into disrepair, as you can see." Francis at first took this assignment literally and began rebuilding the chapel. His vocation, however, was to reform the Christian community by recalling it to the image of Christ in the poor. His story projects his vocation into the present, challenging Christians to make Christ the standard for our lives and calling a spiritually impoverished church to the radical simplicity of the gospel.[46]

The life of Francis provokes our thought, but he was not a thinker; indeed there is an anti-intellectual tendency in Francis. Thomas Aquinas, on the other hand, is renowned as one of the great theologians of all time and is recognized as a Doctor of the church. The life of a scholar, however, is seldom very dramatic; it is Aquinas's thought that is most relevant to Catholic social teaching.

Thomas Aquinas (1225–74)

Thomas was born in southern Italy to a prosperous family who entrusted his care to the local Benedictine monastery in the hope that he would one day become an abbot, a prestigious position that would serve the family honor well.[47] When Thomas decided instead to become a Dominican, his family was aghast at the loss of status implied by this vocational choice. (Apparently the Dominicans were not popular among the upper class.) The family tried to dissuade him, but to no avail.

Thomas was sent to study at Cologne under St. Albert the Great. His classmates called him "The Dumb Sicilian Ox," deriding his size and bulk and his quietness, which they mistakenly took for stupidity. Thomas received his doctorate at the University of Paris, where he also taught. His brilliance quickly emerged in his writing and teaching, and he was in demand, even at the papal court. Thomas taught at several places and traveled widely in Europe, most likely by foot. He produced just over a hundred books, sometimes dictating three different books to three secretaries simultaneously (the original multitasker)! He died at age forty-nine after a brief illness from a blow to the head from a low-hanging branch. Thomas's lifelong study of God drew him closer to God. He had stopped work on his incomplete *Synthesis of Theology* (*Summa Theologiae*) some months before his death after a mystical experience convinced him that what he had written was "so much straw."

Thomas's great contribution was to undertake a systematic exposition of the Catholic faith as a whole in his masterpiece the *Summa Theologiae* (a four-volume compendium or synthesis of theology). Through a series of interrelated questions Thomas tried to show the logic and consistency of the Catholic faith and the compatibility between reason and revelation. The influence of Aquinas's thought on Catholic theology is comparable only to that of Augustine. Pope Leo XIII singled out "Thomism" as a sort of official Catholic philosophy in 1879, and as a result it was almost exclusively taught in seminaries from then until Vatican II (1962–65).

Aquinas was controversial in his own day. While his contemporaries relied heavily on arguments from authority, Aquinas rigorously examined all the arguments before coming to his own position (this is known as the scholastic method). Even more controversial, however, was his systematic incorporation of the newly rediscovered ancient Greek philosopher Aristotle as a basis for Christian theology. In 1270 the bishop of Paris drew up a list of eighteen errors in the writings of Aquinas, and the list was expanded in 1277. This condemnation was not revoked until fifty years later, well after Thomas had died.

Because of the semiofficial status of Thomism after Leo XIII, many of the strengths and limitations of modern Catholic social teaching are rooted in interpretations of Aquinas.[48] A bare outline of some of Aquinas's contributions to Catholic social teaching and of some of the inadequacies of Thomism in the modern age follows.

Aquinas's system of ethics is based in natural law and in virtue theory, and both are fundamental to modern Catholic social teaching. Natural law basically means that reason can comprehend what God expects us to do, that is, follow the eternal law established by the Creator. Papal moral teaching had tended to approach natural law deductively, drawing out absolute moral principles to guide human behavior. An asset of natural law, however, is that it does theoretically allow the church to dialogue with, and speak to, all people of good will on the basis of reason, rather than exclusively to Christians on the basis of revelation (scripture).

Justice is the virtue central to social issues. Aquinas links justice to the common good and defines justice as rendering to all persons what is properly theirs. He distinguished between commutative justice, which governs relations between two persons (such as contracts), and distributive justice, which governs the relation of the individual to society (economic justice and social justice). Modern Catholic social teaching continues this emphasis on justice, fairness, and the common good.

"Catholic social teaching, like much philosophical reflection, distinguishes three dimensions of basic justice: commutative justice, distributive justice, and social justice.

"Commutative justice calls for fundamental fairness in all agreements and exchanges between individuals and social groups. It demands respect for the equal human dignity of all persons in economic transactions, contracts, or promises. . . .

"Distributive justice requires that the allocation of income, wealth, and power in society be evaluated in light of the effects on persons whose basic material needs are unmet. . . .

"Social justice implies that persons have an obligation to be active and productive participants in the life of society and that society has a duty to enable them to participate in this way."

— U.S. Conference of Catholic Bishops,
Economic Justice for All (1968),
#68, 69, 70, 71; see 68–76

There is in Aquinas (and Aristotle) a remarkable balance, the middle way between two extremes, that has characterized Catholic social teaching. It allows the church, for example, to criticize both capitalism (too individualistic) and socialism (too collectivist); to affirm the right of private property, yet insist that it serve the common good; to promote both the principle of subsidiarity (decentralization) and of socialization (state intervention on behalf of the common good); to draw on scripture and tradition, faith and reason.[49]

Thomas's synthesis and development of the just war tradition makes him a significant just war theorist. The position that war can sometimes be morally justified remains the teaching of the Catholic Church today, although pacifism has been recently recognized as an option for individuals.

Aquinas's theory of society was ordered and hierarchical, and his political theory stated that monarchy, grounded in divine authority and committed to following God's will, was the best form of government. These beliefs, which coincided with the church's perceived self-interests in the late eighteenth and nineteenth centuries, inhibited the church from constructively accommodating to modern liberal society and in particular to democratic forms of government and the separation of church and state. Furthermore the concept of human dignity, the foundation of human rights that is so prominent in contemporary Catholic social teaching, is not found in Aquinas, nor is it prominent in Catholic social teaching until John XXIII and Vatican II in the 1960s.[50]

The theological synthesis of Thomas Aquinas in the thirteenth century remains a remarkable achievement, and his thought can still offer insights into today's social concerns and theological controversies. Nevertheless, it may be that Aquinas's tenacious search for truth, incorporating the best ideas available at the time, is a more important lesson for the church today than the conclusions Aquinas arrived at in the medieval era.

The Reformation and the Age of Conquest (1492–1740)

The causes of the Protestant Reformation were theological and political; its tragic result was the violent fragmentation of the church. It was sparked when an Augustinian monk and theologian, Martin Luther (1483–1546), nailed ninety-five theses to the door of a church in Wittenberg, Germany, on October 31, 1517, in an effort to reform the Roman Catholic Church. It is not difficult to be sympathetic with Luther's cause, for the fourteenth and fifteenth centuries were among the worst in the Western church. Church leaders from the pope to the local clergy were corrupt and venal, predominantly characterized by a lust for wealth and power.[51] The match that lit the Reformation was the selling of indulgences in Germany (and elsewhere) to pay for the construction of a new St. Peter's Basilica in Rome. In truth, selling indulgences was theologically indefensible and using German money to build an Italian church was politically insensitive.

Desiderius Erasmus (1466–1536), a Dutch priest (like Luther trained as an Augustinian monk) and itinerant scholar, found himself caught in the middle of the Reformation controversy, although, unlike his English friend Thomas More (1478–1535),[52] he managed to keep his head. The illegitimate son of a priest, Erasmus became the preeminent representative of Christian humanism, with its ideals of reason and dialogue, learning and wisdom, charity and toleration. Unfortunately he lived in a partisan and intolerant age.[53]

A classics scholar and a passionate defender of peace against those who used the New Testament to justify war,[54] Erasmus had used satire, in works like *Praise of Folly* (1511), to confront the greedy clerics, nit-picking theologians, absentee bishops, and power-mad popes in the church. When he read Luther's ninety-five theses, he recognized many of the points he had made himself, and he defended Luther against the charge of heresy. Erasmus called for a prolonged dialogue, in a spirit of charity, aimed at the reform and renewal of the church. The result was that both sides turned on Erasmus, to dash his hope that the church could be reformed without violence or division. Europe dissolved into religious wars between Protestant and Catholic factions and the regional princes and kings who championed their causes. The church split, then splintered, as various reformers differed with one another. The charity and community called for in the gospel were eclipsed by competing theological positions and nascent nationalisms.

One of Luther's theological and ecclesiological principles was the authority of scripture alone. However, when some of his fellow reformers turned to scripture, they found there a nonviolent Christ. These Anabaptists and Mennonites (sixteenth century), Quakers (seventeenth century), and Brethren (nineteenth century) are part of the "radical reformation." They were persecuted and martyred by both Protestants and Catholics, but these "peace churches," as they are known, have endured into our own time. These faith communities generally have a strong sense of social justice and a commitment to nonviolence and peace.

The Catholic Church initiated a Counter-Reformation through the Council of Trent, which met intermittently from 1545 to 1563. The Catholic response to the reformers was to circle its wagons and define itself with a focus on the visible characteristics and practices (such as the pope, seven sacraments, celibate clergy, and so on) that differentiated the Roman Church from the Protestant communities. The Council of Trent required uniformity in rituals and doctrine and froze the church in time. "The Protestant Reformation had placed the Catholic Church on the defensive, and it would remain there until the middle of the twentieth century, fiercely combating the Enlightenment, the French Revolution, Italian nationalism, modern intellectual movements, and especially theological and biblical scholarship."[55] Included in this reaction against the modern world would be the condemnation of freedom of conscience, freedom of religion, and the separation of church and state. Only when John XXIII "opened the windows" of the church by calling the Second Vatican Council (1962–65) would the church enter into constructive dialogue with Protestant communities and the modern world. Benedict XVI, both when he was head of the Congregation for the Doctrine of the Faith under John Paul II and as pope, while not closing the door, has at least dampened this dialogue.

While the Protestant Reformation was raging in Europe, missionaries were planting the cross in the wake of the conquistador's sword in the new world (the Caribbean, Central and South America, and later in Africa and parts of Asia, such as the Philippines) "discovered" by Christopher Columbus (1451–1506) in 1492. In reality, Christian Europe did not so much "discover" a "new world" as *invade* an *old* one, in the spirit of the Crusades and the Inquisition.[56] The Spanish conquerors robbed the native peoples of their gold and silver and of their land. They enslaved the people, and when the indigenous people died from the oppression and the diseases brought by the Europeans, Africans were imported to take their place.[57] The primary motivations for this conquest were greed and power, but the cover story was usually the spread of Christianity and the salvation it brought.[58]

The conquest of the Americas is overwhelmingly a story of oppression, aggressive violence, and slavery, but even here there were voices calling for justice and peace. Perhaps the most significant "voice crying in the wilderness" (Mk 1:2–3) of this period was the Spaniard Bartolomé de Las Casas (1484–1566). For Las Casas there was no salvation apart from social justice. His contemporaries wondered whether the Indians could be saved; Las Casas pondered whether the Spanish, who were persecuting Christ in his poor, could be saved.[59]

Las Casas had himself participated in the oppression of the native peoples. He had served as chaplain for the Spanish conquest of Cuba and received an *encomienda,* a plantation, which he worked with indentured Indians. Converted by Sirach 34:22, "A man murders his neighbor if he robs him of his livelihood, sheds blood if he withholds an employee's wages," Las Casas divested himself of his plantation and began preaching against the exploitation of the Indians. He would devote the rest of his life defending the Indians — traveling back to Spain to lobby church and crown for laws to protect them, then returning to Latin America to try to implement the new legislation.

In his writings, Las Casas, influenced by Christian humanism, developed a political philosophy of universal human rights and a theology of Christ crucified in the poor that would not surface again in the Catholic Church until Vatican II and the Latin American movement called liberation theology. Las Casas and many of his Dominican colleagues argued for the dignity, equality, and full human rights of the indigenous people and for their peaceful conversion. He castigated the conquest and forced conversion of the indigenous peoples, the theft of their wealth, and their exploitation as indentured laborers. He practiced what he preached, refusing to give absolution to oppressive landlords and peacefully settling and converting the Tuzutlán province of Guatemala.

The efforts of Las Casas and others did persuade the church and the king to recognize the rights of the Indians. It must be said, however, that these progressive missionaries were not very successful in actually protecting the majority of Indians or in transforming the exploitative colonial system in Latin America. Nor did Las Casas extend his notion of human rights to the African slaves exported to the Americas to work on the plantations. The consequences of colonialism and its structures of injustice can be found in the gaping inequality and abject poverty that characterize much of Latin America today.

The Church Confronts the Industrial Age (1740–1958)

Earlier in this chapter it was noted that modern popes have been sending encyclicals to the church ever since Benedict XIV revived the custom in 1740, although most scholars date modern Catholic social teaching from Leo XIII's encyclical *The Condition of Labor* in 1891. At least two contemporary commentators, Michael Schuck and Joe Holland, do not wish to lose sight of the social teaching of the popes in the period before the papacy of Leo XIII, from 1740 to 1878.[60] Both of them divide modern Catholic social teaching into three periods — 1740–1878, 1878–1958, and 1958–present — but give different titles to the periods.[61] It seems to me that, in general, the popes were *reacting* against the changes symbolized by the French Revolution and the beginning of the Industrial Revolution in the period from 1740 to 1878; that Leo XIII and his successors tried to *reform* the modern world; and that after 1958, with John XXIII, Vatican II, and Paul VI, the church and the world began to *transform* one another. Thus I prefer to describe these times as the Reactionary period, the Reform period, and the period of Transformation.

The Reactionary Period (1740–1878)

Major world events in the church's Reactionary period include the American Revolution in 1776 with its Declaration of Independence and the development of a democratic republic; the French Revolution of 1789, which overthrew the monarchy under the banner of liberty, equality, and fraternity; the revolutions of 1884; and the beginnings of the Industrial Revolution (1750–1850). The Enlightenment of the eighteenth century had given rise to modern liberalism and then socialism, and the Catholic Church was wary of both. Near the end of this period, Vatican I (1869–70) defined the primacy and infallibility of the pope, officially consolidating the power and authority of the bishop of Rome, and a united and sovereign Italy took the papal states away from the Vatican (1870). While the pope's ecclesial power had never been stronger, the church's political power was waning, and the Vatican struggled to hold on to it against the anticlerical, antiauthoritarian forces of liberalism.

The nine popes of this period produced seventy-seven encyclicals, often addressing social and political issues. These statements condemned the notion of freedom of conscience in religion, vigorously opposed church-state separation, encouraged the censorship of books and the repression of social and theological dissent, and questioned the principle of the consent of the governed — setting the church at odds with most of the major developments of the modern world.[62] (These tendencies of the modern age — including political freedom, the spirit of scientific inquiry, and atheism — would be lumped together under the term "modernism," which was rejected in detail by the church.) The Roman Catholic Church fiercely defended its self-image as the one true church that possessed the truth, and it logically concluded that every state should officially recognize the Catholic Church. No wonder these encyclicals are largely forgotten and most commentators want to begin modern Catholic social teaching with Leo XIII!

It is possible, however, to put a more positive spin on papal social teaching before Leo XIII. John Coleman, a Jesuit professor of religion and society, points out that the church did say a resounding "no!" to excessive individualism, to privatized religion, to civil liberties without corresponding duties, to positivistic science divorced from morality, and to civil rights exclusive of economic rights.[63] Still there is no denying the reactionary defensiveness of the church, which put its own perceived institutional interests ahead of concerns about human suffering.

It is also important to note that what was happening at the Vatican was only a part of the larger, more fertile social thought taking place within the church that was often much more open to the modern world and ameliorative toward the human suffering that abounded.[64] To cite just three examples: religious orders of women were proliferating, such as the Sisters of Charity founded by Elizabeth Ann Seton (1774–1821) in the United States, and they were staffing schools, hospitals, orphanages, and homeless shelters. Frederic Ozanam (1813–53), a professor at the Sorbonne in Paris, founded the St. Vincent de Paul Society to put people in contact with the poor through structured social service. Ozanam was also an important thinker, arguing against the materialism and commodification of persons that characterized liberal capitalism, and for charity and justice through worker associations and state regulation of wages and working conditions.[65] Leon Harmel (1829–1915) was developing his family's textile mill in the Champagne region of France into an experimental Christian corporation that was economically successful and that offered his workers cradle to grave security (albeit in a paternalistic manner).[66] There were wider, less reactionary currents of Catholic social thought and activism swirling through this period.

The Reform Period (1878–1958)

By the end of the nineteenth century, during the papacy of Leo XIII (1878–1903), the Industrial Revolution was in high gear, churning out technological inventions such as electric power, the gasoline engine, the automobile, and the telegraph. From the perspective of the dominant classes, the world was working and improving. The idea of progress fueled a spirit of liberal optimism. The working class, however, was at least partially excluded from all this progress, facing miserable working conditions, and wages that were inadequate for the needs of a family and disproportionate to the profits of employers. The church saw itself as a bulwark of order and authority under attack from the forces of liberalism and revolutionary chaos.[67]

Early in his papacy, Leo XIII gave the Vatican's stamp of approval to Thomism (as interpreted by a small band of scholars of Aquinas and other medieval scholastic thinkers called neoscholastics), and the balanced rationalism found there provided the intellectual foundation for a Catholic critique of both laissez-faire capitalism and collectivist socialism.[68] In his landmark encyclical *The Condition of Labor* (1891), Leo XIII emphatically defended the right to private property as a way forward for the working class (against socialism), but he also insisted (against laissez-faire capitalism) on the social responsibilities attendant to possessing capital, namely, the duty to pay workers a living wage and to respect the right of workers to organize.[69]

Forty years later, Pius XI, at a time of global depression and pessimism, would emphasize even more strongly the social function of private property — the idea that the basic goods of creation should be available to all humanity and that the right of ownership is qualified by the common good and social justice. Pius XI's encyclical *After Forty Years* (1931) also introduced the principle of subsidiarity, which calls for decentralization and an emphasis on the mediating institutions of civil society, such as the family, the church, and other nongovernment organizations. The "corporatism" suggested by Pius XI was an indirect attempt to restore the power of the church vis-à-vis the state through the church's influence on the institutions of civil society, an idea that vanished as Catholic social teaching developed.[70]

In their efforts to bring social reform to the modern world, Leo XIII and Pius XI can be commended for their balanced critique of both capitalism and socialism, for their attention to the suffering of workers, and for their call for respect for the rights of labor. In their 185 encyclicals, however, the five popes of this Reform period never moved from their defensive, triumphalist, hierarchical understanding of the church or toward a genuine appreciation of the possible benefits of the modern world and its liberal values.

The continuity of the church's defensive posture toward the modern world during both the Reactionary period and the Reform period can be seen in the policies of Pius IX, who preceded Leo XIII, and Pius X, who followed Leo (see Table 1.4). Pius IX issued his famous "Syllabus of Errors" (1864), which asserted, for example, that the Catholic Church should be the official religion of the state and denied freedom of religion. Pius X, in the same vein, condemned modernism as "the synthesis of all heresies" in 1907.[71] He instituted an oath against modernism that was required of all clerics and stripped suspect theologians of their teaching positions.[72] Pius XII, the last pope of the Reform period (1939–58), managed to silence or harass most of the major theologians of his time, many of whom would later be vindicated by Vatican II, and two of whom would be made cardinals by future popes.[73] This was a defensive, authoritarian church, closed to dialogue with the modern world.

The Period of Transformation (1958–present)

Thus one can appreciate the sea change for the church represented by John XXIII's convocation of a council of the church, using the metaphor of throwing open a closed window to "let some fresh air in." The windows of the fortress church had been closed since the sixteenth-century Council of Trent. With the papacy of John XXIII (1958–63) and the Second Vatican Council (1962–65), the church began to dialogue with the modern world

Table 1.4. The Modern Popes[74]

Pope	Dates of Papacy	Comments
The Reactionary Period (1740–1878)		
Benedict XIV	1740–1758	
Clement XIII	1758–1769	
Clement XIV	1769–1774	
Pius VI	1775–1799	
Pius VII	1800–1823	
Leo XII	1823–1829	
Pius VIII	1829–1830	
Gregory XVI	1831–1846	
Pius IX	1846–1878	longest papacy in history
Vatican I	1869–1870	
The Reform Period (1878–1958)		
Leo XIII	1878–1903	*The Condition of Labor* (1891) third longest papacy
Pius X	1903–1914	
Benedict XV	1914–1922	
Pius XI	1922–1939	*After Forty Years* (1931)
Pius XII	1939–1958	
The Period of Transformation (1958–present)		
John XXIII	1958–1963	*Christianity and Social Progress* (1961), *Peace on Earth* (1963)
Vatican II	1962–1965	*Pastoral Constitution on the Church in the Modern World, Declaration on Religious Liberty* (1965)
Paul VI	1963–1978	*On the Development of Peoples* (1967), *A Call to Action on the 80th Anniversary* (1971), *Evangelization in the Modern World* (1975)
John Paul I	August 26–September 28, 1978	
John Paul II	1978–2005	*On Human Work* (1981), *On Social Concern* (1987), *On the Hundredth Anniversary* (1991) second longest papacy
Benedict XVI	2005–	*On Christian Love* (2005), *Charity in Truth* (2009)

in a process of mutual transformation. It is a remarkable reversal of course, accomplished by a unique pope. In this period of Transformation the church has embarked upon a continuing and crooked journey.

Angelo Giuseppe Roncalli, the son of peasants, became a highly cultured, well-educated church historian, Vatican diplomat, and patriarch of Venice who was proficient in French, Bulgarian, Russian, Turkish, and modern Greek by the time he was elected pope in 1958, at age seventy-seven. He was expected to be a transitional pope, and he was, but in a different sense.[75]

John XXIII brought a new style to the papacy. In contrast to the aloof Pius XII, he was gregarious and warm, with a keen sense of humor. He created a family atmosphere in the papal household, genially chatting with the gardeners on his daily walks. He was human and humble, becoming in effect everyone's favorite grandfather. He took the role of bishop of Rome seriously, visiting prisoners and sick children on his first Christmas as pope and engaging in pastoral visits throughout Rome. He enjoyed pomp and celebration, but did not stand on protocol.[76] He internationalized the College of Cardinals, dispensing red hats to Africans, Asians, and North and South Americans. He gave greater priority to catechesis than to the magisterium, to communicating the word of God rather than to theological orthodoxy. Two clear themes of his papacy were the unity of the Christian church (ecumenism) and peace among nations; both shine through in his encyclicals and in the documents of Vatican II. He was a pastor to all people, and people loved him.

John XXIII transformed the church through the power of his personal example, and he institutionalized this transformation by conceiving, convoking, and convening the Second Vatican Council (which was completed by his successor, Paul VI). In his opening address to the Council, John XXIII said, "The substance of the ancient doctrine is one thing, and the way in which it is presented is another." He expressed his hope that this Council would be pastoral and ecumenical, that it would promote peace and nudge the church to recognize its true identity and vocation as the church of the poor. Vatican II would commit the church to responding to the "signs of the times," while protecting human dignity and human rights and promoting the common good and solidarity. The Council affirmed the separation of church and state, the freedom of religion, and the propriety of representative government.

In his two social encyclicals, *Christianity and Social Progress* (1961, on the seventieth anniversary of Leo XIII's *The Condition of Labor*) and *Peace on Earth* (1963), John XXIII balanced the principle of subsidiarity with the principle of socialization (which recognized the need for state intervention in a complex and interdependent world), and he recognized human rights and responsibilities as the foundation for world peace. For bringing the church into constructive dialogue with the modern world, with other Christian and religious communities, and with all people of good will; for his advocacy of justice, human rights, and peace; and for his humanity, humility, and holiness, John XXIII rates as one of the two (along with Gregory the Great) truly outstanding popes in history.[77]

John XXIII's successor, Paul VI (1963–78), completed Vatican II and implemented the reforms initiated by the Council, a feat described by Eugene Kennedy, a psychologist and astute observer of the contemporary church, as "something like giving a haircut to a drowsy lion."[78] Paul VI never faltered in the onerous and delicate task of implementing the thrust of the Council. On his watch, there were no excommunications and no theologian was condemned or silenced; only the intransigent conservative dissident Archbishop Marcel Lefebvre was suspended.

Paul VI affirmed that social justice and human rights were central to the mission of the church and essential to the preaching of the gospel. He denounced the gap between the rich and the poor and insisted that the goods of the earth are intended by God for the use of everyone. He said that "development is the new name for peace" (*On the Development of Peoples*, #86), and dramatically pleaded before the General Assembly of the United Nations that there be "never again war." Vatican II renewed the role of bishop within the church and called for greater collegiality among bishops and with the bishop of Rome. Paul VI practiced this principle by holding synods of bishops on particular topics in Rome and by facilitating the development of regional and national conferences of bishops.[79]

"All members of society have a special obligation to the poor and vulnerable. From the Scriptures and church teaching, we learn that the justice of a society is tested by the treatment of the poor. . . . Jesus takes the side of those most in need. . . . As followers of Christ, we are challenged to make a fundamental 'option for the poor' — to speak for the voiceless, to defend the defenseless, to assess life styles, policies, and social institutions in terms of their impact on the poor. . . . As Christians, we are called to respond to the needs of *all* our brothers and sisters, but those with the greatest needs require the greatest response."

—U.S. Conference of Catholic Bishops,
Economic Justice for All (1986),
Introduction, #16; see #24, 48–52, 260.

CELAM (from the Spanish acronym for the Conference of Latin American Bishops) was organized prior to Vatican II, and thus had a head start on episcopal collegiality. The Latin American bishops gathered in Medellín, Colombia, in 1968 to respond to the signs of the times in the spirit of Vatican II. The bishops acknowledged that poverty was the overwhelming reality of their situation — the result of structures of injustice established in colonial times — and that the church was more solicitous of the interests of the rich and powerful than present to and for the poor. At Medellín the Latin American church switched sides, exercising what the bishops called a preferential option for the poor.[80] Latin American theologians were calling for liberation rather than development, and they created a highly influential movement called liberation theology based on the experience and the perspective of the poor.[81]

In a similar spirit, the United States Conference of Catholic Bishops produced two major pastoral letters that have been widely recognized as important, *The Challenge of Peace* (1983) and *Economic Justice for All*

(1986), on the issues of nuclear ethics and economic justice. These statements were noted not only for their content, but also for the consultative process used to develop them. Other national conferences of bishops have made their own contributions.

John Paul II (1978–2005),[82] the first globe-trotting pope, had something of the human touch of John XXIII and the acumen of Paul VI, but he brought a decidedly different spirit to his long reign as pope. In his social encyclicals, John Paul II affirmed and developed Catholic social teaching. He proclaimed the priority of labor over capital and the rights of the worker. He steered a middle course between capitalism and socialism, criticizing the materialism of both. He emphasized the virtue of solidarity and recognized the notion of social sin — that evil can be structural and systematic. Although critical of some aspects of liberation theology, he approved of the option for the poor. He was instrumental in bringing about the fall of communism in his native Poland and in Eastern Europe.

John Paul II was socially progressive, but theologically and doctrinally conservative. He scrutinized, silenced, and disciplined Catholic theologians judged by the Vatican to be less than fully orthodox. He consolidated the authority of the pope and the centrality of the Vatican in the life of the church, reining in the independence of bishop's conferences.[83] He was convinced that the church had to proclaim the gospel of life in the midst of the culture of death that characterized the modern world. Some have interpreted his pontificate as restorationist, a reversion to the defensive, authoritarian style of the pre–Vatican II Catholic Church. Benedict XVI, who was John Paul's right-hand man when he was Cardinal Joseph Ratzinger and head of the Congregation for the Doctrine of the Faith (the former Holy Office), has continued in the direction set by his predecessor.

Conclusion

The development in the content of Catholic social thought will be an ongoing theme of this text. In concluding this first chapter two foundational developments in the history of Catholic social teaching can be highlighted: (1) changes in the theoretical foundations of Catholic social teaching, and (2) different understandings of the church's mission and role (ecclesiology) that are at the base of that teaching.

Changes in the Theoretical Foundations of Catholic Social Teaching

John XXIII could address his encyclical *Peace on Earth* to "all people of good will" because a natural law ethic has been foundational for modern Catholic social teaching. The idea of natural law has a long and complex history that has been interpreted in different and even contradictory ways.[84] For the neoscholastics who so influenced the church, natural law meant that God created human beings for a purpose and that human reason could discover that purpose and lead consciences to an understanding of what is good and right. God's will, then, was accessible to all persons through reason. Thus the church could speak to all people of good will. Although this natural law ethic remains an important source of Catholic social teaching, Vatican II added new sources and shifted the interpretation of natural law.

Natural law, as wielded by Leo XIII and Pius XI (and in the moral encyclicals of John Paul II),[85] was dominated by universal and unchangeable principles and deductive logic. The result was absolute moral norms, certitude, and truth. John XXIII also employed this basic understanding of natural law, but he creatively melded it with the language of human rights, especially in *Peace on Earth*.[86]

The Council's *Pastoral Constitution on the Church in the Modern World*, however, instituted three shifts that dramatically developed the theoretical basis of Catholic social teaching. First, there was a shift from the classical consciousness just described to a historical consciousness that recognized the importance of human experience, culture, and historical change. Thus the church shifted from imposing abstract absolutes on the modern world to responding to the signs of the times from the perspective of the gospel.[87]

Second, new sources of social teaching were added to the almost exclusively philosophical foundations rooted in the doctrine of creation. Vatican II called for greater attention to scripture, and the Council emphasized Christ as the model for a new humanity.[88] Thus biblical studies and Christology become vital sources of post–Vatican II social teaching.

Finally, the Council emphasized the dignity of the human person, rooted in the creation of humanity in the image of God and in Christ's incarnation and redemption of humanity.[89] Human dignity is the basis for the church's affirmation of human rights, which become the minimal standard for evaluating any particular government. The human person is social by nature, and throughout scripture God calls humanity to live in just community. The U.S. bishops capture this fundamental value with the phrase "human dignity, realized in community," in *Economic Justice for All* (#25, passim).

These shifts do not eliminate natural law as a basis of Catholic social teaching, but they do interpret natural law in a more inductive, less absolutist, manner; they also allow other philosophies, such as personalism, to complement natural law and to enrich the theological sources of social teaching through a turn to scripture, Christology, and the dignity of the person. This broadening of the theoretical foundation of Catholic social teaching makes dialogue with the modern world and with other Christian communities realistic and potentially constructive.

Different Understandings of the Church

There is a corresponding development in the understanding of the nature and mission of the church and of the church's relationship with the world. Prior to Vatican II, the popes saw the church as the "perfect society," necessary for the salvation of the world and completely self-sufficient to fulfill its mission. The church, perceiving the modern world as hostile to its mission, thus developed a siege mentality that was exacerbated by the virulent anticlericalism that came in the wake of the French Revolution. Pre-Vatican II popes viewed society as unequal by nature and encouraged the various classes to cooperate with each other for the common good. The church, too, was hierarchical, with authority centered in the pope, who was entrusted with the deposit of faith and who communicated to his obedient flock the knowledge of eternal and natural law sufficient for their salvation. In the Reactionary period, the popes condemned the liberal trends of the modern world and defended Christendom from the revolutions that threatened it. In the Reform period, the popes offered a sinful world an understanding of God's rational, cosmological design to which humanity should conform. Throughout, the church's self-understanding was triumphal and arrogant, and its relationship with the modern world was defensive and paternalistic.[90]

The Second Vatican Council and its two popes brought a dramatic change in the understanding of the nature and mission of the church. The hierarchical perfect society was replaced by the images of an egalitarian people of God and of a pilgrim church journeying toward the kingdom of God. No longer was the church above society, dispensing its truth and wisdom. Now the church was a creative leaven within society, responding to the signs of the times from the perspective of the gospel.

> Thus the Church, at once a visible assembly and a spiritual community, goes forward together with humanity and experiences the same earthly lot which the world does. She serves as a leaven and as a kind of soul for human society as it is to be renewed in Christ and transformed into God's family.... Thus, through her individual members and her whole community, the Church believes she can contribute greatly toward making the family of man and its history more human.... At the same time she is firmly convinced that she can be abundantly and variously helped by the world in the matter of preparing the ground for the gospel. (*The Pastoral Constitution on the Church in the Modern World,* #40)

Thus, in the period of Transformation, the church becomes positively engaged with the world through a dialogue that is mutually transforming.[91]

This new understanding of the church came to fruition in the social teaching and ecclesial practice of Paul VI. In his apostolic letter *A Call to Action* (*Octogesima Adveniens,* 1971, commemorating the eightieth anniversary of *The Condition of Labor*) Paul VI established an open-ended, situation-specific methodology for developing Catholic social teaching that assigns the pope a modest role.

> In the face of such widely varying situations it is difficult for us to utter a unified message and to put forward a solution which has universal validity. Such is not our ambition, nor is it our mission. It is up to the Christian communities to analyze with objectivity the situation which is proper to their own country, to shed on it the light of the Gospel's unalterable words and to draw principles of reflection, norms of judgment and directives for action from the social teaching of the Church. (*A Call to Action*, #4)

Paul VI trusted church leaders and laity to engage in social analysis in light of the gospel and church teaching and to follow through with constructive action to remedy social problems and human suffering. With his blessing the Latin American bishops did just that at their conference in Medellín in 1968, and a Synod of Bishops meeting in Rome produced the significant social statement titled *Justice in the World* (1971).[92] Paul VI implemented the ecclesial vision of *The Church in the Modern World*.

Questions for Reflection and Discussion

1. Were you aware of Catholic social teaching before picking up this book or do you agree that it is the church's "best kept secret?" What can be done to make more Catholics and others aware of Catholic social teaching?

2. Clarence Jordan suggested that his brother was an "admirer" of Jesus, but not a disciple. Do you agree with Jordan that Jesus calls for a radical discipleship? What would such a radical discipleship look like in contemporary American culture?

3. The Fathers of the church, such as Clement of Alexandria and John Chrysostom, counseled compassion and charity toward beggars whom a Christian encounters. Is this advice still relevant today?

4. St. Francis of Assisi pursued "downward mobility," voluntarily giving up his wealth and social status. Is downward mobility possible in our society? Is it a requirement of Christian discipleship?

5. How would you characterize the Catholic ethos (or the relationship between the church and the world) during "the Reactionary period," "the Reform period," and "the period of Transformation?" How would you characterize the Catholic ethos today?

6. How has the changing nature of the social question affected the development of Catholic social thought?

Chapter 2

Faithful Citizenship

The Church and Politics

Since 1976, the United States Conference of Catholic Bishops (USCCB) has issued an election guide for Catholic voters in the year of a presidential election. Several of these were titled *Faithful Citizenship,* and the 2008 version was called *Forming Consciences for Faithful Citizenship.*[1] In these statements the church's bishops relate faith and politics in a manner that can offer guidance to Catholic citizens. These election guides are meant to focus the attention of Catholic voters and the nation on the *moral* dimension of pertinent public policy issues. The Catholic Church rightly believes that faith is relevant to politics and public policy. The relationships between faith and politics and church and state, however, have bedeviled the history of the church and continue to cause controversy.

During the 2004 presidential campaign, for example, first Archbishop Raymond Burke of St. Louis and then a handful of other Catholic bishops declared that they would not give communion to Senator John Kerry, the Democratic candidate and a practicing Catholic, because of his pro-choice voting record on abortion. Bishop Michael Sheridan of Colorado Springs then took the next step and said that Catholics who vote for politicians who support abortion, same-sex marriage, euthanasia, or stem-cell research should not receive communion.[2]

This incident raised a number of questions pertinent to this chapter's topic: Was this inappropriate meddling by the church in political affairs? Do the issues highlighted by Bishop Sheridan, and especially the single issue of abortion, trump all others in the moral discernment of Catholic voters? Is it theologically proper and politically prudent to play politics with the Lord's table? How are citizens and politicians to relate their faith to their decisions about public policy?

This chapter will explore the relationships between church and state, and faith and politics, through the lens of contemporary Catholic social thought in the following way:

- it will establish the theological basis for a relationship between faith and public policy decisions and issues;

36

- it will focus on the dramatic change accomplished at the Second Vatican Council in the church's position on the relationship between church and state;

- it will trace the understanding of the social mission of the church in contemporary Catholic social teaching; and

- it will summarize the principles that Catholic social teaching uses to steer its approach to public policy and offer a more detailed analysis of two cases related to one of those principles, human rights.

The chapter will conclude with snapshots of several organizations involved in political advocacy from the basis of faith. The intent of this chapter is to probe the meaning of faithful citizenship.

A Theological Basis for a Relationship between Faith and Politics

There are two temptations in the relationship between faith and politics: *privatization* and *politicization*. The latter is what happens to the church when it becomes a secular power, when the church tries to rule in the temporal sphere as well as in the religious. History demonstrates that whenever the church yields to this temptation corruption soon follows.

Privatization is the tendency to separate faith into a sphere separate from the rest of life, to ignore the communal and public ramifications of our relationship with God. Privatization is a form of theological individualism where faith is private; faith is only about me and God. Privatization might be more of a temptation for some Protestant communities, with their emphasis on salvation by faith alone, than for the deeply communitarian Catholic tradition, which has included works as a necessary result of faith.[3] The individualism ushered in by the Enlightenment, however, infected Catholic spirituality as well, and perhaps especially in American culture.

Privatization will be the focus of this section of the chapter. Politicization, which has certainly characterized the Catholic Church in history, will lead us into the next section on the relationship between church and state.

A Private Faith versus a Public Faith

There is a temptation to separate one's spiritual life and one's secular life into two separate and unrelated spheres. There are cultural and historical reasons for this unfortunate, even heretical, separation.

There are a number of trends in modern American culture that tend to privatize faith into a sphere separate from the rest of life. *Individualism*, when applied to faith, puts the focus on my personal relationship with God.

Faith is personal, but this does not mean that it should be private. Furthermore, contemporary life is *fragmented*. We tend to live in separate worlds at work, at home, at school, at the fitness center, and so on. Thus it becomes easy to think of prayer as something we do on Sunday morning and forget about the rest of the week (unless we have a test or a big presentation or a decisive meeting or become ill). Secularization has appropriately removed most aspects of social life from religious control, but it tends toward *secularism,* which denies the reality of transcendence, that there is more to life than what appears on the surface. These trends push faith and religion into a separate sphere on the margins of everyday life.[4]

Moreover, the United States was basically a Protestant country at its founding, and the Catholic Church, swelled by a stream of immigrants, created something of a ghetto for self-protection.[5] In the 1950s Catholic parishes, which usually included an elementary school, became cocoons where the young were socialized into a distinct subculture. Catholic identity was established as a somewhat defensive posture in a rather hostile social environment. The Catholic Church itself in the nineteenth and the first half of the twentieth century took a defensive stand against "modernism" and the modern world. "The Roman Catholic spirituality of the late 1950s, in general, did not take the temporal order very seriously."[6] The church fostered a spirituality of detachment from the allure of the modern world. One result of these various trends was a temptation to compartmentalize faith into a sphere separate from the rest of life, to have a private spiritual life unrelated to one's secular and public life.

Arthur Simon, one of the founders of the Christian citizens' lobby group Bread for the World, says, "The separation of religion from life is pure heresy."[7] Faith (one's relationship with God) should be the center of a person's life, affecting every dimension of life, including where we live, what kind of car we drive, and how we vote. Christianity is intended to be a philosophy of life, a way of living.

Certainly this was the way that the people of Israel understood their covenant with God, the liberator of the oppressed and the defender of the poor. Being God's people affected the whole of life. God's people were to worship Yahweh alone, and they were to live righteous lives in a just community. The Torah (God's law) touches on every aspect of life — including diet, sex, Sabbath rest, land distribution, and conflicts in the community. Israel's prophets called the people back to this all-embracing covenant, castigating them for their idolatry and for their injustice and immorality.

Jesus preached to a people who took for granted the connection between faith and politics. Israel had been taken over by the Roman Empire, and the Jews expected God to send a political messiah, like their great king David, who would conquer the Romans and reestablish the state of Israel. The Romans, like all conquerors and oppressors, had to watch their backs.

This is the context, for example, of the question that was put to Jesus by his adversaries, "Should we pay taxes to Caesar?" It was a seditious question. In responding, Jesus asked to see a coin that bore the image of Caesar. Then he said, "Render unto Caesar the things that are Caesar's, and unto God the things that are God's."[8] It is a clever answer because it is ambiguous and subject to interpretation. It is a prudent response because it keeps Jesus from being arrested for sedition, yet it is also prophetic, in that the Jewish faith would call a person to render everything, one's entire life, to God.

In the long run Jesus did not manage to avoid arrest. His teaching about the compassion, mercy, and nearness of God and his own messianic claims contradicted the legalism of the Jewish leaders and stirred their resentment. They decided that he was dangerous and had to be silenced. They had him arrested, convicted him in a kangaroo court of blasphemy under Jewish law, and then convinced Pilate, the Roman procurator, that Jesus was also a threat to Rome. The Romans tortured and executed him by crucifixion under the charge, "Jesus of Nazareth, King of the Jews." This is hardly a story devoid of politics, but it is also a story of faith that transcends politics.

Pope John Paul II directly addresses privatization in his 1988 apostolic exhortation in response to a Vatican Synod on the laity, *On the Vocation and the Mission of the Lay Faithful in the Church and in the Modern World (Christifideles Laici)*:

"There cannot be two parallel lives in [the laity's] existence: on the one hand, the so-called 'spiritual' life, with its values and demands; and on the other, the so-called 'secular' life, that is, life in a family, at work, in social relationships, in the responsibilities of public life and in culture. The branch, engrafted to the vine which is Christ, bears its fruit in every sphere of existence and activity. In fact, every area of the lay faithful's lives, as different as they are, enters into the plan of God, who desires that these very areas be the 'places in time' where the love of Christ is revealed and realized for both the glory of the Father and service of others. Every activity, every situation, every precise responsibility — as, for example, skill and solidarity in work, love, and dedication in the family and the education of children, service to society and public life and the promotion of truth in the area of culture — are the occasions ordained by Providence for a 'continuous exercise of faith, hope and charity.'" (#59)[9]

The Christian "Way" embraced all of life. The poetic first lines of *The Pastoral Constitution on the Church in the Modern World (Gaudium et Spes, 1965)* put it this way, "The joys and hopes, the griefs and the anxieties of the men of this age, especially those who are poor or in any way

afflicted, these too are the joys and hopes, griefs and anxieties of the followers of Christ. Indeed, nothing genuinely human fails to raise an echo in
their hearts" (#1).[10] Thus, the Second Vatican Council reversed the defensive
posture of the Catholic Church and brought it into a mutually transforming
dialogue with the modern world.

Faith is like salt in saltwater or light in a room; it permeates our existence,
influencing every decision and every act. Faith, then, is personal and public;
it is related to politics and public policy, as it is related to every aspect of
life. The question now becomes *how* is faith related to politics?

The Politicization of the Church

Politics, in its various forms, is universal. Whenever humans gather in
community of various types and sizes, there is a need for order and for
governance of some kind. Politics is inevitable; it is a feature of community. Religion is also universal and diverse. Our concern is the relationship
between the Christian community and the political order. This is a complex
relationship in history. The purpose of this section is to shed some light
on the current situation through a broad understanding of how the church
arrived at this place.

The early Christian community was persecuted by the Romans. This
reality obviously signals an uneasy relationship between Christians and
the "principalities and powers."[11] Paul, falsely hoping that his status as
a Roman citizen might protect him from martyrdom and realizing that
political authorities are necessary under God, counseled obedience and
accommodation in his Letter to the Romans (13:1–7). The apocalyptic vision
of the Book of Revelation, however, understandably envisions God crushing
the oppressive powers persecuting the church (Rv 13) and establishing a new
Jerusalem, a utopian rule (Rv 21). As is usually the case with the oppressed,
this sentiment had to be expressed in code, the symbolic language found in
Revelation.

After the conversion of the Roman Emperor Constantine in 313 C.E.,
Christianity was made the official religion of the Roman Empire by an edict
of the emperors Theodosius and Gratian in 380. In effect, the status of the
church changed from a persecuted sect to a power and principality itself.
Some argue that this was a fall from grace for the church, which caused
Christianity to compromise its ideals of humility, service, and nonviolence.
Others contend that this allowed Christian values to become profoundly
integrated into Western civilization, a graced opportunity indeed. Both
perspectives contain some truth.

There is no doubt, however, that the church succumbed too often to the
temptation of politicization, which might be symbolized by the scene of
Pope Leo III crowning Charlemagne as emperor of the Romans in 800. For
example, popes called for a series of crusades to reclaim the Holy Land, and

the church established the Inquisition, which tortured those suspected of heresy and sometimes executed them. The church itself became a warmonger and a persecutor. Not only did the pope, bishops, and priests influence princes and kings; they became rulers themselves, owning large estates, accompanying conquistadors (the cross and the sword), administering large plantations in the "new world," and commanding armies and governing the papal states in Italy. This politicization of the church resulted in debauchery, nepotism, corruption, exploitation, greed, and hunger for power. The spiritual and social mission of the church has often been eclipsed by greed and power.

This tragic story of the Christian church has to be balanced by the martyrs and saints (some of whom have been popes, bishops, and priests) and the ordinary faithful whose hospitality, kindness, service, and courage really have instilled gospel values into global culture. Nevertheless, we have to remember both St. Francis of Assisi (1182–1226), who inspired the church to recover the values of simplicity, service, and nonviolence, and Pope Innocent IV (papacy 1243–54), who approved of the use of torture in the Inquisition, raised nepotism to a high art, and erased the distinction between church revenues and personal income.[12] The church should celebrate the saints and repent for the sins.

John Courtney Murray
and the Contemporary Relationship
between Church and State

The first chapter noted that the church reacted against the revolutionary changes in the political order symbolized by the American and French revolutions in the late eighteenth century. It proved difficult for the church to let go of the Christendom of the Middle Ages, the time when the church oversaw both the spiritual and the temporal spheres. It is only with the papacy of Pope John XXIII and the legacy of the Council he called — the Second Vatican Council — that the church officially entered into a new relationship with the state. An American Jesuit, John Courtney Murray (1904–67), was a central figure in this transformation of the position of the Catholic Church.

Murray was a prototypical academic. He entered the Society of Jesus in 1920, when he was sixteen. After receiving his B.A. from Weston College and an M.A. from Boston College, he spent three years teaching English and literature at the Jesuit-run Ateneo de Manila in the Philippines. Murray was ordained in 1933, received his doctorate in theology from the Gregorian University in Rome in 1937, and returned to teach theology at Woodstock College in Maryland, where he would spend nearly his whole teaching career. He was the first priest to be a visiting professor at Yale University in 1951–52. He became editor of the journal *Theological Studies* in 1941 and was instrumental in its becoming the premier journal for Catholic theology in the United States. For a time he also served as an associate editor of the Jesuit magazine *America.*[13]

Like Thomas Aquinas, Murray led a life dedicated to learning and scholarship. Murray's ideas generated conflict and debate, and eventually they resulted in Vatican II's *Declaration on Religious Freedom (Dignitatis Humanae,* 1965), a milestone in Catholic political theology. During Murray's lifetime, Catholics were gradually assimilated into American culture, culminating in the election of John F. Kennedy as president in 1960. Murray constructed an intellectual framework, a Catholic public philosophy, that enabled Catholics to be unabashedly American.

In the 1940s Murray engaged in a lively debate with Fr. Paul Hanley Furfey in the pages of academic journals on the topic of intercredal cooperation, that is, whether Catholics could cooperate with Protestants in organizations aimed at social improvement, trade unions, and the like. Although this topic was transient, it gives a sense of the times, and it prepared Murray for the more substantial academic debate in the 1950s with Fr. Joseph Clifford Fenton, a professor at Catholic University and editor of *The American Ecclesiastical Review,* and his colleagues, Frs. Francis Connell and George Shea, on religious liberty and the relationship of the church and the state.[14]

Murray's opponents held to the official position of the church at the time: Since the Roman Catholic Church is the one true church, and since the state is under God, the state must worship God through the Roman Catholic Church. Therefore, it is ideal for the Catholic Church to be the established church in every state. Since error has no public rights, the state should ideally repress other religious beliefs and support those of the Catholic Church. In less than ideal circumstances (where Catholics are a minority, for example), the church can tolerate different arrangements in the interests of the common good, but the ideal remains.[15]

This position is obviously in tension with the first amendment of the U.S. Constitution, which guarantees the freedom of religious practice and prohibits the establishment of any religion.[16] Murray argued that the separation of church and state and religious liberty were both acceptable in Catholic thought. Predictably, Murray's position got him in trouble with the Vatican, but he was vindicated by the Second Vatican Council.

Murray's complex and sophisticated argument, developed over a decade (1945–55) and put forward in a series of articles primarily in *Theological Studies,* contains the following elements:[17]

1. On the basis of a Thomistic interpretation of natural law, Murray distinguished between the supernatural or spiritual order and the natural or temporal order. He maintained that the *sacred and the secular orders of life* should work in harmony with one another. They are united in the conscience of the individual who is both a Christian and a citizen. These are, however, two separate societies, a diarchy, and they should not be confused. The church has competency and authority in the spiritual, transcendent realm,

and the state must recognize and protect the freedom and autonomy of the church in spiritual matters.

2. Murray also distinguished between *society and the state*. The state is an agency with a limited role within society, and the state should have the freedom and autonomy to exercise its limited role. The church also has a role in society, but it is not to be identified with the state.

3. Murray further distinguished between the *common good and the public order*. The common good includes all the social goods — spiritual, moral, material — pursued by humanity. The common good is a goal of both the spiritual and secular realms, of the church, society, and the state. The public order, which includes public peace, public morality, and justice, is the purview of the state. Concern for public order can sometimes justify state intervention to limit religious freedom. For example, it can prohibit religiously motivated child sacrifice or polygamy. Otherwise, the state should protect religious freedom.

4. A right can be understood as an empowerment or an immunity, and Murray understood *religious liberty* to be a double immunity existing within civil society: no one can be forced to act against one's conscience in religious matters, and no one can be restrained from acting according to one's conscience. The right to religious freedom is limited only by a legitimate concern for public order. Liberty was Murray's passion, both religious freedom and civil liberties in general. "His was a single complex insight: the free person under a government of limited powers."[18] Thus Murray's thought is consonant with the human rights revolution in Catholic social thought that was accomplished by John XXIII's *Peace on Earth* and the Second Vatican Council and continued by John Paul II.

5. Murray brought to his argument and its defense a sense of *historical consciousness and the development of doctrine*. He distinguished between universal principles and their contingent, historical applications.[19] When his critics kept quoting Leo XIII and Robert Bellarmine in opposing him, Murray undertook a strenuous historical analysis of the issue in five articles published in *Theological Studies* from 1952 to 1954. He found the basis of the proper relationship between church and state in the teaching of Pope Gelasius I (494) and of John of Paris in the thirteenth century, who proposed two great societies, the religious and the civil, with different competencies and legitimate authority each in its proper sphere. He interpreted Leo XIII as doing his polemical best in his historical situation where the Catholic Church was confronted by continental liberalism and extreme individualism. Faced with atheistic secularism, which reduced the church's role to the realm of the private, Leo defended a confessional state (in other words, the establishment of a particular religion by the state) and denied religious freedom. However, Murray argued that (at that time) limited constitutional governments presented the church with a new challenge that required a different response. The Catholic tradition of two societies, religious and civil, guided this new response. There is no ideal state, and thus there is no universal or

ideal relationship between church and state. This relationship will change over time, guided by the universal principles of the priority of the spiritual over the temporal, and the church's freedom to exercise its salvific role.[20]

In 1955 the Vatican prohibited Murray from further publication on the issue of church and state just as his sixth article carefully interpreting Leo XIII was set to be published in *Theological Studies*. He accepted his silencing in the conviction that truth would win out and turned his attention to an analysis of American culture and the American proposition of pluralist democracy. In 1960, in the run-up to the election of John F. Kennedy, Murray published a collection of essays on these topics titled *We Hold These Truths: Catholic Reflections on the American Proposition;*[21] the book garnered considerable positive attention, including a cover story in *Time* magazine (December 12, 1960).

Murray was conspicuously not invited to the first session of the Second Vatican Council in 1962, but Cardinal Spellman of New York included him in the second session of the Council in 1963 as his personal theologian. Murray later became an official theological *peritus* (expert), one of a number of *periti* who had previously been silenced by the church, and he co-authored, with Fr. Pietro Pavan, the various versions of the *Declaration on Religious Freedom,* which was officially approved by the Council on December 7, 1965.[22]

The Declaration on Religious Freedom basically affirmed Murray's position on religious liberty and the separation of church and state. This was a radical departure from Leo XIII's insistence on a confessional state and the denial of religious freedom. Indeed, it was this realization that religious freedom represented an apparent reversal of church teaching, that is, the idea of the development of doctrine, which was perhaps the most controversial aspect of the document.[23] Murray's painstaking and brilliant work on the history of church-state relations and on the teaching of Leo XIII served him well in this regard. Murray stated that a task of theology "is to discern the 'growing end' of the tradition; it is normally indicated by the new question that is taking shape under the impact of the historical movement of events and ideas."[24] In Murray's hands the "growing end" of the Catholic understanding of church-state relations and religious freedom flourished.

Murray's articulation of the necessity for religious freedom and for a relationship between church and state appropriate for the modern world, and his understanding (along with many of his theological contemporaries) of the development of doctrine and historical consciousness are enough to solidify his position as the most significant American Catholic theologian of the twentieth century. Murray, however, made another major contribution to American Catholic public theology. On the basis of natural law, Murray argued that the American proposition of a constitutional, democratic state with a limited government centered on protecting human rights and public order was fully consistent with Catholic social thought. He also used natural law and Catholic thought to critique American culture.[25]

Murray claimed that natural law is the only way to defend Western constitutionalism and pluralistic democracy. He may have overreached here, but his argument certainly affirms that one can be Catholic and American. Murray further argued that human rights are derived from natural law. He quite consciously developed a public *philosophy*, based on natural law and reason, rather than a public *theology* that incorporated revelation or Christian symbols in public dialogue. Murray believed that reason is the only language allowed in public discourse because of the pluralism of the public forum.[26] This is a controversial position today, but it continues to have adherents, such as Fr. J. Bryan Hehir, who is one of Murray's many theological beneficiaries.[27]

On the basis of natural law and what he called an "incarnational humanism," Murray highlighted common values that provide a shared meaning in a pluralistic context. Murray saw three threats to these shared values and thus to the American proposition of pluralistic democracy: (1) technological secularism, which excludes values from public discourse; (2) practical materialism, which locates human happiness in consumerism; and (3) philosophical relativism, which contends that there is no objective truth and all ideas are equal in value.[28] Active respect for the shared values of human dignity, freedom, and human rights can shield against these threats.

Murray suffered a series of heart attacks in the last years of his life. He died on August 16, 1967, in a New York taxi, less than two years after the close of the Council. During that time as his health permitted he had given presentations and published articles commenting on and defending the *Declaration on Religious Freedom*. Several times in his life he had been hospitalized for exhaustion. He was only sixty-three when his heart finally gave out.

In 1955, the year he was silenced by the Vatican, Murray received from St. Louis University the first of several honorary degrees. At Fordham University, Murray-Weigel Hall is named in honor of Murray and his Jesuit friend and colleague, Gustave Weigel. The Catholic Theological Society of America has named a prestigious award for contributions to theology after John Courtney Murray. This American Jesuit is further honored in that his thought is a touchstone for contemporary Catholic political theology. His ideas continue to be critically discussed, and theologians across the liberal-conservative spectrum consciously claim to be the heirs of Murray. Due in large part to the scholarship of Murray, the Catholic Church turned its back on a history of politicization and coercion (Christendom, crusades, conquest, and inquisitions) and embraced religious freedom.[29] As a result Catholics can be proudly (but critically) American.

There are a number of critiques of the subtleties of Murray's thought; Murray was an important voice, but hardly the last word.[30] What I find lacking in Murray is a more active engagement with the overwhelming civil liberties issue of his day — race relations. Today Murray's focus seems too parochial. He speaks out about the constitutionality and justice of state aid for Catholic schools, but he is silent on the civil rights movement. Given the signs of his times (the Montgomery bus boycott was in 1955, and Martin Luther King Jr. was assassinated less than a year after Murray's death), it seems strange that a man with a passion for freedom and civil liberties would not add his powerful voice to the cause of black freedom in America.

The Church and the World:
The Social Mission of the Church

The *Declaration on Religious Freedom* was part of the revolutionary turning of the church toward the modern world that was engineered by Pope John XXIII and implemented by his successor Paul VI. Pope John accomplished this through two social encyclicals and the Second Vatican Council. When we remember that John XXIII was pope for only four and a half years (October 28, 1958–June 3, 1963), we see how truly revolutionary this was. In less than a decade the Catholic Church underwent a metamorphosis from a reactionary, insular, conservative institution to a progressive pilgrim people of God in constructive dialogue with all aspects of the modern world. This is warp speed in church time, and it is no wonder that the change left many Catholics reeling.

Christianity and Social Progress

Pope John's first social encyclical, *Christianity and Social Progress (Mater et Magistra)*, commemorated the seventieth anniversary of Leo XIII's *On the Condition of Labor (Rerum Novarum, 1891)*. Although dated May 15, it was released on July 15, 1961. Much of its content focused on economic issues, which is the subject of the next chapter. Both its context and its tone, however, are relevant to the relationship of faith and politics.

Angelo Roncalli's formation in the faith and his diverse ministry as a priest and bishop prepared him to turn the church toward the world.[31] Angelo was the fourth of thirteen children born (in 1881) to a peasant farmer in a village in the diocese of Bergamo in northern Italy. The local bishop had launched a campaign of social action in response to Leo XIII's *On the Condition of Labor,* and Angelo's great-uncle participated in it. Angelo was formed in a family and faith community that realized the social dimension of the gospel.

After ordination in Rome he returned to serve as secretary to a new bishop of Bergamo, Radini Tedeschi, who believed that Christ had a preference for the marginalized and the oppressed. Fr. Angelo served as a hospital orderly and a chaplain in World War I, an experience that hammered home the evil of war. Roncalli was then posted as a papal diplomatic representative first in Bulgaria (1925–34) and then Turkey and Greece (1934–44), where he became schooled in both interfaith and ecumenical relations. He was then sent to France as a papal ambassador (1944–53). There he encountered the worker-priest movement, in which priests ministered by working alongside of laborers, and Pax Christi, a Catholic peace organization. Bishop Angelo briefly served as the Vatican observer to UNESCO, the social arm of the United Nations.

In 1953 Archbishop Roncalli was appointed the patriarch of Venice and made a cardinal. Given his formation in the faith and his diverse ministry, it is not surprising that in his first radio broadcast a day after being elected pope (October 29, 1958), he identified the two major concerns of his papacy as the unity of the Christian church and peace in the world.[32] John's two social encyclicals flowed out of his personal experiences and formation.

As pope, John steered the Catholic Church into a new relationship with the Italian state. He disentangled the church from direct involvement with party politics and promoted a reserved collaboration with the government that was focused more on the common good and human rights than party politics. In doing so Pope John rebuffed the position of some of the cardinals in the Vatican bureaucracy under whose leadership the church had habitually interfered in Italian politics. In changing the relationship between the Vatican and the Italian state from indirect control to collaboration for the common good, John anticipated Vatican II's *Declaration on Religious Freedom*. This was the local context of Pope John's first encyclical.[33]

Christianity and Social Progress was the first step in implementing John XXIII's vision of opening the church to the modern world. He had taken the curia (Vatican bureaucracy) and the world by surprise in announcing his intention to convene a council in 1959. Now he produced a document that was modern, accessible, open and optimistic in tone, and inductive in methodology.[34] Although Pope John established continuity with his predecessor Leo XIII, he also innovatively addressed the social questions of the day. He was factual in his appraisal of scientific and technological developments, new social and economic realities, and the radical changes in post-war politics, but he was not defensive or pessimistic. He did not dwell on the negative or what was wrong with the world, but pointed to human progress and the hope for further achievement.[35] In this encyclical Pope John planted the seed of openness to and dialogue with the modern world that would come to fruition at Vatican II.

Especially in the fourth part of the encyclical (#212–265) there are several themes that would receive further development at Vatican II and beyond:[36]

◆ Human dignity and its realization in community are the twin foundations of Catholic social teaching (#219). These two principles would be the theme of the first two chapters of part 1 of *The Pastoral Constitution on the Church in the Modern World*.

◆ Action on behalf of justice is essential, and it is the most effective way to *teach* the social dimension of faith (#231, 232). "In other words, Pope John emphasized that the Christian is not only educated *for* action but *by* action."[37] Service and advocacy are essential for internalizing the social gospel, and such witness will move others in the same direction.

- Pope John emphasized the "noble task" of the *laity* in translating the church's social teaching into action (#241). He stressed that Catholic social doctrine is an integral part of the Christian message (#222) and essential to living a good Christian life. John XXIII renounced privatization and a spirituality of detachment and replaced it with a *spirituality of engagement* that called on Christians to transform the world.

- Finally, Pope John recommended the three-step method developed by Cardinal Cardijn of *see, judge, act* as a way of implementing the church's social teaching in society (#236). This method of social analysis and action would be further developed in papal social teaching and in liberation theology.

Thus *Christianity and Social Progress* set the tone for Vatican II to emphasize Christian humanism and the church's dialogue with the world.

Peace on Earth

John XXIII's second social encyclical, *Peace on Earth* (*Pacem in Terris*), was issued on April 11, 1963, in between the first and second sessions of the Council and just two months before John died. It continued the accessible, personalist, and optimistic tone of *Christianity and Social Progress*, and it was also a precursor for some of the themes developed by Vatican II and in later Catholic social thought. For example, it recognized religious freedom, a pluralism of forms of government, and a distinction between state and society — all themes developed by John Courtney Murray and integrated into the *Declaration on Religious Freedom*. The fifth and final part of *Peace on Earth* continues the themes noted above by urging the participation of informed and professionally competent Catholics in public life, and by allowing Catholics to cooperate with non-Catholics in social and economic affairs.[38]

Taken together, *Peace on Earth* and Vatican II's *Pastoral Constitution on the Church in the Modern World* are the fullest treatment of political morality in modern Catholic social teaching. Pope John's *Peace on Earth* develops a distinctively Catholic approach to peacemaking and international relations, which calls for the protection and promotion of the full spectrum of human rights, at every level of social and political life, as the foundation of peace and the specific purpose of all governments. John made human rights the backbone of political morality in church teaching. This constructive shift in Catholic teaching has had the effect of putting the Catholic

Church and Catholics on the front lines of the struggle for justice through-out the world. "For following the publication of this encyclical, Catholics in Chile, South Africa, South Korea, Poland, Guatemala, El Salvador, the Philippines, Mexico, East Timor, and elsewhere marched at the forefront of human rights movements."[39] Indeed Nobel laureates such as Adolfo Perez Esquivel in Argentina, Lech Walesa in Poland, Kim Dae Jung in South Korea, Mairead Corrigan Maguire in Northern Ireland, and Felipe Ximenes Belo in East Timor are part of the legacy of Pope John and *Peace on Earth*.

Vatican II's Pastoral Constitution on the Church in the Modern World

The first part of *The Pastoral Constitution on the Church in the Modern World* (*Gaudium et Spes,* 1965), which consists of four chapters, provides the theological basis for Christian humanism and for a faith that is engaged with the world. The first two chapters address the twin foundations of Catholic social teaching, human dignity (#12–22) that is realized in com-munity (#23–32). The third chapter (#33–39) underscores the humanism of the document's opening lines (quoted above), and the fourth chapter (#40–45) discusses the interaction of the church and society, highlighting a mutually enriching dialogue. *The Pastoral Constitution* says that "the split between the faith that many profess and their daily lives deserves to be counted among the more serious errors of our age" (#43).

The second part (five chapters) addresses specific áreas of some urgency — marriage and family, culture, economic issues, politics, and peace and inter-national relations. The fourth chapter (#73–76) on political life is our concern in this chapter. *The Pastoral Constitution* echoes the themes of the *Declaration on Religious Freedom*. Political authority is rooted in the social nature of human beings and thus is under the authority of God the creator (#74). There can be a pluralism of forms of government, and the government should protect the rights of people to participate in society (an affirmation of democracy) and enjoy religious freedom. "In their proper spheres, the political community and the Church are mutually independent and self-governing" (#76). Both are commissioned to serve the common good and to foster human flourishing.

The *Pastoral Constitution* made two notable contributions to Catholic social teaching. This document in particular, but the Second Vatican Coun-cil as a whole, introduced a *new methodology or approach to Catholic social ethics*. Previous social teaching was rooted almost exclusively in a deduc-tive, natural law approach. The *Pastoral Constitution* is more inductive and directly theological. It begins with a term used by Pope John, the "signs of the times," that is, a realistic analysis of what is going on. In respond-ing to the "signs of the times," it is more biblical and christological, as well as philosophical. The Council brings the gospel and faith in Christ to bear on what is actually happening in the world. This is a more historically conscious approach that takes human experience seriously, and it is more properly theological. The approach is both natural law and revelation, both reason and faith. This is an important corrective for a teaching that had been too abstract and overly philosophical.[40]

Second, *The Pastoral Constitution on the Church in the Modern World* was key to accomplishing the dialogue between the church and the modern world that was the vision of Pope John in calling the Council. The relationship between the church and the world is neither oppositional (Christ against culture) nor one of identity (Christ above culture). Rather it is a *relationship of mutual interaction and dialogue* (Christ transforming culture) in which the church listens to and learns from society and also speaks to, criticizes, and changes society.[41] The church's mode of operation in society is now more collaborative than controlling. The church is like yeast, leavening society and raising it toward the kingdom of God. This begins a new chapter in the history of the Catholic Church.

Paul VI and A Call to Action

In 1967, Paul VI published his encyclical *On the Development of Peoples* (*Populorum Progressio*) on economic justice, the topic of the next chapter. To commemorate the eightieth anniversary of Leo XIII's *The Condition of Labor* in 1971, he published an apostolic letter addressed to Cardinal Maurice Roy, president of the Pontifical Commission for Justice and Peace, titled *A Call to Action* (*Octogesima Adveniens*).[42] There were some minor advances in *A Call to Action,* including one of the first acknowledgments of environmental problems, attention to urbanization, recognition of varieties of socialism, and an emphasis on action as a requirement of faith. This brief document, however, achieved three major innovations regarding faith and politics.[43]

First, Paul VI, in contrast to his predecessors, asserted that the *local church has the primary responsibility* for assessing social injustice in light of the gospel and the teaching of the church, and for working to remedy it. It is not the role of the pope to put forth universal answers for complex, specific problems (#4). Pope Paul's disclaimer regarding papal authority and power was consistent with the collegiality and the historical consciousness confirmed by Vatican II.

Second, Paul VI affirmed that contemporary aspirations for *equality* and for *participation* are rooted in human nature itself, and he added these to the list of human rights that have become so basic to Catholic social teaching (#22). Although it took the church a long time to recognize the innate equality of all human beings, it finally did so. As with the first point, Paul's affirmation of human equality was in contrast to the social hierarchy accepted by his predecessors. Paul's emphasis on participation, that is, shared responsibility for decision making and for creating justice in every aspect of life, was just as compelling. It was an endorsement of democracy in politics and of the empowerment of the poor.

Finally, Pope Paul *shifted the emphasis from economics to politics* in the struggle for justice (#46). The pope clearly recognized that poverty is a matter of structural injustice and that changing structures and systems involves politics and the intervention of the state and of international authorities. Christians need to use political power to achieve the common good.

John Paul II: Unimplemented Innovations

Pope John Paul II (papacy, 1978–2005) clearly confirmed and clarified this last point: the need for structural change and for political involvement to accomplish it. The innovative approach of *A Call to Action* regarding collegiality, equality, and participation, however, failed to take root. "It has had a very limited impact on the way the official Church acts either internally or externally in the world, and has effectively become a dead letter in the domain of the hierarchy."[44] One reason for this has been the reinterpretation and resistance of John Paul II, but the seeds of ambiguity regarding an implementation of a historically conscious understanding of Catholic social teaching were sown by Paul VI himself, and they were present in the Council as well.

There is no denying that John Paul II took dramatic stands on behalf of human rights, promoted social justice, castigated a consumerist society, and affirmed and developed the central principles of Catholic social teaching. He hardly turned his back on the social tradition of the church. His reputation as an advocate for the poor and oppressed and as a peacemaker is well deserved.

The project of John Paul's papacy, however, in some ways seemed out of tune with the spirit of Vatican II and the direction set by John XXIII and Paul VI. The collegiality called for by Vatican II and practiced by conferences of bishops in the years after the Council was reined in and replaced by a centralization of authority in the pope and the Vatican. The spirit of dialogue with other Christian churches and other faiths and with the world was trumped by an assertion of the truth of the Catholic Church and of the absolute, universal principles taught by it. Even within the church dialogue yielded to silencing and removing theologians who dared to seek truth beyond the church's official teaching, the reprimanding of bishops who questioned the party line, and the appointment of bishops and other authorities on the basis of their loyalty to Rome and its teaching.[45]

Paul VI had maintained that Catholic social teaching was historically constructed and that local Christian communities could contribute to its ongoing development by creatively and faithfully responding to new and complex situations (*Call to Action*, #4). John Paul II, in contrast, stressed the continuity of Catholic social *doctrine* (not teaching)[46] and its universal principles, taught consistently by the *magisterium,* and simply applied by the laity to new situations.[47] John Paul II's few references to paragraph 4 in *A Call to Action* amount to a distortion of the meaning of the text and at least an unconscious shift from its historically conscious methodology.[48]

With regard to the church and the world, a shift took place during the papacy of John Paul II "from an ecclesiology which saw the Church as a pilgrim people in the world to an ecclesiology of the Church as the guardian of truth which it dispenses to the world"; the shift was from historically contextualized methodologies to "theologies built on ahistorical truths, universally valid principles, and a suspicion of the material, historical world."[49] This shift further undermined Paul VI's emphasis on participation by halting its application to the church itself and hindering its application in the world through a suspicion of the effectiveness of democracy as a way of arriving at the truth already possessed by the church.[50]

The seeds of this failure to implement the innovations indicated in *A Call to Action,* however, can be found in the document itself and in the compromises that took place at the Council that resulted in ambiguities. Paul VI called for participation in every aspect of the world, but not in the church itself. "There can be no question of a contradiction between asserting that participation in decision making in economic, social, and political affairs is a requirement of human dignity, and that the exclusion of the laity from decision making within the Church is ongoing."[51]

Because the entire work of the Council involved a series of compromises between divergent understandings of human nature and the church, this contradiction runs through Vatican II itself. Paul VI saw his role as assuring the unity of the church, and thus he intervened in places during the Council to engineer compromises that resulted in near consensus acceptance of the Vatican II documents. This was both an achievement and a liability. "If in Vatican II the Church opened its door to historicity, Paul nevertheless attempted to preserve some small space for stasis."[52] Even during the Council, Karol Wojtyla, archbishop of Krakow in Poland, offered interventions during the discussion of the *Declaration on Religious Freedom* that emphasized truth over freedom, and when he became pope this was a consistent theme.[53] The gulf between participation in the world and in the church widened under John Paul II, but it began with Vatican II and Paul VI himself.[54]

A similar contradiction can be seen in Paul VI's application of equality to women "to participate in cultural, economic, social and political life" with his understanding of "woman's proper role...at the heart of the family as well as within society" (#13), and the exclusion of women from leadership roles and decision making within the church.[55] This incomprehensible gap between the vision of *A Call to Action* and its implementation within the church leaves the post-Vatican II Catholic in an ambiguous, even untenable, place.

Justice in the World

A Call to Action was published in May of 1971. In the fall of the same year a Synod of Bishops[56] met in Rome to address two topics, the ministerial priesthood and the role of the church in working for justice. On December 7, 1971, this synod published in its own name the fruits of its discussion on the latter topic, *Justice in the World (Justitia in Mundo)*. Most of the 190 bishops at the synod had been elected to represent their local episcopal conferences, and more than half were from developing countries. Thus the synod was truly global, reflecting the influence of the "third world."[57] Although brief and schematic, *Justice in the World* was a powerful statement regarding the importance of action for justice in the mission of the church, and it made at least four important contributions to Catholic social teaching.

The document has an introduction and four chapters.[58] In the introduction *Justice in the World* makes its first important contribution by proclaiming *the essential connection between Christian faith and justice,* and in the second chapter by developing *the biblical and theological basis for the social mission of the Church.* The introduction ends with these oft-quoted words: "Action on behalf of justice and participation in the transformation of the world fully appear to us as a constitutive dimension of the preaching of the gospel, or, in other words, of the Church's mission for the redemption of the human race and its liberation from every oppressive situation" (289). Although the term "constitutive" was not controversial during the synod, its exact meaning became a topic of discussion in the years following the release of *Justice in the World*.[59] In the end, it is clear that the term signals an intimate connection between justice and the gospel, one that is far more than a moral implication, but is instead at the core of the gospel. The social mission of the church is neither peripheral nor optional; it is central to the identity, vocation, and the work of the church.[60]

The second chapter of the document provides an outline of the theological basis of the connection between faith and justice. "The Church's mission on behalf of justice is ultimately grounded in the nature of God as disclosed in the Hebrew Scriptures ['the liberator of the oppressed and the defender of the poor' (293)] and in the actions and teachings of Jesus as recounted in the Christian Scriptures."[61] Jesus inseparably linked love of God and love of neighbor, especially love of the least of these (Mt 25:40). The bishops conclude, "Christian love of neighbor and justice cannot be separated. For love implies an absolute demand for justice, namely a recognition of the dignity and rights of one's neighbor. Justice attains its inner fullness only in love" (293).

The bishops are tapping the roots of Catholic moral theology here. Moral action and good works, like worship, are motivated by gratitude for God's mercy and love; righteousness and justice are responses of the beloved to the lover. Justice is the minimum measure of love of neighbor. Action on behalf of justice and the effort to transform the world toward the kingdom of God are essential to Christian discipleship.

Second, *Justice in the World* insists that *the church itself must be just.* "While the Church is bound to give witness to justice, she recognizes that anyone who ventures to speak to people about justice must first be just in their eyes. Hence we must undertake an examination of the modes of acting and of the possessions and life-style found within the Church itself" (295). The church should respect human rights, including fair wages, suitable freedom of expression, the right to participate, the rights of women, and judicial rights (295). In order to credibly proclaim the gospel to the poor and to the rich, the church should exercise a "sparingness" in its consumption and use of material possessions (295). The lifestyle of all disciples, from bishop to layperson, should be a witness to the gospel.

The influence of the Medellín meeting of the Latin American Bishops' Conference (CELAM) in 1968 can be seen here. Many clergy and religious in Latin America were now living with the poor and sharing in their suffering and powerlessness. It must be said, however, that the church still struggles mightily with being a credible witness to justice, human rights, and voluntary poverty. The church's exclusion of women from leadership and decision-making positions is, for example, one glaring counterwitness. Nevertheless, it was refreshing to see the synod address the issue of internal justice.

Third, the synod bishops affirm the existence of a "right to development" (290). The first chapter of the document is a reading of the signs of the times and suggested responses. The bishops note the paradox of the greater unity of a global village and an increasing division between the rich and the poor. Respect for human rights is the key to the flourishing of the human family. The right to development is not simply an addition to the list of human rights but a kind of integration of the interlocking constellation of economic rights — food, shelter, clean water, health care, education, adequately paid employment — necessary for justice. The bishops are clear that social sin has created structural injustice, and justice demands structural transformation, which requires political involvement. They also insist that the poor and developing countries must participate in their own development (291). Indeed, overcoming marginalization through participation is the essence of the right to development.[62]

Finally, the third chapter of the document sketches specific *strategies for acting on behalf of justice.* The bishops call for new methods of education for justice that yield not only information but the transformation of persons, who then work to change society (296). Their suggestions have an affinity with the "conscientization" or consciousness-raising methods developed by Paulo Freire in Latin America and adapted by liberation theology.[63] The synod document calls for cooperation between rich and poor parishes and dioceses as a way to redistribute wealth and resources (297), and for ecumenical and interfaith collaboration, both in working for justice and in studying the social implications of the gospel (297–98).

Furthermore, the practice of justice requires international action, and the synod offered eight specific recommendations: (1) support for human rights, (2) the constructive participation of all nations in the United Nations, (3) concrete steps toward economic development (such as today's Millennium Development Goals), (4) fostering inclusive decision making and equal participation of all nations in international organizations related to development and trade, (5) just and multilateral aid, (6) reduced consumption by the rich in light of poverty and environmental destruction, (7) respect for cultural diversity, and (8) the right to participate in society and decision making (298–99).

Justice in the World ends with a word of hope based in the eschatological idea that humanity is cooperating with God by working for a society that is more just and peaceful. "It is not that all must be done by dint of human action; it is enough that human action for justice provides the soil for the coming reign of God 'to take root' in human hearts."[64] This synod document, along with the documents by John XXIII, the Second Vatican Council, and Paul VI, stimulated a surge of interest in matters of global justice in church circles and a rise in personal commitment to action for justice. This is its lasting legacy.[65]

Paul VI's Evangelization in the Modern World

In 1975, Paul VI published an apostolic exhortation titled *On Evangelization in the Modern World* (*Evangelii Nuntiandi*) in response to the 1974 Synod of Bishops on the theme of evangelization. This document has also been widely influential, perhaps even more significant than Vatican II's *Decree on the Missionary Activity of the Church* (*Ad Gentes*).[66]

In his apostolic exhortation, Paul VI returned to the question of the relationship between liberation and evangelization raised above. His goal was to avoid the two extremes of (1) reducing the mission of the church to liberation and (2) of unduly separating the spiritual redemption proclaimed by the church from the social justice aspects of that proclamation.[67] The relationship between liberation and evangelization was being debated in light of the rising influence of Latin American liberation theology,[68] and in light of *Justice in the World*'s affirmation that action on behalf of justice is a "constitutive dimension of preaching the gospel."

In his discussion of this question (chapter 3, #25–39), Paul VI achieved the remarkable balance that characterizes Catholic social teaching at its best. There are profound links between evangelization and human advancement — in the anthropological order "because the [person] who is to be evangelised in not an abstract being but is subject to social and economic questions," and in the theological order "since one cannot dissociate the plan of creation from the plan of redemption" (#31). "The Church...has the duty to proclaim the liberation of millions of human beings, many of whom are her own children — the duty of assisting the birth of this liberation, of giving witness to it, of ensuring that it is complete. This is not foreign to evangelization" (#30). "Nevertheless she reaffirms the primacy of her spiritual vocation and refuses to replace the proclamation of the kingdom by the proclamation of forms of human liberation; she even states that her contribution to liberation is incomplete if she neglects to proclaim salvation in Jesus Christ" (#34). The church calls for both personal conversion and social transformation.[69]

> The church considers it to be undoubtedly important to build up structures which are more human, more just, more respectful of the rights of the person and less oppressive and less enslaving, but she is conscious that the best structures and the most idealized systems soon become inhuman if the inhuman inclinations of the human heart are not made wholesome, if those who live in these structures or who rule them do not undergo a conversion of heart and outlook (#36).

Even as Christians work to change the social structures that oppress human beings, they are aware that no social system will ever be the kingdom of God. Christians minister to the whole person, doing both the corporal works of mercy and the spiritual works of mercy. Human dignity is the link between liberation and evangelization.[70]

Benedict XVI: Charity Is Constitutive of the Church's Mission

These documents published during the papacy of Paul VI integrate action for justice into the mission of the church in a careful but clear way. The first encyclical of Pope Benedict XVI, *On Christian Love* (*Deus Caritas Est,* released Christmas 2005) upends this hard-won, balanced integration by making charity, not justice, constitutive of the church's mission.[71]

Benedict is the first to use the term "constitutive" in an official church document since the Synod of Bishops famously did so in 1971 in *Justice in the World*. He uses it twice in paragraph 20, but to refer to the ministry of service or charity (*diakonia*), which was one of three essential characteristics of the early church, along with proclaiming the word of God (*kerygma-martyria*) and celebrating the sacraments (*leitourgia*) (see also #25a). Benedict summarizes his point: "For the Church, charity is not a kind of welfare activity which could equally well be left to others, but is a part of her nature, an indispensable expression of her very being" (#25a).

Following Augustine and Vatican II, Benedict distinguishes between the church and the state, two distinct spheres that are always interrelated (#28a).

> The just ordering of society and the State is a central responsibility of politics.... The church cannot and must not take upon herself the political battle to bring about the most just society possible. She cannot

and must not replace the State. Yet at the same time she cannot and must not remain on the sidelines in the fight for justice. She has to play her part through rational argument and she has to reawaken the spiritual energy without which justice, which always demands sacrifice, cannot prevail and prosper. A just society must be the achievement of politics, not the Church. (#28a)

Whereas charity is the proper task of the church, "the direct duty to work for a just ordering of society, on the other hand, is proper to the lay faithful" (#29). It is the laity then who keep the church in the battle for justice.

In paragraph 27, Pope Benedict acknowledges in a general way that Catholic social teaching has developed over time. Then he proceeds to substitute charity for justice as constitutive of the mission and identity of the church (surely it is both charity and justice), and to divide the people of God into the church and the laity. Of course the laity have an important role to play as faithful citizens, but bishops are citizens as well. As official spokesmen for the church, bishops have a responsibility to directly address the state on issues of morality and justice. The U.S. Catholic bishops, through the United States Conference of Catholic Bishops (USCCB), have fulfilled this role well in the past through their pastoral letters on nuclear ethics (1983) and economic justice (1986) and many other statements. Pope John Paul II also exercised this responsibility behind the scenes in regard to the liberation of Poland and Eastern Europe.

The USCCB had already taken this shift in its guide to the 2008 election issues. Quoting Benedict XVI's encyclical *On Christian Love* (#28), the bishops distinguish between their role to teach, guide, and encourage the laity, and the laity's role of direct engagement in political life. Indeed, they title the document *Forming Consciences for Faithful Citizenship*. Perhaps one of the best ways for bishops to help form consciences is to lead by example. As we have seen, the relationship between faith and politics and church and state is a complex and controversial area. It seems to me, however, that Pope Benedict has drawn a new line and in the wrong place.[72] Paul VI articulated a more faithful balance in his position. Justice and love are intrinsically related to one another, and both are the essential responsibility of the whole church.

Values and Principles That Guide
the Church's Approach to Public Policy

Given the development in Catholic social teaching that began with Pope John XXIII, it is now possible to outline the values that comprise a Catholic vision of social, political, and economic life. These seven principles are so interrelated with one another that they should be viewed as a cluster or a cohort rather than a list. They often reflect the balance (both/and, rather than either/or) that is deeply characteristic of the Catholic vision.

1. Human Dignity, Realized in Community

As noted above, the twin foundations of Catholic social teaching are human dignity and the social nature of humanity.[73] Human beings are sacred and social. Human dignity and the call to community are rooted in both reason and revelation.

Observation and reflection on human nature can result in an appreciation of the dignity of the person. Although other creatures can be amazing, it seems that it is only humans who are capable of the kind of amazement at the workings of nature of someone like Sir David Attenborough (who has produced nature programs for the BBC for years) or someone like Charles Darwin, who can observe nature and discover the process of evolution. Humans create complex cultures and can compare them. Through science humans have gradually come to an understanding of the world, and through technology they have begun to transform it. Humanity is capable of appreciating beauty, of doing good, but also of creating destruction and experiencing depravity. Each person is unique and unrepeatable. Humans enter into relationships and mourn the death of loved ones. These observations and many others point to the value and worth of human beings.

The biblical concept of human dignity, however, is not based only on the sense of the self, rationality, or other human quality, but on humanity's relationship with God. It is theocentric. The person is created by God, in the image of God, for relationship with God, called by God, accepted by God, redeemed by God. This human dignity is not earned, but a gift of creation. It is thus inalienable; it cannot be taken away. Persons are ends in themselves, not a means to some end or purpose.[74] Each and every human being has tremendous worth and value and should be treated with great respect. Every human person has an *equal* dignity. Appreciation and respect for human dignity is the basis for the church's social teaching.

Human beings are innately social. Humans are born dependent on others for survival, and we remain interdependent throughout our lives. Not only are we in each other's debt; we find ourselves fulfilled and happy in relationship with one another.

God entered into a covenant with a certain people and called them to create a just community where the widow, the orphan, and the stranger — the marginalized and vulnerable — would be protected. "This communitarian character is developed and consummated in the work of Jesus Christ."[75] Jesus called a community of disciples to follow him, and his message and ministry also focused on the poor and marginalized (see Mk 2:13–17). Jesus defined our relationship with God in terms of our relationship with each other. Love of God and love of neighbor are two sides of the same coin.

This call to create a just and nurturing community is also a basis of Catholic social teaching. From these twin foundations — human dignity, realized in community — flow the other values that comprise the Catholic vision of a good society.

2. The Common Good

As we have seen, Catholic social teaching holds that the common good is the goal and purpose of society and the state and an abiding concern of the church. The concept of the common good incorporates the values of human dignity and of community. John XXIII described it as "the sum total of conditions of social living, whereby persons are enabled more fully and readily to achieve their own perfection,"[76] and he later states that it is "chiefly guaranteed when personal rights and duties are maintained."[77] Thus respect for *human rights* becomes a criterion for honoring the common good.

The idea of the common good is that the good of each person is bound up with the good of the community; all are responsible for all.[78] The Catholic Bishops' Conference of England and Wales describes the common good as "the whole network of social conditions which enable human individuals and groups to flourish and live a fully, genuinely human life."[79] Human flourishing is connected to the health of the community and the creation of a good society. All persons should share in this social reality through their *participation* in it, contributing to the community and reaching their full potential through it.[80] The common good is neither simply an aggregate sum as in utilitarianism (the greatest good for the greatest number), which can be blind to the well-being of individuals and minority groups, nor a disaggregate as in individualism, which de-links personal flourishing from the health of the community or from a good society. Human flourishing and the quality of common life are linked by the common good.[81] In the contemporary world, which is increasingly interdependent, the common good has a global dimension.

Jimmy Carter, former U.S. president, Nobel Peace Prize recipient, and a model of a healthy relationship between faith and politics, gives a clear illustration of the common good in describing how an encounter with a young woman afflicted with guinea worm disease transformed his perspective and his work for justice.[82] Carter tells of visiting a village in Ghana with his wife, Rosalyn, in 1988. As they approached a small cluster of villagers, a young woman appeared to be in excruciating pain. It looked as if she were cradling a baby in her right arm, but closer inspection showed it to be her grossly swollen right breast from which a guinea worm was emerging through her nipple, causing her fiery pain as it migrated through her body. Carter later discovered that this was the eleventh worm to infect the young woman that season, and that she was one of two hundred in her village of five hundred afflicted with guinea worms. "Villagers of all ages were too weak to walk or permanently scarred and crippled. As a result, a community would go hungry because its farmers were too sick to work in the fields."

Carter explains that before this encounter and as president he had tended to see global matters in a macro way, focusing abstractly on world leaders and international politics. "Having seen her that day in 1988, I came to examine life differently — in a micro way. I now believe that the vitality of one person's life has an impact on the health and harmony of the surrounding world." In response, the Carter Center, along with other organizations such as the World Health Organization, UNICEF, the Centers for Disease Control and Prevention, and the Peace Corps, working with the villagers themselves, have nearly eradicated guinea worm disease worldwide. As a result more people and their communities are healthy and flourishing. This is what it means to work for the common good.

3. Participation

Participation is key to the realization of the common good. "The person is called to participate in shaping society in such a way as to promote the well-being of its members, and it is in this act of participation that the essential dignity of the person is both achieved and realized."[83] To a great extent the goal of respect for human rights is to allow and enable persons to participate in the community, create a good society, and thus to flourish as human beings.

Civil rights, such as freedom of speech, of the press, of assembly, and so on, allow persons to participate in the public policy decisions that shape society. Social and economic rights, such as education, work, and health care, enable persons to contribute to the common good and to realize their human potential. Freedom of conscience and freedom of religion enable a person to respond to the transcendent dimension of human life. Participation, then, is a significant value for Catholic social teaching and a criterion for assessing the health of a community and for leading a fully human life.

4. Solidarity, Subsidiarity, and Socialization

Pope John Paul II recommended solidarity as the virtue and the attitude fitting for our interdependent age. Solidarity is rooted in the oneness of the human family with God as our common parent. As Martin Luther King Jr. put it, "All life is interrelated. All men are caught in an inescapable network of mutuality, tied in a single garment of destiny."[84] We now know that all humanity is genetically related and that we are all composed of stardust. We are theologically and physically brothers and sisters. Moreover, we are dependent on one another and affected by each other's choices and action. Our breakfast table can encompass labor and resources from all over the world — milk from Wisconsin, grain from Kansas, a banana from

Guatemala, sugar from the Philippines, coffee from Ecuador, delivered to us using oil from Nigeria or Saudi Arabia. Farm subsidies in the United States or Europe affect farmers in other parts of the world: for example, they can cripple the ability of farmers in Africa to compete on the world market, pushing them more deeply into poverty. The fact of our global interdependence, says John Paul II, calls us to the virtue of solidarity if we are to work for justice and live in peace.[85]

> When interdependence becomes recognized in this way, the correlative response as a moral and social attitude, as a "virtue," is solidarity. This then is not a feeling of vague compassion or shallow distress at the misfortunes of so many people, both near and far. On the contrary, it is a firm and persevering determination to commit oneself to the common good; that is to say, to the good of all and of each individual because we are really responsible for all. (#38)

Solidarity is the proper perspective and the appropriate virtue for living in a global village.

Subsidiarity and *socialization* are principles that pertain to the role of the state and government in working for the common good. Pius XI articulated the principle of subsidiarity (from the Latin for "help") in his social encyclical *After Forty Years* (*Quadragesimo Anno,* 1931) as a guiding norm, rooted in natural law, for restoring the social order.

> Just as it is gravely wrong to take from individuals what they can accomplish by their own initiative and industry and give it to the community, so also it is an injustice and at the same time a grave evil and disturbance of the right order to assign to a greater or higher association what lesser or subordinate organizations can do. For every social activity ought of its very nature to furnish help to the members of the body social, and never destroy and absorb them. (#79)

Subsidiarity, then, means decentralization. Government should not usurp the autonomy and authority or civil organizations; national government should not interfere with competent and effective local government, and so on.[86] Subsidiarity is a check on tyranny and an aid to participation. (Pius XI hoped it would restore some of the authority of the church that had been appropriated by the state.)

Thirty years later, in different circumstances, John XXIII affirmed the necessity of the principle of subsidiarity, but balanced it with what he called "socialization." In a more complex and interdependent world, John saw the legitimate need for state intervention in society on behalf of the common good.[87] Socialization recognizes that there is a place for national and even international governing bodies to remedy structural injustices and to guarantee human rights such as education and health care. Subsidiarity limits the role of the state in working for the common good of society, and socialization recognizes the legitimacy of that role, depending on the circumstances.

5. Social Sin and Structures of Injustice

In the same section of *On Social Concern* where John Paul II discusses solidarity, he also discusses "structures of sin" (#35–40). John Paul had also discussed the concept of social sin and its relationship to personal sin in his 1984 post-synodal apostolic exhortation titled *Reconciliation and Penance* (#16). This has led contemporary moral theologians to probe the relationship between personal sin and social sin.[88] Although sketching the details of this discussion would take us too far afield, it is important to acknowledge that the ideals toward which it is aimed, expressed in notions such as the common good, participation, solidarity, and human rights, are never fully realized in history and that humanity continually falls short.

The contemporary world is wounded, characterized by oppression, exploitation, and injustice. This social evil tends to take on virtually an independent existence, to infiltrate the structures and institutions of social life. The human condition is embedded in a situation of guilt (original sin) and a state of spiritual enslavement (the sin of the world) that affects and conditions all human actions in a manner. This tragic state of affairs is a given of human existence:

> But at a deeper level [disturbances in the social order] flow from man's pride and selfishness, which contaminate even the social sphere. When the structure of affairs is flawed by the consequences of sin, man, already born with a bent towards evil, finds there new inducements to sin, which cannot be overcome without strenuous efforts and the assistance of grace.[89]

Unjust social structures oppress their victims and crush their spirits, and they become internalized by both victims and those who benefit from them. These structures generate a false consciousness of acquiescence to injustice and of privilege that blinds everyone to the sinfulness of the situation. And such structures tend to be self-perpetuating, leading to a spiral of sin and evil.[90] John Paul II accentuates two examples of structures of sin, "the all-consuming desire for profit" (or greed) and "the thirst for power (#37 in *On Social Concern*)." Other examples would include racism and sexism.

The Christian response to this realistic analysis of the human situation calls for both personal conversion and the transformation of social structures. This will be the ongoing response of the church until God decisively establishes the kingdom of God. This process is also a spiral, but one that moves in the direction of the common good and the reign of God. The reform of public policy and social institutions will be incomplete without a change of heart. The U.S. civil rights movement, for example, dismantled the structures of segregation, but it did not eradicate racism. And personal conversion always propels one into action for justice and participation in the transformation of the world. As the refrain of a recent hymn puts it, "God in your grace, God in your mercy, turn us to you to transform the world."[91]

6. Option for the Poor

Derived from Latin American liberation theology and incorporating a major biblical theme, "option for the poor" will be further developed in the next chapter on economic justice, but it is included here for the sake of completeness. The option for the poor means that all members of society and society itself have a special obligation to the poor and vulnerable; the justice of a society is measured by its treatment of the poor. In the words of the U.S. Catholic bishops, "Decisions must be judged in light of what they do *for* the poor, what they do *to* the poor, and what they enable the poor to do *for themselves*. The fundamental moral criterion for all economic decisions, policies, and institutions is this: they must be at the service of *all people, especially the poor.*"[92] A good society is one where there is no debilitating poverty, where everyone can participate and realize his or her human potential. In order to realistically move toward such a society, the poor and marginalized persons must receive privileged attention.

7. Human Rights

While the language of rights has never been absent from contemporary Catholic social teaching, it was Pope John XXIII who brought human rights to center stage in the church's strategy for working for justice.[93] Two great global institutions, the United Nations and the Catholic Church, latched on to human rights as a way to champion justice and critique injustice in a pluralistic world.[94] There are remarkable parallels between the United Nations' Universal Declaration of Human Rights (1948) and John XXIII's elucidation of human rights in *Peace on Earth* (1963).[95] For both institutions human rights became a normative framework that established minimal conditions for a just society no matter what form of government or economic system a nation adopted.

The language of rights, a product of the Enlightenment, emerged in the contemporary world in two strands or traditions. Liberalism and capitalism emphasized freedom and thus civil and political rights, such as the right to political participation, juridical rights, the rights of economic initiative and private property, and the rights to freedom of the press, of assembly, and of religion, and so on. Marxism and socialism emphasized equality and thus social and economic rights, such as the rights to food, shelter, education, and health care, and to work and a just wage.

Civil and political rights are generally immunities that are more readily subject to incorporation into law. Social and economic rights are empowerments or entitlements that require government policies and subsidies. During the Cold War period (1945–91), these different emphases hardened into an aspect of the ideological struggle between the democratic West and the communist East.[96] Each side accused the other of neglecting human rights.

The Catholic vision of human rights (and that of the United Nations) is inclusive and integrates both civil and political rights and social and economic rights. The Catholic vision is rooted in the dignity of the human person who is created in the image of God (*imago Dei* in Latin, Gen 1:26–27), a *trinitarian* God, that is, a God who is essentially relational and self-gift. Thus, "The fundamental human right is the right to give oneself away to another and ultimately to the Other."

At its foundation, the Christian tradition of human rights rejects both the individualism and the collectivism that can distort an ethic of human rights. The Christian understanding is essentially communitarian: the individual and the community give life to one another. The goal is neither the autonomous individual of liberalism nor the submersion of the individual into a commune or the state of collectivisim, but persons flourishing through relationships and community. Freedom is freedom for self-giving and freedom for participation in community, and the purpose of community is the enrichment of the person.[97]

Thus, human rights can give specific meaning to human dignity, the common good, and solidarity, and the protection and promotion of human rights can establish the minimal conditions for a just social order irrespective of how the society is structured. The Catholic Church was slow to embrace human rights, but they have now become central to the church's work for justice. Moreover, the Catholic vision of human rights offers a profound grounding of the concept in "human dignity, realized in community," a coherent integration of political and economic rights, and a balanced appreciation of both rights and duties.

There remains some controversy about human rights. Some contend that human rights are a Western construct imposed on other cultures, and others argue that cultural diversity and pluralism make a *universal* declaration of human rights theoretically impossible. Nevertheless, through the United Nations and dedicated nongovernmental organizations, human rights have become widely known and mostly accepted moral standards. Groups such as Amnesty International and Human Rights Watch monitor and publicize violations of human rights. Yet despite the widespread acceptance of the concept of human rights, glaring violations remain routine and ubiquitous. In our world women are trafficked as virtual sex slaves, workers toil in sweatshops for wages insufficient for life, and tyrants rule through oppression, torture, and murder. Such conditions are not morally ambiguous according to the standards of human rights, but egregious abuses.

Torture: A Clear Violation of Human Rights

The practice of torture is an example of the flagrant violation of human rights.[98] Torture is intentional cruelty aimed at destroying the sense of identity, meaning, and purpose of the victim in order to procure information from the victim, to punish the victim, and/or to establish a political atmosphere of fear and intimidation. Torture violates human dignity by brutalizing the victim and dehumanizing the perpetrator. Torture shatters solidarity and community. Even when torture leaves no lasting physical marks, it leaves irreparable psychological damage by obliterating the mutual trust essential for communal life.[99]

On October 4, 2007, the *New York Times* broke the story of secret U.S. Justice Department memos that permitted torture in fighting the "war on terror." President George W. Bush responded the next day, saying once again, "This government does not torture people."[100] The scandals of Abu Ghraib and the like, the CIA torture program based on secret detention and extraordinary renditions, the Guantanamo Bay prison, and the release of the Justice Department memos in the early months of the Obama administration are convincing evidence, however, that the United States *did* engage in the shameful and illegal practice of torture.

Americans, by and large, are not ashamed that our government cruelly treated detainees in the war on terror. Surveys of American public opinion suggest that about half of Americans think torture is justified in some circumstances. A Pew Research Center survey in October 2006 found that Catholics approve of its use by a slightly wider margin than the general public, and another survey in April 2009 found that the more people attend church, the more likely they are to condone torture.[101] Fear, sparked by 9/11 and fanned by the Bush administration, seems to have persuaded the majority of American Christians that state security can justify torture. This is the way torture is usually rationalized.

Besides the state security argument (torture is a necessary tool in the "war on terror"), the Bush administration used two other justifications for torture. The president and his loyal lawyers argued that "unlawful enemy combatants" are not covered by the Geneva and U.N. Conventions or U.S. law and that "enhanced interrogation techniques" (so-called "torture lite" or "coercion") were not torture.

Standing against this defense of torture are Christian ethics and pragmatic self-interest (not to mention international and U.S. laws that unequivocally prohibit torture and cruel, inhuman, and degrading treatment of prisoners). Beyond the implausibility of the Bush administration's legal argument was its blindness to the ethical reason that prohibits torture — it violates human dignity. Even a captured terrorist who has been involved in the slaughter of innocents is a human being, sacred in God's sight, someone for whom Christ died. The litmus test of a commitment to human rights is how a society treats the weak and marginal, the guilty and despised.[102] Since Jesus was tortured and crucified, it would seem that Christians would see Christ in the victim of torture.

Although the Bush administration was vague about the definition of "enhanced interrogation techniques," coercion commonly includes sleep deprivation, hooding, forced nakedness, exposure to heat and cold, withdrawal of food and water, the use of drugs to cause confusion, rough treatment (slapping, shoving, or shaking), sensory deprivation or assaults with loud noise, forcing a prisoner to stand for days at a time or to sit in uncomfortable positions, prolonged interrogations, use of threatening dogs, waterboarding (dripping water from a wet cloth on the face, creating the sensation of drowning), religious or sexual humiliation, playing on the prisoner's fears for himself and his family, and the use of several of these techniques in combination.[103] Would any of us want these techniques used on us or a loved one? Can anyone deny the cruelty of these techniques?

When our government engages in torture, it is done in our name, for our protection. We are the perpetrators of this cruel treatment, and we are spiritually diminished by the practice. Torture drives a stake into the soul of any society. The United States is now in the same moral league (although there is a difference in degree) with the Saddam Hussein government in Iraq, and our global reputation reflects this reality. It is ironic and tragic that American torture happened at Abu Ghraib, the site of some of the worst atrocities of Saddam's regime.

There are also several practical reasons to oppose torture. Tortured innocents (most of the prisoners at Abu Ghraib and some of the prisoners at Guantanamo Bay and those caught up in the program of secret rendition were innocent) are prone to become terrorists and insurgents. Furthermore, torture seldom works: it is less effective than humane methods and thus unnecessary, it does not yield credible information, and its use prohibits the lawful prosecution of the victim and nullifies his or her value as a witness.[104] Interrogators and intelligence agencies have long known that torture and humiliation are counterproductive and unreliable.[105] Building a relationship with the detainee based on respect is generally more effective in yielding information. Those who are tortured or coerced will often tell the interrogator anything to stop the pain and duress. Indeed, such false information was used by the Bush administration as part of its justification for the war on Iraq.[106] This is also why coerced confessions are not admissible in court, and why it would be virtually impossible to prosecute detainees who have been tortured. Finally, if the United States condones torture, American prisoners are more likely to be tortured. This is a reason why former Secretary of State General Colin Powell and the Pentagon have been critical of Bush administration policies.

Although the Catholic Church is admittedly burdened with its past history of practicing torture itself during the Inquisition, the contemporary church is on record as absolutely condemning torture. The hypocrisy of the Bush administration on this issue (saying one thing and doing another) and the popular support of Americans for a policy of torture may have made it difficult for the church to speak out. Most church leaders, including Catholic bishops, have been silent, in effect disappearing on this issue. The only direct statement by a church body that I am aware of is the fine *Resolution on Human Rights in a Time of Terrorism and Torture* approved by the General Assembly of the Presbyterian Church USA in 2006. Officially the Catholic Church and the churches in general were not much of a counterweight to the Bush administration's torture policy.[107]

The National Religious Campaign Against Torture (*www.nrcat.org*) is an important movement against torture, the abuse of detainees, and the erosion of due process of law in the United States. NRCAT released a statement signed by American religious leaders, including Bishop William Skylstad, president of the USCCB, on November 2, 2006. The statement says,

> Torture violates the basic dignity of the human person that all religions hold dear. It degrades everyone involved — policymakers, perpetrators, and victims. It contradicts our nation's most cherished values. Any policies that permit torture and inhumane treatment are shocking and morally intolerable. Nothing less is at stake than the soul of our nation. What does it signify if torture is condemned in word but allowed in deed? Let America abolish torture now — without exception.

Anyone can sign on to the statement at the campaign's website.

The torture and abuse of powerless detainees and the erosion of due process of law condoned by the United States government during the Bush-Cheney years were morally outrageous violations of basic human rights. Silence and subtlety were not the right responses. The people of God and their leaders should have been more vocal and more active in opposing the repugnant practice of torture. It should never happen again.

Immigration: A Case of Human Rights in Conflict

Particular human rights, however, are not absolute, and human rights can conflict with one another. The right to migrate in search of basic sustenance, for example, can conflict with the right of a nation to secure its borders. Immigration is a global problem that is also a much debated political issue in the United States. It is an example of a conflict of human rights that can result in a certain ambiguity. Paradoxically, despite the apparent conflict among human rights, the American Catholic bishops have exercised clearer and more persistent moral leadership on immigration than on torture.[108]

Hospitality toward strangers is a consistent biblical theme (see Deut 10:17–19 and Mt 25:35–36), and it is a feature of Catholic social teaching.

As might be expected, the right to migrate is clearly expressed by Pope John XXIII in *Peace on Earth:* "Every human being has the right to freedom of movement and of residence within the confines of his own country; and,

"For the Lord your God is God of gods and Lord of lords, the great God, mighty and awesome, who is not partial and takes no bribe, who executes justice for the orphan and the widow, and who loves the strangers, providing them with food and clothing. You shall also love the stranger, for you were strangers in the land of Egypt."

— Deuteronomy 10:17–19

"Then the king will say to those at his right hand, 'Come, you that are blessed by my Father, inherit the kingdom prepared for you from the foundation of the world; for I was hungry and you gave me food, I was thirsty and you gave me something to drink, *I was a stranger and you welcomed me*, I was naked and you gave me clothing, I was sick and you took care of me, I was in prison and you visited me.' "

— Matthew 25:34–36

"Migrants should be met with a hospitable and welcoming attitude which can encourage them to become part of the Church's life, always with due regard for their freedom and their specific cultural identity."

— John Paul II, *The Church in America,* #65

when there are just reasons for it, the right to emigrate to other countries and take up residence there. The fact that one is a citizen of a particular state does not detract in any way from his membership in the human family as a whole, nor from his citizenship in the world community" (#25).[109]

In January 2003 the Catholic bishops of Mexico and the United States published a joint pastoral letter titled *Strangers No Longer: Together on the Journey of Hope,* the product of two years of broad consultation and study on the topic of immigration. They enunciated five principles based on Catholic social teaching to guide a nation's immigration policy (#34–38): (1) persons have the right to find opportunities in their homeland; (2) persons have the right to migrate to support themselves and their families; (3) sovereign nations have the right to control their borders; (4) refugees and asylum seekers should be afforded protection; and (5) the human dignity and human rights of undocumented migrants should be respected. To these could be added another consistent theme of the bishops: the value of the family, which is put under duress by the reality of immigration (#64). The bishops responded to the apparent conflict between human rights on this issue with this conclusion:

The Church recognizes the right of a sovereign state to control its borders in furtherance of the common good. It also recognizes the right of human persons to migrate so that they can realize their God-given rights. These teachings complement each other. While the sovereign state may impose reasonable limits on immigration, the common good is not served when the basic human rights of the individual are violated. In the current condition of the world, in which global poverty and persecution are rampant, the presumption is that persons must migrate in order to support and protect themselves and that nations who are able to receive them should do so whenever possible. It is through this lens that we assess the current migration reality between the United States and Mexico. (#39)

Basic human rights receive priority, and the principle of the common good serves to mediate in this situation.[110] It is not a choice between immigration or secure borders, but both immigration and secure borders.

Although many Americans seem to be up in arms over the immigration issue, the church quite rightly wonders what the fuss is about.[111] Certainly the United States must work hard to keep terrorists at bay, but building a wall between the United States and Mexico is an expensive and ineffective response to this need for security. Moreover, migration benefits both the immigrant and the United States. The United States needs skilled and unskilled labor, and Mexicans and others need work. Hospitality and decency require that these vulnerable workers be treated with respect and with justice.

It is possible that an influx of migrants can burden the infrastructure and social services of particular communities, but the United States surely has the resources to respond constructively. In providing opportunities for immigrants the United States will benefit from their contributions and eventually assimilate them into the national "melting pot," as it has done throughout its history. Among the ten goals that the U.S. bishops highlighted for the 2008 presidential election is the following: "Achieve comprehensive immigration reform that secures our borders, treats immigrant workers fairly, offers an earned path to citizenship, respects the rule of law,[112] and addresses the factors that compel people to leave their own countries" (#90 in *Forming Consciences for Faithful Citizenship*). This seems imminently reasonable and clearly faithful.[113]

These brief analyses of two contemporary human rights issues facing citizens in the United States give a sense of how human rights can be central in the church's involvement with the world. Since the 1960s when it embraced human rights, the Catholic Church has an impressive, but hardly unblemished, record of standing for human rights. Catholics participated in the U.S. civil rights movement, for example, but it was the black Protestant churches that were in the *forefront* of the movement.[114] After a presentation on "Law and Human Rights," I asked the speaker (who had dedicated his law career to working for human rights because of his Christian faith) about the record of the Catholic Church in this area. He agreed that the Catholic Church was often an ally on behalf of human rights but bemoaned the church's blindness especially regarding justice for women and homosexual persons. Granted the complexity of both issues, from a human rights perspective the church has been a countersign regarding women and homosexuals.

Political Advocacy

Because faith has a public and political dimension, Christians are required to be active as citizens. This is especially so if one is fortunate enough to live in a democracy that depends on the political participation of everyone. Christians are called to be both charitable (direct service to those in need) and just (advocacy and empowerment).

Throughout its history the church has practiced the works of mercy as enunciated in the parable of the last judgment (Mt 25:31–46): feeding the hungry, giving drink to the thirsty, welcoming the stranger, sheltering the homeless, caring for the sick, visiting prisoners. One thinks of Mother Teresa of Calcutta, Albert Schweitzer bringing health care to Africans, and Mother Antonia's contemporary mission to prisoners in Mexico.[115] This direct service has even been institutionalized through hospitals, schools, nursing homes, hospices, and credit unions sponsored by the church. It is not controversial to say that charity is a requirement of faith.

Social ministry also requires work for justice, which can be controversial. Charity is like a Band-Aid or stitches that stop the bleeding, while justice is like surgery to respond to the cause of a condition. Thus shelters are needed for the homeless, but it is only affordable housing, programs for drug addiction and for mental health, and jobs that pay a living wage that will reduce the number of homeless persons.

Since Vatican II, Paul VI's *A Call to Action* and the Synod of Bishops' *Justice in the World,* there have been a number of Catholic organizations founded especially to lobby for public policies that benefit the poor and the voiceless, to enable the poor to speak for themselves, and to work for justice and peace. There are also similar ecumenical organizations in which Catholics play a significant role. This section will provide snapshots of several of these organizations in order to indicate how this dimension of social ministry can be fulfilled.

Catholic bishops exercise leadership on matters of morality and public policy through the *United States Conference of Catholic Bishops* and its various committees.[116] The bishops, of course, have a significant teaching role. They exercise this through pastoral letters such as *The Challenge of Peace* (1983), *Economic Justice for All* (1986), and *Strangers No Longer* (2003), as well as various other statements and teaching documents, such as the quadrennial political responsibility statements.

Sometimes these documents themselves have a public policy impact. The Peace and Economics pastorals, for example, were developed through a process of broad consultation that included government experts and leaders, and they received wide coverage in the media, including a cover story in

Time magazine. One could argue that the just war criteria and analysis in the Peace pastoral, for example, has shaped the discussion of war in the United States since then.

The bishops also directly lobby Congress and the president through official letters, public testimony before Congress, and the staff of the USCCB. Regarding public policy, four of the USCCB committees that represent the bishops' positions before Congress are especially relevant: Social Development and World Peace (SDWP), the Committee for Pro-Life Activities, the Committee on Migration, and the Office of Government Liaison (OGL). Most dioceses have an office set up to lobby state legislatures and governments regarding the moral and institutional concerns of the church and also have committees, such as Justice and Peace Commissions, committed to educating the church about Catholic social doctrine and putting it into practice.

Because the USCCB is the official voice of the church in the United States, it has rigorous processes to make sure that it is representing a near consensus of its over two hundred bishops who chair and constitute its various committees. Although collaboration on particular issues is not unheard of, the nature of the USCCB makes joining coalitions rare. The USCCB is consciously nonpartisan, and it is aided in this by its consistent ethic of life (see chap. 5), which tends to make it, and Catholics in general, partially out of step with both of the major political parties in the United States. Catholic principles and the stances of the USCCB challenge those on the right (to be effectively concerned for the poor) and on the left (regarding the right to life). At its best, the USCCB focuses on the moral dimension of public policies.

Catholic social teaching, to which it contributes, yields the principles that are the foundation and parameter of the teaching and stances of the USCCB. In the spirit of Vatican II, the American bishops give due regard to scripture and theology in their statements, and they are also convinced of the need to be understood and persuasive in a pluralistic public context. The bishops also do their homework, drawing on the insights of the social sciences and the church's pastoral experience with the poor and marginal. The USCCB recognizes the difference between its firm commitment to principles and its more tentative public policy stances. The bishops are primarily pastors. They struggle with the tension between the call to be prophetic and the need to compromise sometimes in the political realm.

The USCCB sponsors or collaborates with three organizations that are directly involved in the church's social ministry: the Catholic Campaign for Human Development, Catholic Relief Services, and Catholic Charities USA. All three include justice education and public policy advocacy in their mission, and all three have web pages.

The Catholic Campaign for Human Development (CCHD) is the domestic economic development arm of the USCCB. It fosters local and national empowerment projects for the poor primarily through start-up grants to community organizations. Since its founding in 1969, CCHD has provided more than seventy thousand eight hundred grants to self-help projects developed by grassroots groups of poor persons. Each year CCHD distributes national grants to more than three hundred projects based in local communities. In addition, hundreds of smaller projects are funded through the 25 percent share of the annual CCHD collection retained by dioceses.

Catholic Relief Services (CRS) was established in 1943 to provide assistance to refugees during World War II. It now provides emergency or disaster relief and funds for economic development projects throughout the world. Although independent of the USCCB, CRS is overseen by the American Catholic bishops. CRS provides aid and development assistance to all persons in need. Its community-based, sustainable development programs include agricultural enterprises, community banks, health education, clean water projects, and peace-building initiatives. The goal is always to make the local population the central participant in its own development. Similar to secular programs such as Oxfam, CRS enjoys a reputation for efficiently using contributions to aid those in immediate need and to empower some of the world's most destitute communities.

Catholic Charities USA is a network of seventeen hundred agencies and institutions nationwide aimed at reducing poverty, supporting families, and empowering communities. Catholic Charities is involved in a broad spectrum of assistance efforts from emergency relief to adoption to legal assistance for immigrants. Founded in 1910, it is the nation's largest private assistance and antipoverty program, providing help and hope to more than 7.8 million people of all faiths each year. Its agencies are supported by bishops in their local dioceses. It is, in a sense, the social work arm of the Catholic Church in the United States.

The Center of Concern in Washington, D.C., was founded in 1971 as a joint venture of the Jesuits and the USCCB. It functions as an independent Catholic think tank providing resources that analyze global and national social problems and offer constructive solutions from the perspective of Catholic social teaching.[117] The Center is involved in both advocacy and justice education, but not in direct service. It develops position papers, treatises, and educational materials on social justice issues, conducts a variety of workshops and institutes on themes linking faith and justice, and publishes a free bimonthly newsletter titled *Center Focus*. The Center of Concern website, for example, had a link titled "Election 2008: Voting the Common Good" focusing on the common good, international relations, immigration, and (in collaboration with Pax Christi USA) the Iraq war, meant to provide a variety of resources (fact sheets, position papers, questions for candidates) on important justice and peace issues in the 2008 presidential election.

NETWORK is a national Catholic social justice lobby. It was founded at a meeting of forty-seven religious sisters in Washington, D.C., in December 1971. The mission and purpose of religious orders of women uniformly respond to the call of the gospel to serve those in need. The sisters who came together to found NETWORK had come to believe that providing the immediate needs of the poor (charity and direct service) was not enough, that faithfulness to the gospel also demanded work to transform unjust systems that perpetuate economic injustice. Thus NETWORK "educates, lobbies, and organizes for economic and social transformation."[118] Structural change through public policy advocacy is at the heart of NETWORK's mission. It focuses on economic and social justice issues, including environmental issues. Peace is a tangential concern. It focuses its lobbying on Iraq, for example, on reconstruction and economic development. NETWORK has chosen not to lobby regarding abortion, in part because other organizations have embraced that focus.

NETWORK, based in congregations of religious women, brings three lenses to its work for justice: Catholic social teaching, the life experiences of the poor, and feminism.[119] Its staff (who are paid uniform salaries) and board are comprised of sisters and lay women, and the organization consciously seeks to collaborate on justice issues and build coalitions. Its membership of twelve thousand includes both individuals and organizations, such as religious congregations of women and men, parishes, and so on, and thus represents over a hundred thousand people. It publishes a bimonthly newsletter, *NETWORK Connection,* and sends out legislative alerts to its members. There are also full-time registered lobbyists on its staff. NETWORK also sponsors local and regional workshops on legislative issues and the connection between faith and justice and collaborates on national conferences on these topics.

Bread for the World (BFW or Bread) is similar to NETWORK in its goals and method, but it is ecumenically Christian and includes Catholic participation and membership on its board. Established in 1974, Bread aims to be "a collective Christian voice urging our nation's decision-makers to end hunger at home and abroad."[120] Through the Bread for the World Institute, it engages in policy analysis and education. BFW publishes an annual Hunger Report, briefing papers on hunger issues, and a newsletter, *Bread,* nine times a year. BFW members are organized according to congressional district, and Bread operates primarily through churches and campuses. It sponsors an annual offering of letters to elected representatives in its member churches, focused on a particular issue related to hunger. Bread primarily lobbies Congress through the active participation of its fifty-eight thousand members who e-mail, write, and call their representatives in response to legislative action alerts.

Bread for the World has a respectable record of success in Congress. Bread had a hand, for example, in the U.S. government's doubling its development assistance during the Bush administration. Bread for the World has also helped to strengthen national nutrition programs, assisting millions of the families in this country who struggle to feed their children. Bread collaborated with Bono's "One" program to "make poverty history," and with the Jubilee initiative to reduce the debt of the poorest nations.

Neither Bread nor NETWORK engages in direct service; both groups lobby to change public policy as a way of feeding the hungry and empowering the poor. As Bread for the World points out, government funding for national and international aid usually dwarfs the amount of private aid. As an ecumenical organization, Bread attracts a broad membership, but its focus on hunger is somewhat narrower than NETWORK's concern for social and economic justice. Both groups work effectively to make the connection between faith and action for justice and to empower their members to participate in shaping public policy toward justice for the poor. Through these organizations Christian citizens continue to make a difference.

The Interfaith Center for Corporate Responsibility (ICCR) is an interfaith organization of institutional investors who promote justice by working for corporate social responsibility. ICCR now includes 22 Protestant denominations, 2 Jewish groups and over 250 Roman Catholic orders, dioceses, health groups, and others, representing over $80 billion in investments.[121] These faith-based investors press companies to be socially and environmentally responsible by sponsoring over two hundred shareholder resolutions annually and by lobbying CEOs and corporate directors.

In the early 1970s, at the initiative of the National Federation of Priests' Councils, a number of Catholic religious communities began to apply the principles of Catholic social teaching to the question of their investments. The formation of the National Catholic Coalition for Responsible Investment (NCCRI) under the leadership of Capuchin Father Michael H. Crosby resulted from a number of meetings and regional symposia. The ICCR and NCCRI developed on parallel tracks before most of the Catholic organizations joined the more inclusive ICCR located in New York at Riverside Church, leaving the NCCRI in a sort of dormant mode.[122] Responsible investing and advocacy for corporate responsibility are other ways of connecting faith and justice.

Which of the national or international agencies listed here are active in your local community? What other justice and peace organizations are active in your area? How are they organized? What sort of activities are they engaged in? Join in their work or start a local group on your campus, at your church, or in your community.

Pax Christi USA (PCUSA), an affiliate of Pax Christi International (PCI), is a Catholic peace organization that focuses on peace education, advocacy, and witness on behalf of nonviolence and justice, and opposition to violence and war.[123] Pax Christi International was founded in France in 1945 to work for the reconciliation of France and Germany in the wake of World War II. In 1963 it accepted John XXIII's *Peace on Earth* as its charter, and it affirms Paul VI's statement, "If you want peace, work for justice."[124] Thus Pax Christi is committed to human rights and justice as the basis for peace. PCUSA addresses a broad range of issues similar to the USCCB's consistent ethic of life, including abortion and ecology, but with a focus on peace, and it partners frequently with other justice and peace groups in its work. Although it is not technically a pacifist organization, Pax Christi clearly promotes a commitment to nonviolence, supports conscientious objectors, advocates disarmament, and opposes war and violence.

> In a world that settles differences by armed violence or the threat of it, Pax Christi offers a nonviolent alternative. In a world that too often defines "justice" as "revenge," Pax Christi breaks the cycle of violence by fostering reconciliation. In a world where countries invest more money in weapons than in the well-being of their people, Pax Christi calls individuals to disarm their hearts and work toward a world free of nuclear and conventional weapons.[125]

Its tactics include prayer, study, and action, which can range from lobbying elected representatives to protests and civil disobedience.

PCUSA was begun in 1972 by a small group of lay Catholics, including Gordon Zahn and Eileen Egan. Like its parent organization, it is a model of episcopal and lay collegiality. It is led by a national executive director, a bishop president, and a national council, with its national office in Erie, Pennsylvania. Among PCUSA's over twenty thousand members are 120 U.S. Catholic bishops. Its membership includes parishes, religious communities, and colleges. It encourages grassroots action by its 340 local groups. PCUSA publishes a quarterly periodical, *The Catholic Peace Voice,* and a variety of books, pamphlets, and study guides on peace and nonviolence. PCUSA shares the hope for reform that characterizes the other organizations we have examined, and there is among many of its members and some of its leaders a strong sense of resistance to the culture of violence that appears to pervade America. PCUSA tends to be more radical than some other groups in its approach to justice and peace, in the spirit of Gandhi and Martin Luther King Jr., and of Jesus.

A more ecumenical and interfaith counterpart to PCUSA is the Fellowship of Reconciliation (FOR), headquartered in the United States in Nyack, New York. FOR is an international pacifist organization with Christian roots.

Besides these national organizations (some of which have local affiliates), there are likely local groups in your state, city, diocese, place of employment, or university dedicated to addressing public policy from a faith perspective.[126]

In my hometown, for example, there is *CLOUT* (Citizens of Louisville Organized & United Together), an organization of religious congregations and neighborhood groups that work together to improve the community through direct advocacy. CLOUT is currently a Christian grassroots organization composed of eighteen congregations, half of which are Catholic parishes. The co-presidents in 2008 were a Catholic pastor and the bishop of the Baptized Pentecostal Church of Holiness. The member congregations are urban and suburban, and the participants are multicultural and interracial.

In the fall, members of the participating congregations meet in small groups to discuss local issues of injustice. These issues are grouped under topics, and there is a preparation assembly that chooses a topic for the year. A committee of volunteers with some expertise in the topic does further research and narrows the focus to a specific issue. In 2008 the topic was health care and the issue became "Catch a Falling Child." Approximately thirteen thousand low-income children in Louisville who were eligible for the Kentucky Children's Health Insurance Program (KCHIP) were not enrolled because of lack of outreach and cumbersome application requirements including an annual face-to-face interview.

This issue then became the focus of the spring "Nehemiah Assembly," which is patterned on the assembly called by the Jewish lay administrator, Nehemiah, who was sent by the Persian king to rebuild and restore Jerusalem after the Babylonian exile (Neh 5). At that assembly Nehemiah confronted the powerful elite of Jerusalem who were exploiting their fellow citizens. Nehemiah got a commitment from the powerful to change their behavior. This is the goal of the Nehemiah Assembly. Local and state health care leaders were "invited" to attend the assembly in front of over a thousand people from CLOUT. They were confronted with the injustice of the situation and asked to commit to specific steps toward fixing it. Such a large crowd chanting slogans in the round can be quite persuasive, as the representative of the governor's office discovered. These same leaders are called to report back to the following fall assembly about progress that has been made on the issue.[127]

Since its beginning in 1991, CLOUT has addressed issues such as traffic signals and bus shelters, a police crackdown on drug dealers and programs for drug addiction, bilingual interpreters at family health centers, supervised suspensions and direct instruction in Jefferson County Public Schools, and the creation of an affordable housing trust fund. CLOUT is a faith-based organization that is making concrete, constructive changes in the community.

Conclusion

This chapter has presented Christian action on behalf of justice as a "constitutive dimension" of the mission of the Catholic Church and a requirement of faith. It has shown the development of Catholic social teaching regarding faith and politics and articulated some principles based on that teaching. And, finally, it introduced some organizations that are responding to the call to act for justice in the public realm.

Questions for Reflection and Discussion

1. Do you think that privatization — the tendency to separate faith from the rest of life — is a real temptation today? Give some examples of privatization. Is it too strong to label privatization a "heresy?" Are actions on behalf of justice and participation in the transformation of the world *constitutive* of the mission of the church and of discipleship?

2. Since the emperor Constantine made Christianity the official religion of the Roman Empire, the politicization of the church has been a constant temptation. Did Vatican II's *Declaration on Religious Freedom*, which implies separation of church and state, finally lay this temptation to rest? What do you think is the proper relationship between church and state?

3. In the years prior to the Second Vatican Council the Jesuit theologian John Courtney Murray was silenced by the church, prohibited from speaking or publishing about religious freedom and church-state relations. The church continues to silence theologians who are discussing controversial issues. What do you think of this practice?

4. The chapter notes a tension between the church's call for participation and democracy *and* the church's claim to possess the truth revealed by Jesus Christ on the one hand and the church's own hierarchical and centralized structures on the other. Is participation a human right? Can we vote on the truth?

5. The synod document *Justice in the World* insists that the church itself be just. Is the church fulfilling this challenge today?

6. How does "the common good" differ from the utilitarian principle of "the greatest good for the greatest number"?

7. How do the principles of solidarity, subsidiarity, and socialization complement each other? How might these principles influence a particular public policy discussion (of your choice)?

8. Since World War II a remarkable consensus has emerged around human rights as minimum moral standards for a just society, yet human rights are widely violated. Identify some violations of human rights today. Is torture "a clear violation of human rights"? Should the United Nations (or the United States) intervene in the internal affairs of a state on behalf of human rights (humanitarian intervention)?

Chapter 3

Economic Justice

As we have seen, modern Catholic social teaching began with Pope Leo XIII's *The Condition of Labor* (*Rerum Novarum*) in 1891. Since Leo's successors have chosen to mark the fortieth, sixtieth, eightieth, ninetieth, and hundredth anniversaries of that encyclical with documents of their own, there is a focus in Catholic social teaching on the rights of workers and economic justice. The story of César Chávez and the struggle for justice for migrant and seasonal farm workers in the United States, known as *la causa*, is a good entry point into the topic of economic justice from a Christian perspective, the theme of this chapter.

César Chávez and *La Causa*

César Chávez (1927–93) was born near Yuma, Arizona, in a farmhouse that was built by his grandfather in the style of a Mexican hacienda in order to house three generations.[1] César spent the first ten years of life on this farm with his parents, Librado and Juana, his two brothers and two sisters, and their extended family. In 1938, however, the Chávez family lost their farm because of unpaid taxes and became migrant farm workers who turned to the fertile fields of California to earn a living. Librado had repeatedly sought to obtain a federal loan to pay the back taxes and interest on the farm, but the loan application was blocked by the local bank president, a wealthy landowner and grower who owned land adjacent to the Chávez farm. This man eventually bought the farm for half the value of the back taxes owed.

The Chávez family's experience as itinerant farm laborers illustrates the suffering and injustice imposed on the workers who are essential to putting food on our tables. The family followed a circuit through California, planting, nurturing, and harvesting fruit and vegetables for the multi-billion-dollar agribusiness corporations. Much of the labor is called "stoop work" because of the posture required to do it. César suffered his whole adult life from back trouble. Substandard housing that is crowded and often without running water, sanitation, or cooking facilities is a constant problem for migrant workers. The Chávez family spent their first winter on the circuit in tents pitched in a muddy field.

Migrants face the constant strain of moving on in search of uncertain, backbreaking work for meager wages at the hands of corrupt contractors. After World War II, migrant workers faced the competition of *braceros,* Mexican contract workers brought to the United States to work for even lower wages (1942–64).

Agriculture is consistently ranked in the top three most hazardous occupations in the United States. Not surprisingly, seasonal workers do not receive any benefits from their employers, and their mobility means they can seldom access government programs even when they are eligible for assistance. Often neither potable water nor sanitation facilities are provided in the field, and the workers are susceptible to pesticide poisoning. Migrant farm workers can't afford to take a day off if they are sick, and they seldom have access to health care.

The migratory life is especially hard on children. César dropped out of school after the eighth grade, having attended thirty-seven different schools. Instead of going to school, children often have to work in the fields. It was in school, where English was a second language for Spanish-speaking children, that César first experienced the prejudice and discrimination that characterize the experience of Chicanos (Mexican Americans) in the United States. Chávez family members, for example, were routinely denied service at restaurants. César was even arrested while home on leave from the Navy during World War II for refusing to comply with segregated seating in a movie theater.

The World War II veteran married Helen Fabela in 1948. César and Helen would raise eight children. Their first winter together was spent in a one-room shack with no electricity or running water. César bummed rides to the fields. When it became nearly impossible to find farm work because of the low-wage *braceros,* César found work in a lumber yard.

César had befriended Fr. Donald McDonnell, a labor priest, who told him about the church's teaching on the right to organize and the right to earn a living wage. A few years later, Fr. McDonnell recommended César to Fred Ross, a community organizer who was trying to establish the legendary Saul Alinsky's Community Service Organization (CSO) on the West coast.[2] César worked for CSO for ten years, rising to the position of national director, with a steady salary and a decent income.

In 1962 Chávez, along with Dolores Huerta,[3] quit the CSO to organize a union for farm workers. César had become frustrated with the CSO's refusal to try to organize farm workers and had grown wary of its power and professionalism, which seemed to distance the organization from those it was supposed to serve. César and the other members of the staff of the National Farm Workers Association (NFWA) worked for $5.00 a week plus their modest expenses.

For three years the NFWA staff worked to establish the foundation of a viable union. Then, in 1965, Filipino farm workers associated with the Agricultural Workers Organizing Committee (AWOC) walked out of the vineyards in Delano, California, and the NFWA voted to join the strike against growers of grapes. In the first year of the strike the two organizations merged to form the United Farm Workers Organizing Committee (UFWOC) under the leadership of Chávez. The strike spread throughout California and lasted five years. After a two-year nationwide boycott of California table grapes, the growers finally recognized the union and negotiated contracts in 1970.

Almost before the victory party ended, California vegetable growers entered into "sweetheart contracts" with the Teamsters Union. A sweetheart contract is one between an employer and a union that does not truly represent the interests of the workers. The farm workers had not voted to have the Teamsters represent them, and the Teamsters were clearly in bed with the growers. Thus the UFWOC, which in 1972 became the United Farm Workers of America (UFW), chartered by the AFL-CIO, entered into a struggle with a rival union as well as with the growers. This established a pattern for *la causa* that persists today — one step forward and two steps backward.

When the contracts with grape growers expired in 1973, these corporations also entered into sweetheart deals with the Teamsters. The UFW workers went on strike again and renewed and expanded the boycott to include lettuce and eventually some brands of wine, most notably Gallo. Teamster thugs roamed the strike zones and picket lines, beating and threatening the UFW strikers. The police often favored the growers, turning a blind eye to the violence or joining in themselves.

National labor legislation almost always excludes farm workers: they are not covered by minimum wage legislation, for example, or in legislation that protects the right of workers to organize and to vote to be represented by a union. Thus it was a historic breakthrough when the California legislature passed the Agricultural Labor Relations Act (ALRA) in 1975 and Democratic Governor Jerry Brown signed it into law. It specifically guaranteed farm workers the right to organize and bargain collectively, and it set up the Agricultural Labor Relations Board (ALRB) to administer the law and monitor union elections. The ALRB worked well for about a year, but then lobbying by agribusiness managed to weaken the law and turn the ARLB into an obstacle to union organizing. Again it was one step forward and two steps backward.

César Chávez and the UFW struggled for justice for farm workers throughout the 1980s. Strikes and boycotts seemed almost constant. Pilgrimages, from Delano to Sacramento, the capital of California, for example, were organized periodically to rally the workers and their allies and to focus attention on the cause. In 1988, in the midst of a grape boycott focused on the danger of pesticide use for the workers and for the environment, César engaged in his third and longest public fast. It lasted for thirty-six days. César fasted as a sign of penance and purification, as opposed to a pressure tactic, and this fast did seem to renew and reinvigorate the UFW.

César died in his sleep on April 23, 1993, at the house of a union friend in Arizona, not far from the adobe farmhouse where he was born. He is buried at La Paz, California, the site of the UFW offices. Over forty thousand people participated in his funeral procession.

The UFW continues in the up-and-down struggle for justice for migrant farm workers. Today there are over 3 million migrant workers in the United States. Their labor cultivates and harvests the fruit and vegetables of a 28-billion-dollar industry that nourishes you and me. Migrant workers, however, remain among the most impoverished and powerless people in our country. Most farm workers earn less than $10,000 a year. Farm workers still suffer from substandard housing, inadequate health care, unsafe working conditions, lack of education, and racial discrimination.[4] On Thanksgiving Day, 1960, the renowned television journalist Edward R. Murrow (1908–65), shocked the nation by broadcasting a documentary titled *Harvest of Shame* about the plight of migrant farm workers. Unfortunately, despite the commitment of César Chávez and the UFW, not much has changed in fifty years.

César Chávez brought a moral vision to his leadership of the UFW and *la causa*. Chávez was influenced by Gandhi and Martin Luther King Jr., and he was absolutely committed to nonviolence. The labor movement primarily uses nonviolent techniques such as marches, picketing, strikes, and boycotts, and labor protestors have often been the victims of violence. Some labor activists, however, have been known to use violence in their cause — destroying machinery, for example, or assaulting strike-breakers brought in to take the jobs of those on strike. The UFW, under the leadership of César Chávez, consciously employed and developed the philosophy of nonviolence.

César tapped into the religiosity of the farm workers, over 85 percent of whom are Catholic, reflecting their mostly Mexican, but also Latino or Filipino, heritage. There are interesting parallels between civil rights movement's roots in the Protestant black church and *la causa*'s reliance on Catholic piety. UFW marches were called pilgrimages (*peregrinaciones*), and they were invariably accompanied by banners of Our Lady of Guadalupe. Mass was often celebrated at the sites of strikes or picket lines from the back of a pickup truck. César and most of his partisans worked for justice because of their faith.

The faith that motivated *la causa* was nurtured by prayer and included a strong sense of service and sacrifice that is integral to Mexican religious tradition. Chávez led an ascetic and contemplative lifestyle, rising at 4:30 in the morning for a couple of hours of meditation before attending daily Mass when possible. César learned service from Juana Chávez, his mother, who never refused hospitality to a needy stranger and who sent her children to invite the hungry and homeless to their table. A sense of sacrifice can be seen in the willingness of the already poor to engage in strikes, to undergo three-hundred-mile pilgrimages for the cause (in one picture César is supporting himself on the shoulders of two colleagues because of his blistered feet), and in César's penitential fasts. When César died in 1993, he did not own a house or a car, and he made just over $5,000 a year working indefatigably as president of the United Farm Workers. Early on César experienced the freedom that came from extricating himself from the trap of the affluent version of the American dream.[5] Instead he embraced the "justice for all" version of the American dream, as did his nonviolent contemporary, Martin Luther King Jr.

César was strongly influenced by the principles taught by the church concerning human dignity, solidarity, the option for the poor, and the rights of workers, but he found that the official church was slow and spotty in putting its own principles into practice. In 1968 Chávez asked the U.S. bishops to endorse the grape boycott. The bishops, who recognized that many of the growers were wealthy and influential Catholics, issued a statement that asserted the rights of the workers to organize and to a just wage, and it recognized the value of family farms. It neither endorsed nor condemned the grape boycott. While some priests, religious women, and Protestant ministers stood with the farm workers, many others supported the status quo.

A year later, the U.S. Catholic bishops appointed an ad hoc committee, chaired by Bishop Joseph Donnelly of Hartford, Connecticut, and including two labor priests, George Higgins and Roger Mahony (who eventually became the cardinal archbishop of Los Angeles), to mediate between the workers and the growers, and this committee was rather effective in doing so.[6] In 1972, the U.S. bishops did endorse the UFW's lettuce boycott. It can be said that eventually bishops, priests, and laity, including Dorothy Day (whom we will meet in the chapter on peace), took the side of justice for the farm workers and transformed Catholic social teaching into Catholic social action.[7]

The story of César Chávez and *la causa* is a fitting introduction to the four prominent themes of Catholic social teaching on the topic of economic justice — the rights of workers, the idea of a social mortgage on private property and material possessions, the option for the poor, and authentic development as a response to global poverty. The remainder of this chapter will explore these four themes in the development of Catholic social teaching.

The Dignity of Work, the Priority of Labor, and the Rights of Workers

The English title of the encyclical that began the modern tradition of Catholic social teaching is *The Condition of Labor*. It addressed the appalling working conditions that resulted from the Industrial Revolution. Since many of the documents of Catholic social teaching have commemorated the anniversaries of the 1891 document, they too have addressed the rights of workers in the changing circumstances of the time (see Table 3.1). Since the most comprehensive treatment of work in Catholic social teaching is John Paul II's *On Human Work* (*Laborem Exercens,* 1981),[8] we will use it to trace the development of the Catholic tradition on work.

On Human Work was John Paul's third encyclical. It marked the ninetieth anniversary of *On the Condition of Labor.* Written by the pope himself, its scheduled publication date was delayed by the assassination attempt against the pope by Mehmet Ali Agca in St. Peter's Square on May 13, 1981. John Paul II revised the document as he recuperated, and it was published on September 14, 1981. *On Human Work* was influenced by the pope's own experience of manual labor in a stone quarry during the Nazi occupation of Poland and by his philosophical background in Thomism, phenomenology, and personalism. After an introduction that connects *On the Condition of Labor* with the contemporary social question, each of the four sections presents a major theme of the encyclical — the personal nature of work, the priority of labor over capital, the rights of workers, and the spirituality of work.

Table 3.1. The Documents of Catholic Social Teaching That Significantly Address Economic Justice

Year	Author	Latin Title	English Title
1891	Leo XIII	*Rerum Novarum*	*The Condition of Labor*
1931	Pius XI	*Quadragesimo Anno*	*After Forty Years*
1961	John XXIII	*Mater et Magistra*	*Christianity and Social Progress* (70th Anniversary)
1965	Vatican II	*Gaudium et Spes*	*Pastoral Constitution on the Church in the Modern World*
1967	Paul VI	*Populorum Progressio*	*On the Development of Peoples*
1968	CELAM		Medellín Conference Documents
1971	Paul VI	*Octogesima Adveniens*	*A Call to Action* (80th Anniversary)
1979	CELAM		Puebla Conference Documents
1981	John Paul II	*Laborem Exercens*	*On Human Work* (90th Anniversary)
1986	USCCB		*Economic Justice for All*
1987	John Paul II	*Sollicitudo Rei Socialis*	*On Social Concern* (20th Anniversary of *On the Development of Peoples*)
1991	John Paul II	*Centesimus Annus*	*On the Hundredth Anniversary*
2009	Benedict XVI	*Caritas in Veritate*	*Charity in Truth* (Intended for the 40th Anniversary of *On the Development of Peoples* in 2007, but was delayed.)

The Dignity of Human Work as Based in the Dignity of the Worker

In the second section the pope grounds the dignity of human work in the creation stories of Genesis that announce that human persons are created in the image of God and given the task of subduing the earth. Human beings share in the creative activity of God through work (#4). Furthermore, Jesus the carpenter provides an eloquent "gospel of work" that witnesses to the truth that "the value of human work is not primarily the kind of work being done, but the fact that the one doing it is a person" (#6). Work is for humanity, not humanity for work. John Paul II clearly gives priority to the subjective dimension of work. A worker should never be reduced to a cog in a machine; the whole purpose of the machine (the economy) is the flourishing of human persons (#7).

This vision of work would seem to run counter to the treatment of workers in the mills and mines of the Industrial Revolution, the contemporary sweatshops in Central America or New York City, the fertile fields of California, or the orderly rows of cubicles in an insurance company in Hartford. The dignity of human work and the priority of the personhood of the worker challenge the morality of the modern economy.

John Paul shows that work is valuable and meaningful in three spheres (#9–10). Through work humans participate in God's creative activity and realize their human potential. Despite the toil that work involves, it is good for a person (the personal sphere). Work provides sustenance for individuals and the resources necessary for family life (the material and family sphere). Through work persons contribute to the community, participate in society, and establish the common good (the social sphere). Thus work is essential for a meaningful life; it is a human obligation, and a human right.

The Priority of Labor over Capital

In the third section (#11–15), John Paul affirms a principle consistently taught by the church: the priority of labor over capital. This follows logically from the primacy of persons over things established in the first section.[9] This principle should resolve both the class conflict asserted by Marxism and the exploitation of labor that characterizes a rigid capitalism. Capital is produced by labor, and thus labor and capital cannot be separated from one another. A just economy is shaped by the value of work and the dignity of the worker, the priority of labor, and the participation of the worker in the process of production. Since John Paul II maintains that the participation of the worker in the process of production is key to a just economy, he (rather vaguely) recommends proposals in which workers share in the ownership, management, or profits of the business (#14). The U.S. Catholic bishops are more explicit about new forms of partnership between workers and managers in their pastoral letter *Economic Justice for All* (#298–306).

And Benedict XVI calls for new forms of business enterprise that combine private and public, profit and nonprofit, all in the conscious interest of solidarity and the common good in *Charity in Truth* (#41, 46). While the Christian tradition has affirmed the right to private property, this right has been conditioned by the common good and the common purpose of created goods. Thus, "one cannot exclude the socialization, in suitable conditions, of certain means of production" (*On Human Work*, #14).

Again this Catholic principle of the priority of labor over capital would seem to challenge the modern corporation's relentless search for the cheapest labor and the greatest profit and the resulting "race to the bottom" that undermines protection of workers, product safety, and environmental responsibility.[10]

The Rights of Workers

The fourth section of the encyclical (#16–23) elaborates on the rights of workers in the broad context of human rights that establishes the minimum conditions for a just society.[11] If one is obligated to work in order to fulfill one's human potential, meet the material needs of oneself and one's family, and contribute to society, then work is a human right, and society has a responsibility to provide the opportunity for every person to work.

In this context John Paul II distinguishes between the "direct employer" and the "indirect employer." The direct employer enters into a contract with a worker. The indirect employer refers to the other factors that influence employment and the conditions of employment, such as labor legislation, industrial development, training and education, transportation systems, and so on (#16–17). The pope insists on the indirect but real responsibility of society, including the state or government, to develop policies and institutions that support full employment and healthy conditions for work. John Paul was aware, in 1981, that the indirect employer is not only national, but global, that is, a responsibility between governments and involving international organizations such as the United Nations and what is now called the World Trade Organization. Providing the opportunity to work is an essential element in the common good, which is the goal of a good society.

John Paul II recognizes that just remuneration for work is key to workers' rights. He defines a just wage as a "family wage," that is, compensation sufficient for maintaining a family and providing for its future. Leo XIII had called for a living wage that would support the wage earner and his family in reasonable and frugal comfort and allow him to purchase property. Leo considered private property as the antidote to poverty. Leo insisted that wages were not merely a matter of a contract or of market forces, but that they were tied to human dignity and human need (*On the Condition of Labor*, #34–35, #4–5). Forty years later, Pius XI developed a more complex calculation for just remuneration, considering not only the need of the worker and his family, but also the financial condition of the employer and the welfare of the whole society (*After Forty Years*, #63–75). John XXIII added considerations for the contribution of the worker and for the global common good (*Christianity and Social Progress*, #71) to this calculation, and he suggested profit sharing and partnership arrangements of various kinds (#84–103).[12] John Paul II seems to have returned to the simpler, more worker-focused approach of Leo XIII in his discussion of just remuneration.

The struggle for a fair and living wage continues today in both developed and developing counties, and the principles of Catholic social teaching offer some guidance.[13] Catholic social teaching, however, does not directly address the current reality of the U.S. economy, which is characterized by the ballooning salaries of chief executive officers (CEO), stagnant wages for ordinary workers, and increasing inequality — the rising gap between the very rich and the rest. The ratio between the highest-paid and the average-paid worker was 42 to 1 in 1980. By 2005 it had mushroomed to 411 to 1. The median American family made nearly $1000 *less* in 2006 than in 2000, even though the U.S. economy had a healthy rate of growth in that period. Between 2002 and 2006, 75 percent of all income gains went to the top 1 percent — households making more than $382,600 a year. The United States is now the third most unequal industrial society, after Russia and Mexico.[14]

Some argue that the extravagant wealth of a few does not necessarily hinder the flourishing of the majority. The extreme economic inequality found in the United States, however, concentrates power in the hands of a wealthy few and thus erodes democracy and participation; it also seriously undermines solidarity. The super-wealthy have extraordinary political clout through campaign contributions that influence politicians or by running for office themselves. This legal distortion of the political process provokes cynicism and disengagement among ordinary citizens. Moreover, the very wealthy tend to isolate themselves from common life in gated communities and elite country clubs. They take care of their own needs privately and thus disinvest from public education, transportation, libraries, recreation, and policing.[15] Extreme inequality runs counter to the major principles of Catholic social teaching — the common good, solidarity, participation, and the option for the poor.

Besides a living wage, workers have a right of association so that they can form unions or professional associations to defend their interests. The right to organize unions has been a mainstay of Catholic social teaching from Leo XIII (*On the Condition of Labor*, #36–44) through John Paul II (*On Human Work*, #20) and Benedict XVI (*Charity in Truth*, #64). The tradition has consistently upheld the right to strike, although it has cautioned that this extreme measure not be abused (*On the Condition of Labor*, #31; *On Human Work*, #20).

Workers also have a right to a safe work environment, to health care, to rest during the week and during the year, to provision for retirement in old age, and security in case of injury at work (*On Human Work*, #19). Disabled persons have the same rights as other workers (#22). Workers have a right to emigrate in search of a better life, and immigrant workers have all the rights discussed thus far (#23). Immigrants should be treated with respect and hospitality, not discrimination and exploitation.

Leo XIII warns that children can be harmed by hard work disproportionate to their level of maturity, like rough weather's impact on the buds of spring, but he does not condemn child labor. Both Leo (in 1891) and John Paul (in 1981) think that the primary work for women should be in the role of a mother who rears and educates her children. They think it best that women not work outside of the home (*On the Condition of Labor*, #33; *On Human Work*, #19). This consistent papal position has been criticized as unrealistic and sexist. The popes do not seem to realize that many women work out of necessity, and that women have the same need for personal fulfillment and social participation as does any human being.[16]

A Spirituality of Work

The final section of *On Human Work* (#24–27) returns to some of the biblical themes of the second section. It reinforces the theme that work is a participation in the creative activity of the Creator, that humanity is a co-creator with God. John Paul II highlights work as a theme, metaphor, and topic in the New Testament and makes the connection with the work of both Jesus and the apostle Paul. The pope also relates the toil aspect of labor with the redemptive work of the cross. Surprisingly, John Paul does not develop a spirituality of solidarity in the struggle for social justice connected to the labor movement.[17] On this point César Chávez can make a definite contribution to a spirituality of work.

The Social Purpose of Private Property and Material Possessions

The *Compendium of the Social Doctrine of the Church* includes "the universal destination of goods and private property" among the five (or so) key principles of Catholic social teaching (#176–84), and John Paul II titles the fourth chapter of his encyclical *On the Hundredth Anniversary* (*Centesimus Annus*, 1991) "Private Property and the Universal Destination of Material Goods" (#30–43). The pope addresses economic issues in that chapter, and he begins by tracing this principle through the teaching of his predecessors and in his own thought in his two prior social encyclicals (#30).

John Paul II emphasizes the consistency of Catholic social teaching rather than its development. Thus he makes the case that Leo XIII recognizes that the right of private property is conditioned by the common good (#30).

Many other commentators suggest that Leo XIII was so insistent that private property was part of the solution to the poverty of workers and an answer to socialism that he nearly neglected to put any social limits on it (*On the Condition of Labor,* #30, 35).[18] Pope Leo had a very individualistic understanding of private property, which is generally out of step with the Catholic tradition. With the possible exception of Leo XIII, however, what John Paul II calls "the social mortgage" on private property (*On Social Concern,* #42) is found throughout modern Catholic social teaching,[19] and it is deeply rooted in Christian tradition.

That principle, which can be stated as the universal destination of created goods or the social purpose of private property and material possessions, is an example of the balance characteristic of Catholic social teaching, but it also contains an emphasis. Catholic social teaching affirms both the right of private property and the common good. When these values are in conflict, however, the common good takes priority, or trumps private property.

The social mortgage (social "lien" might also be a good metaphor) on private property is rooted in the doctrine of creation, and thus also in natural law. God has created the material world for the good of all. Therefore created goods have a universal destination. Although private property can be an effective social arrangement, the earth and its resources are owned by God and are gifted to all of humanity. Humans are stewards of this creation, not owners in any ultimate sense (see chapter 5 below). Thus the common good and the needs of the poor take precedence over any surplus private possessions.

The Hebrew laws regarding the sabbatical year, when the land was given rest, and the Jubilee Year (the fiftieth year), when the land was restored to its original owners and slaves were freed (Lev 25 and Deut 15), are expressions of this principle. The earth is the Creator's, and God sets limits on its use and establishes rules for its fair distribution.

This principle is evident in the teaching of the New Testament as well, not least in the parable regarding the fates of poor Lazarus and the rich man at whose gate he begged (Luke 16:19–31).[20] It can also be seen in the practice of the Christian community in Jerusalem of holding all their possessions in common and distributing them according to need (Acts 2:43–47; 4:32–37).

In his reflection on this principle in *On the Development of Peoples,* Paul VI refers to the 1 John 3:17, "If someone who has the riches of this world sees his brother in need and closes his heart to him, how does the love of God abide in him?" Pope Paul then quotes St. Ambrose (340–97 C.E.), as representative of the Fathers of the church, to the effect that aiding those in need is not a matter of charity but of justice, because God's gift of creation is for the common use of all. Paul VI concludes, "No one is justified in keeping for his exclusive use what he does not need, when others lack necessities" (#23). This is a moral challenge indeed for North American Christians who have so much when two-thirds of humanity is without basic necessities.

According to this principle rich Christians in a hungry world are a scandal and should be an anomaly.

The social purpose of material possessions is also a logical conclusion of other major principles of Catholic social teaching, especially solidarity and the option for the poor. As John Paul II points out in *On the Hundredth Anniversary*, this principle applies not only to natural resources but also to the works of human hands, such as the information, technology, and skills that are so essential to the modern economy (#31–32).[21]

Sharing information, technology, and skills for the common good raises interesting questions and some moral dilemmas. Not so long ago it seemed that the scientific community, for example, readily shared research with one another with the goal of the progress of science itself. Now many scientists seem more entrepreneurial and competitive. Scientific and technological developments are often funded with public money. Should a scientist receive a patent for a mouse created for cancer research? Should drugs for HIV positive people in developing countries be made widely available to the poor? If corporations cannot profit from their investments in research will they stop investing in research? What sort of public policy will enhance the common good in this area?

The Preferential Option for the Poor

The option for the poor was listed among the key principles of Catholic social teaching in chapter 2. It is a principle that directly pertains to economic justice and to human rights. This section will trace its place in Catholic social teaching and expand upon its meaning.[22]

The concept of a "preferential option for the poor," a contribution of the Latin American church to Catholic social teaching, has strong biblical roots. In the Hebrew scriptures this theme is prominent in the story of the Exodus (Ex 1–15), which is the foundational story of the covenant between God and the Hebrew people. When the Hebrews fell into slavery in Egypt, God heard their cries of distress and saved them from their oppression through the intercession of Moses. God is a liberator of the oppressed. And when the Hebrews began to oppress one another after settling in the promised land (Israel), God sent prophets (messengers) who denounced the injustice and idolatry of the people and called them back to the covenant with God that demands justice.

Jesus himself was one of the common people, born in a stable under embarrassing circumstances and welcomed by lowly shepherds. He was a refugee before settling in an obscure village, a carpenter's son. Jesus proclaimed good news to the poor, the release of captives, and freedom for the oppressed (Lk 4:18–19), and he ministered to those on the margins of society — the lepers, tax collectors, prostitutes, the sick in body and spirit and the disabled. Among his closest followers were fisherfolk, a reformed tax collector, and some women "who provided for them out of their resources" (Lk 8:1–3). His message so disturbed the powerful that he was crucified as a revolutionary. Jesus was clearly committed to the poor and the marginalized, to liberation for the oppressed.

There is another related biblical theme that is also important for understanding the option for the poor: God chose the weak to confound the strong, the foolish to fluster the wise, the despised to bring down the powerful (1 Cor 1:27–28). God called Israel to be God's special people, hardly the obvious political choice. God chose a man with a speech impediment (Moses) to tell the Egyptian pharaoh to let the Hebrews go (Ex 4:10–16). God chose the cowardly Gideon to be God's champion against the powerful Midianites, and then dismissed all but three hundred of the troops (Jgs 6–7). And God anointed David, Jesse's youngest son, who was out watching the sheep, to be Israel's king (1 Sam 16). Then God chose Mary of Nazareth, an ordinary, unmarried young woman to bear Jesus, the son of God, into the world (Lk 1:26–56). As we have seen, Jesus collected a motley crew of the marginalized to be his disciples and the founders of the church.[23] There is a definite pattern here, and there is no reason to think that God has changed it in acting in contemporary history.

In its response to the Second Vatican Council (1962–65), the church in Latin America tapped into this biblical vein that privileges the poor. The bishops of Latin America and the Caribbean had formed into a conference (called CELAM from the acronym in Spanish) and held a general meeting in Rio de Janeiro in 1955, well before Vatican II. When CELAM held its second general meeting in Medellín, Colombia, in 1968, the Latin American bishops were consciously seeking to respond to the "signs of the times" in the spirit of Vatican II. The overwhelming reality of their people was poverty. Thus at Medellín the church in Latin America committed itself to respond pastorally to the needs of the poor. The phrase "preferential option for the poor" was not used explicitly in the Medellín documents but the idea is clearly there.[24]

Leo XIII alludes to God's special concern for the poor in *On the Condition of Labor* (#29), and John XXIII states that the church wishes to be the "church of the poor" in an important speech given a month prior to Vatican II, an idea that finds its way into *The Pastoral Constitution on the Church in the Modern World* (1965, #1, 29, 63–72, passim).[25] The term "preferential option for the poor" was coined by Peruvian theologian Gustavo Gutiérrez in the period following the Medellín conference in 1968, and it was used by the Latin American bishops at their Puebla conference in 1979.[26] Paul VI develops the theme of the option for the poor throughout *On the Development of Peoples* (1967, #12) and in *A Call to Action* (1971,

#23).[27] It is used by the American Catholic bishops in *Economic Justice for All* (#16, 24, 52, 87–88), and in the *Compendium of the Social Doctrine of the Church* (182–84, 449). In *On Social Concern* (#42) and *The Hundredth Anniversary* (chapter 6, #57) John Paul II confirmed the idea, but he had difficulty using the term. John Paul prefers "preferential but not exclusive love of the poor" or something similar. The preferential option for the poor was reaffirmed by the fifth general conference of CELAM in Aparecida, Brazil, in May, 2007.[28] It has become a defining characteristic of contemporary Catholic social teaching.

The idea needs to be "unpacked," and this may signal that the phrase is somewhat confusing.[29] The "poor" refers to those who are *materially* impoverished, powerless, and marginalized. Both poverty and prejudice render a person marginal and powerless. This concept refers to those whose basic needs are unmet or whose human rights are crushed through discrimination.

God has a preference for or privileges the poor. God is on the side of the poor, working in history to free people from oppression and exploitation. Because God stands with the poor, so should Christians.[30] Thus the preferential option for the poor is first of all a perspective and an attitude that results in concrete movement and action. It means seeing reality the way the poor see it and responding appropriately. For example, when bus fares inch up because of higher gas prices, the poor who depend on public transportation and who are barely scraping by may find their monthly budgets devastated. The decision whether to buy milk for the children or pay the increased bus fare to work is on a different order from the higher cost of filling up the SUV or Hummer.

> As individuals and as a nation, therefore, we are called to make a fundamental "option for the poor." The obligation to evaluate social and economic activity from the viewpoint of the poor and the powerless arises from the radical command to love one's neighbor as one's self. Those who are marginalized and whose rights are denied have privileged claims if society is to provide justice for *all*. (*Economic Justice for All*, #87)

John Paul II was afraid that "preferential" might be misunderstood to mean an exclusive concern or to countenance class conflict. God created us all and loves every one of us, but God pays special attention to those who are vulnerable and needy, just like parents do. Privileging the poor does not exclude anyone else from concern. Nevertheless, the litmus test for the justice of a society is how the poor are faring, not how many yachts there are per thousand of the population.

John Paul's wariness of class conflict is understandable given his formation in communist-controlled Poland. The pope is correct that the option for the poor does not necessitate violence. Catholic social teaching, however, has been rightly criticized for not taking seriously enough the reality of conflict.[31]

Given original sin and human nature, oppressors seldom change their behavior simply on the basis of awareness. There is a conflict between the interests of the poor and the interests of their oppressors that can be resolved only through confrontation, dialogue, and direct action. John Paul acknowledges that justice requires both personal conversion and social transformation (*On the Hundredth Anniversary,* #57–58).

An "option" for the poor does not mean that Christians can choose whether or not to be on the side of the poor. Rather, it means a *commitment* in favor of the poor. Such a commitment is unlikely to be sustained without solidarity with the poor, that is, a lifestyle that includes increasing experience with the poor and sharing the lot of the poor. The result of such a commitment includes political action for justice. This involves empowering the poor to act on their own behalf and accompanying them on this journey. César Chávez is a model of the option for the poor. He understood the plight of farm workers from the inside. When he had the opportunity for economic security as a community organizer, he instead decided to commit himself to *la causa.*

"Central to the biblical presentation of justice is that the justice of a community is measured by its treatment of the powerless in society, most often described as the widow, the orphan, the poor, and the stranger (non-Israelite) in the land."

"The way society responds to the needs of the poor through its public policies is the litmus test of its justice or injustice."

— *Economic Justice for All,* #38, #123

One way of grasping the option for the poor is by considering the saints and contemporary witnesses who have lived in solidarity with the poor and ministered to and been empowered by the poor.[32]

• *Francis of Assisi* (1182–1226) is renowned for responding literally to Jesus' call to the rich young man to "go, sell what you own, and give the money to the poor, and you will have treasure in heaven; then come, follow me" (Mk 10:21). Francis spent the rest of his life pursuing downward social mobility, letting go of material possessions and of power and prestige (see chapter 1 above.)

• *Angela Merici* (1474–1540) was moved by the poverty and ignorance of her neighbors in northern Italy and began to educate their children, especially the girls. Soon others were inspired to join in this work. Shortly after her death the church officially recognized her group of followers as the Ursulines, one of the first religious communities of women to live and work in the community rather than the enclosure of a convent.

• *Martin de Porres* (1579–1639), a Dominican lay brother in Lima, Peru, offered charity and healing to all those who counted as nothing in the city — Indians, the poor, the sick, especially African slaves, and even the animals. He was recognized as a living parable of God's kingdom.

• *Frédéric Ozanam* (1813–53) lived at a time of social chaos in Paris and France. An intellectual and distinguished professor at the Sorbonne, the University of Paris, Ozanam sought to defend Christianity and the church from the secularization initiated by the French Revolution and to reconcile the church with the positive values of liberty and democracy espoused by the Revolution. He soon realized that intellectual arguments were insufficient without witness, without acts of charity and justice. Thus he formed a fellowship of lay Christians to minister to "Les Misérables," the victims of the Industrial Revolution who lived in densely populated, disease-ridden slums and labored in dangerous, debilitating conditions. The St. Vincent de Paul Society continues to serve the poor and witness to the credibility and integrity of the gospel.

• *Peter Maurin* (1877–1949) was a French peasant who immigrated to North America and became an itinerant laborer. He developed a vision that related the gospel to society in a way that would "build a new society within the shell of the old." Fortuitously he was directed to *Dorothy Day* (1897–1980), a journalist and recent Catholic convert who had a history of involvement in radical social movements and was seeking a way to apply the gospel to issues of social justice. Within a year they had established the *Catholic Worker,* a newspaper and a movement dedicated to Christian non-violence and to practicing the works of mercy through houses of hospitality. Catholic Worker communities, which are committed to living in solidarity with the poor and oppressed and working for social justice and peace, continue to witness to the option for the poor throughout the country today.

• On September 10, 1946, the woman who would become known as *Mother Teresa of Calcutta* (1910–97) experienced what she referred to as a call within a call. Known then as Sister Agnes, a Loretto missionary from Albania who had spent twenty years teaching middle-class students in India, she suddenly felt that God "wanted me to be poor with the poor and to love him in the distressing disguise of the poorest of the poor." She received permission to move outside the walls of the convent to the streets of Calcutta and began teaching the children and ministering to those who were dying pitiful deaths in the gutters. When others joined her in this work she established the Missionaries of Charity who continue to live simple lives among the poorest people throughout the world and offer small acts of charity with great love.

• The small country of El Salvador in Central America, in the period from the mid-1970s through the 1980s, exemplifies a new kind of Christian martyr common in our age. These martyrs were murdered by those who professed to be Christians, not only because they clung to their Christian faith but also because they advocated for the poor and for social change.

During this period of civil unrest and government repression, it is estimated that death squads in El Salvador killed over seventy thousand peasants out of a population of under 5 million. Among the first priests killed for their commitment to the poor was *Rutilio Grande* (1928–77), a native Jesuit who had come to redefine his vocation after Vatican II in terms of service to the poor rather than as an exemplar of Christian perfection.

• The newly appointed, shy, and conservative archbishop of San Salvador, *Oscar Romero* (1917–80), officiated at the funeral of his friend and was himself radicalized by the experience. Romero distanced the church from the corrupt government, decried its repression, criticized U.S. military support, and sided decisively with the poor. He was assassinated while saying Mass in 1980.

• Later that year four American women — Maryknoll Sisters *Maura Clarke* and *Ita Ford,* Ursuline Sister *Dorothy Kazel,* and lay missioner *Jean Donovan* — were raped and killed by Salvadoran military officers. Jean Donovan, aged twenty-seven, was from a privileged background and had embarked on a successful accounting career before finding her materialistic lifestyle empty and unfulfilling. Her pursuit of a deeper response to the gospel led her to El Salvador and a commitment to the poor despite the clear risks of solidarity with the poor — capture, torture, and disappearance.[33]

• And then in November 1989 six Jesuit priests associated with the University of Central America in San Salvador, their housekeeper, and her sixteen-year-old daughter were forced to lie down in their garden and were shot in the back of the head by an elite antiterrorist unit of the army. The Jesuits in El Salvador had articulated and implemented a theology of liberation centered on the option for the poor. They shared the fate of the "crucified peoples" of Latin America.

• *Helen Prejean,* a Sister of St. Joseph of Medaille, recounts her own call within a call in her best-selling book *Dead Man Walking.*[34] She grew up in a privileged family in segregated Baton Rouge, Louisiana, in the 1940s and 1950s. In 1980 she experienced a radical shift in perspective at a conference that was part of the reform movement in the Catholic Church exploring the connection between religious faith and social justice. A talk by Sister Marie Augusta Neal convinced her not only of Jesus' option for the poor but of the impossibility of being nonpolitical. If one is not challenging an unjust system, one is supporting the status quo and thus is not neutral. Within a year she moved from teaching in the suburbs to pastoral ministry in St. Thomas, a New Orleans housing project of poor black residents. There she continued her education regarding the systematic oppression of the poor. At the request of a friend, she also agreed to become a pen pal to a death row inmate. This led to a ministry to the poor on death row and to advocacy against capital punishment.

Each of these people opted for the poor and became part of the "cloud of witnesses" (Heb 12:1–2) who live in solidarity with the poor, offer direct service to the poor, and advocate the transformation of social structures that repress and oppress people in response to the gospel. The church has further clarified its commitment to the poor and to overcoming poverty in its teaching about authentic development, our next topic.

Authentic Development as a Response to Global Poverty

On July 7, 2009, Pope Benedict XVI released his third encyclical, *Charity in Truth* (*Caritas in Veritate*), on the eve of a summit hosted by Italy for the G8, a group of eight economically powerful nations. On that occasion the pope met with U.S. president Barak Obama and presented him with a copy of the new social encyclical. The G8 summit addressed issues such as food security and climate change, which are touched on in the encyclical.

This deft timing by the Vatican culminated a process that had been delayed for over two years, in part by a global economic recession. Pope Benedict planned *Charity in Truth* to mark the fortieth anniversary of Paul VI's *On the Development of Peoples* (*Populorum Progressio*, 1967). John Paul II had observed the twentieth anniversary with his *On Social Concern* (*Sollicitudo Rei Socialis*, 1987). *Charity in Truth* is the first social encyclical since John Paul II's *On the Hundredth Anniversary* (*Centesimus Annus*, 1991). These four documents address the gap between the rich and the poor and between developed and developing countries. This section will focus on Benedict XVI's *Charity in Truth*, the most recent word from the church on global poverty and the alleviation of the suffering of the poor, which consciously depends on and recapitulates the thought of Paul VI.

The subtitle of *Charity in Truth* is "On Integral Human Development in Charity and Truth." Integral or authentic human development, a concept that Benedict borrows from Paul VI (*On the Development of Peoples*, #14–21, 34, 42–43),[35] has been the church's response to global poverty. Whereas economists tend to focus on economic growth as the key to economic development and the alleviation of poverty, the church sees this as a necessary, but insufficient, condition for human development. Paul VI and Benedict XVI have offered a holistic vision of integral human development, one that is material and spiritual, secular and transcendent.

Authentic human development entails the economic growth manifested by greater production *and* the just redistribution of these goods and services to benefit the common good. Human development includes the economic, political, cultural, moral, and spiritual realms. It involves the principles of human rights, the option for the poor, and an ethic of solidarity and fraternity, participation, and social justice. Although social and economic structures and institutions are important, authentic human development happens ultimately through the responsible exercise of human freedom (*Charity in Truth*, #17). It is a vocation (#11, 16) that is rooted in a deep

Christian humanism (#78). Integral human development is the genuine and realistic antidote to global poverty. It is the framework for both Paul VI's *On the Development of Peoples* and Benedict XVI's *Charity in Truth*. This concept integrates the church's mission for evangelization and spirituality with its concern for social justice and its duty to engage in social action.[36]

This holistic concept of authentic human development allows Benedict XVI to make some insightful and challenging remarks about the economy and economic development. Benedict observes that "as society becomes ever more globalized, it makes us neighbors but does not make us brothers" (#19). Then he catalogs some of the causes of poverty and the consequences and challenges of globalization (*Charity in Truth*, chapter 2, #21–33):

- increasing inequality between the rich and the poor;

- government and corporate corruption (#22);

- the weakening of social protection through outsourcing, failure to respect the rights of workers, undermining labor unions, and the mobility of labor (#25);

- loss of cultural identity through commercialization (#26);

- food insecurity and hunger (#27);

- disrespect for the right to life (#28);

- a focus on short-term profit or purely technological solutions to human problems (#32);

- high tariffs imposed on goods from developing countries as well as lingering neocolonialism (#33).

In the third chapter of *Charity in Truth* (#34–42), the pope makes some fundamental observations and highlights some basic Christian values to give direction to the economy so that it might aid in achieving integral human development. Basically Benedict replaces the greed that characterizes much of modern capitalism with a sense of gratuity and with the requirement that the economy serve the common good. Profit cannot be the sole measure of a business enterprise's value. Rather business must be guided by a "person-centered ethic (#45)" that recognizes human dignity and builds genuine community. Economic decisions should express "fraternity," that is, genuinely personal relationships, and they should be guided by charity and gratuity. The primary purpose of business and of the economy is to serve the common good: to create a society conducive to human flourishing and to contribute directly to integral human development. This message reinforces and goes beyond the idea of corporate social responsibility. "Benedict is not simply suggesting a moral yardstick for the marketplace. He is claiming that every communal exchange needs to become a loving act modeled on the gratuitous gift of Jesus Christ."[37]

Paul VI has an *articulated vision of human development.* He understood the term to indicate the goal of rescuing peoples, first and foremost, from hunger, deprivation, endemic diseases, and illiteracy. From the economic point of view, this meant active participation, on equal terms, in the international economic process; from the social point of view, it meant their evolution into educated societies marked by solidarity; from the political point of view, it meant the consolidation of democratic regimes capable of ensuring freedom and peace. (*Charity in Truth,* #21)

The second truth is that *authentic human development concerns the whole person in every single dimension.* Without the perspective of eternal life, human progress in this world is denied breathing-space. Enclosed within history, it runs the risk of being reduced to the mere accumulation of wealth; humanity thus loses the courage to be at the service of higher goods, at the service of the great and disinterested initiatives called forth by universal charity. (ibid. #11)

Development must include not just material growth but also spiritual growth, since the human person is a "unity of body and soul," born of God's creative love and destined for eternal life.... A prosperous society, highly developed in material terms but weighed heavily on the soul, is not of itself conducive to authentic development.... *There cannot be holistic development and universal common good unless people's spiritual and moral welfare is taken into account,* considered in their totality as body and soul. (ibid. #76)

Benedict gives concrete direction to this basic insight in two ways. While he appreciates the utility of a market economy (#35), he distinguishes a capitalist economy, governed by the pursuit of profit for shareholders, from a civil economy that is focused on the common good of all its "stakeholders — namely the workers, the suppliers, the consumers, the natural environment and broader society" (#40).[38] He affirms the latter, and he applauds hybrid business enterprises "of the so-called 'civil economy' and the 'economy of communion'" (#46, 41, 38) that use their profits to enhance the common good.[39]

Second, Benedict confirms the role of the political community in regulating and managing the economic order so that it serves the common good (#36). The nation-state has a role in governing national economies and directing them toward integral human development. He also calls for an international supervisory agency, logically linked to the United Nations, "to manage the global economy; to revive economies hit by the crisis; to avoid any deterioration of the present crisis and the greater imbalances that would result; to bring about integral and timely disarmament, food security and peace; to guarantee the protection of the environment and to regulate migration" (#67). Political communities, the pope reminds us, are to be guided by the principles of subsidiarity (#47, 57, 60, 67) and solidarity (#47, 48, 58 passim), but both of these principles agree that global problems require international institutions to organize and to focus international cooperation.[40]

The great challenge before us, accentuated by the problems of development in this global era and made even more urgent by the economic and financial crisis, is to demonstrate, in thinking and behavior, not only that the traditional principles of social ethics like transparency, honesty and responsibility cannot be ignored or attenuated, but also that in *commercial relationships* the *principle of gratuitousness* and the logic of gift as an expression of fraternity can and must *find their place within normal economic activity.* (*Charity in Truth,* #36)

Thus Benedict XVI is consistent with Paul VI's *On the Development of Peoples* in using the concept of authentic human development as a framework for responding to global poverty. Within that framework he innovatively addresses globalization[41] and the current economic crisis. The expected critical discussion about Benedict's ideas and teaching on the topic of development has already started.[42]

A Tough Read

Peter Steinfels, a religion writer for the *New York Times,* forthrightly addressed one early criticism of *Charity in Truth* by asking why the encyclical was so poorly written.[43] Steinfels is not trying to dismiss this "remarkable document, brimming with profound ideas and moral passion and issued at a time when it could hardly be more relevant," but to raise an honest, serious question. "Of course," Steinfels admits, "not everyone will agree that *Caritas in Veritate* is hard going. Some people, after all, enjoy visits to the dentist, and besides there are many crystalline sentences that can be yanked from the molasses-like text."

Benedict acknowledges that the church does not offer technical solutions to social and economic problems, but rather a Christian vision regarding integral human development and moral principles to guide solutions (#9).[44] Nevertheless, the abstract generality, obscurity, and sheer density of the prose in the encyclical make its meaning ambiguous and open to misinterpretation. The encyclical attends neither to the victimization of women by poverty and exploitation nor to the role of women in development. This is not surprising; after all, the sexist language of the document consistently excludes women.

An encyclical is among the most authoritative exercises of the teaching and pastoral role of the pope. Given the realities of globalization, environmental adversity, and the current economic crisis, the Christian community and the world need the wisdom, guidance, and encouragement of the church. A nearly unintelligible document is a pastoral and educational tragedy. For example, I would be reluctant to assign *Charity in Truth* to my undergraduate students lest it undermine respect for the church's social teaching by being all but indecipherable by the educated general reader. One wonders whether political leaders and academic experts in the social sciences will wade through such a ponderous document. If the church wants to be influential and effective in relating the gospel to social issues, its teaching should be clear and accessible.[45]

Bono: Activist for a World without Poverty

Economic development is a complicated and contested matter. Christians are encouraged to put their faith into action through advocacy organizations such as NETWORK and Bread for the World and to make financial donations to organizations such as the Catholic Campaign for Human Development and Catholic Relief Services (see chapter 2 above). There are, however, some individuals whose commitment to the poor has had dramatic results. Former President *Jimmy Carter* has worked through the Atlanta-based Carter Center to eradicate tropical diseases that devastate whole villages and to promote fair democratic elections all over the world. *Paul Farmer,* a professor of medical anthropology at Harvard University and attending physician at Brigham and Women's Hospital in Boston, has been a public-health pioneer in rural Haiti. He founded Partners in Health in 1987 to fight infectious diseases and to bring health care to the world's poorest people.[46] Another such individual is Bono, the lead singer for the Irish rock band U2.[47]

For decades Bono has been using his charm, charisma, and celebrity status to "Make Poverty History." In 1985 U2 played in Live Aid, a concert dedicated to famine relief organized by his friend and fellow Irishman Bob Geldorf. After the concert Bono and his wife, Ali Hewson, spent six weeks volunteering at an orphanage in Ethiopia. Bono was overwhelmed by the hunger, war, and corruption he experienced in Africa, but he put his concern on the back burner while U2 catapulted to world recognition for its music. Then in 1997 a British development advocate, Jamie Drummond, contacted Bono with the message that, while Live Aid raised $200 million, Ethiopia alone paid $500 million in annual debt service to the world's lending institutions. Drummond invited Bono to be a spokesperson for Jubilee 2000, a church-based campaign to persuade governments to cancel third-world debt in honor of the new millennium. In accepting this role, Bono began to immerse himself in the facts, causes, and remedies regarding global poverty,

especially in Africa. As he went from fluency to mastery, under the tute-
lage of friends such as Drummond and economist Jeffrey Sachs,[48] he found
his voice.

Early in the new millennium Bono founded an advocacy organization
called DATA, a Geldorf-inspired double acronym meant to position the
group at the nexus of the nonprofit development world (debt, AIDS, trade,
Africa) and the results-oriented world of politics and corporations (democracy, accountability, transparency in Africa). Bono is an ace networker
for the cause of the poor with a knack for fostering effective relationships across the political and social spectrum. On at least this issue, Bono
believes, everyone can break bread together. He effectively lobbied the Clin-
ton administration on debt relief, and he persuaded George W. Bush to
triple foreign aid for AIDS relief in Africa and to launch the Millennium
Challenge Corporation, which rewards countries with development aid for
being accountable. He appealed to President Bush and to some of his key
aides on the basis of softhearted faith (the biblical imperative to help the
poor) and on the basis of hardheaded national interest (eradicating poverty
opens up markets and improves the American image).

Bono is comfortable talking to church groups, telling them about Christ
and the lepers to stimulate compassion for AIDS victims and noting that
there are 2,103 passages in scripture about taking care of the poor. Born to
a Protestant mother and a Catholic father, Bono strives to live his faith more
than talk about it. He is convinced that God cares about the development
of humanity, both individually and collectively.[49] He brings to the cause of
the poor a passion born of faith and a pragmatism rooted in reason and
experience. He realizes the complexity of the problem and the inadequacy
of our efforts, but he is willing to nudge governments to take incremental
steps in the right direction.

When the G8 countries met at Gleneagles, Scotland, in early July 2005,
Bono and the human development community of activists sensed an opportunity to accomplish something significant. The then prime minister of Great
Britain, Tony Blair, and his chancellor of the Exchequer, Gordon Brown,
were committed to alleviating global poverty, and they announced challenging goals for the summit in regard to debt relief and development aid. The
development community worked together on an integrated awareness campaign called "Make Poverty History" in the UK and the ONE Campaign in
the United States. Over two hundred thousand people dressed in white cir-
cled Edinburgh to encourage the G8 leaders meeting nearby to make poverty
history. On the twentieth anniversary of Live Aid, free concerts were held
in each of the G8 countries to raise awareness about global poverty and the
importance of the G8 summit. Bono personally met with the leaders of five
of the eight countries at the summit to persuade them to make a significant
commitment. In the end the leaders agreed to cancel the debt of the eighteen
poorest African countries and to commit to increase development aid by
$50 billion by 2010.

Such commitments, while significant, are also fragile. In order to take strides in making poverty history, Bono and the development community realize that there needs to be an international *movement* of millions of concerned citizens willing to raise our voices and lobby our governments to sacrifice on behalf of the poor. When election campaigns begin to turn on the issue of global poverty and the necessity of development aid and of fair trade policies, we will know that progress is being made in forming a movement for integral human development.

Bono is a complicated man. In March of 2005, U2 was inducted into the Rock and Roll Hall of Fame. He is a talented singer and songwriter and an international rock star. He is also a savvy capitalist with celebrity tastes for the good life. He owns expensive homes in Dublin, Manhattan, and the south of France, and orders thousand dollar bottles of wine in expensive restaurants. He has not exactly embraced the downward mobility of Francis of Assisi. Yet he has also directed his capitalist instincts into the creative (and controversial) Red Campaign, which tries to harness consumers and corporations into contributing to aid the poor. And he is a tireless campaigner and effective advocate on behalf of the poor in Africa. His depth of knowledge and understanding, genuineness, and passion have persuaded the powerful to subsidize medicines for AIDS victims, to work toward the eradication of infectious diseases, to cancel the debt of struggling countries, to ease trade barriers for products from developing countries, and to feed the hungry. Rock on!

Conclusion

Catholic social teaching on economic justice focuses on four themes — (1) the rights of workers, (2) the idea of a social mortgage on private property and material possessions, (3) the option for the poor, and (4) authentic human development as a response to global poverty. Each of these themes calls the human family toward solidarity — into genuine relationship with each other. Christians are to work for a world where each person and everyone can flourish, where every person's basic needs are met, and where meaningful work allows a person to make a living and to contribute to the common good. Economic justice requires changes in lifestyle, personal sacrifice, and generosity. It also requires a transformation of social structures so that they foster fairness and a real opportunity for human development.

Questions for Reflection and Discussion

1. What can be done to ensure justice for migrant farm workers? What are the rights of workers? How should a just wage be calculated? The issue of migrant farm workers is connected to the question of justice and hospitality for immigrants (chap. 2). What sort of immigration policy should the United States have?

2. Is there a social lien on private property and material possessions? What would you be willing to sacrifice for those whose basic needs are not being met? Would you vote for a candidate who proposed higher taxes in order to increase foreign aid, unemployment benefits, and support for the needy?

3. Does God take the side of the poor? Mother Teresa, who was "poor with the poor and who loved Jesus in the distressing disguise of the poor," has been criticized because she did not advocate for social policies and structural change that would benefit the poor. What do you think of this criticism? Is advocacy for justice a necessary complement to direct service to the poor? How would an option for the poor change your lifestyle?

4. Discuss the principle of authentic or integral human development as a response to global poverty.

5. Is there a disconnect between Bono's rock star lifestyle and his advocacy for a world without poverty? Does Bono need to be poor with the poor and involved in direct service to the poor in order to be an effective advocate for and with the poor?

Chapter 4

War and Peace

In 1965, the Second Vatican Council felt compelled "to undertake an evaluation of war with an entirely different attitude."[1] The primary reason for this was that the nature of war itself changed in the twentieth century. War became more devastating and deadly. Of the approximately 18.5 million deaths in World War I (1914–18), over half were soldiers. It is estimated that 40 million people died in the Second World War (1939–45), and nearly 60 percent were civilians. In recent conflicts, such as those in Bosnia, Rwanda, Sudan, Afghanistan, and Iraq, 75 to 90 percent of the victims have been civilians.[2] In 1945, the United States used atomic weapons on Hiroshima and Nagasaki, leveling both Japanese cities. Since then, such weapons have been refined into weapons of unimaginable power, and now nine countries possess them. A fresh appraisal of war is indeed in order.

This chapter will examine the morality of war and the search for peace in Catholic social thought. It will briefly recount the church's history regarding war and peace, analyze this theme in modern Catholic social teaching, and set forth the state of the question today.

A Brief History of Christian Thought on War and Peace

The church's teaching on war and peace can serve as a case study in the development of doctrine. Its evolution is contextual and complex, that is, it takes place in response to particular historical situations, and the church's response is usually multifaceted. This tradition continues to develop today. It is possible, however, to highlight three basic approaches regarding the morality of war in Christian tradition — pacifism or nonviolence, just war, and crusade.[3]

Pacifism/Nonviolence

During its first three centuries, the Christian community did not participate in war. The Fathers of the church during this period, such as Tertullian (160–220) and Origen (185–254), viewed nonviolence as a requirement of the countercultural way of life that was Christian discipleship. This repudiation of warfare was consistent and unanimous among these early Christian writers. Being a soldier was generally seen as incompatible with the Christian faith because of the love preached by Jesus and because of the idolatry practiced by the Roman army. Until the Roman emperor Constantine converted to Christianity in 313, the church was a marginalized and persecuted religious sect. During this period Christians were pacifists for a variety of reasons, not least the perceived incompatibility between discipleship and killing.[4]

After Constantine, the status of Christianity changed, as did its relationship with the state. As the power of the Roman Empire ebbed and Rome came under threat from barbarians attacking from the north, Ambrose (340–97) and Augustine (354–430) drew on the Greek and Roman concept of "just war" to justify Christian participation in war. Augustine's political theology and his acceptance of just war would come to dominate Christian tradition from the fifth century to the present.[5]

Just War

The just war tradition has developed considerably through history. Thomas Aquinas (1225–74) considered "whether it is always sinful to wage war." His response consolidated Augustine's thought on just war and gave it more coherence. Thomas also expanded on the conditions for going to war, giving more attention to the morality of fighting a war.[6] Further significant expansion of the just war theory took place in the sixteenth and seventeenth centuries in the writings of the Spanish Dominican Francisco de Vitoria (1492–1546), the Spanish Jesuit Francisco Suarez (1548–1617), and the Dutch Protestant Hugo Grotius (1583–1645), who consolidated the beginnings of international law.[7] The changing nature of war led to further developments in the just war tradition in the twentieth century.

The U.S. bishops offer a contemporary statement of the criteria for a just war in their 1983 pastoral letter, *The Challenge of Peace: God's Promise and Our Response*.[8] The bishops strongly affirm that there is a presumption for peace and against war. Thus the burden of proof rests with those who wish to justify the morality of a particular war. The purpose of the just war tradition is to prevent war and, if war becomes justified, to restrain or limit war. Traditionally the criteria have been divided into two groups: *jus ad bellum*, the reasons why and when a war might be morally justified, and *jus in bello*, principles that regulate the conduct of war (#80–84). *All* of the criteria must be met for war to be justified, and during the prosecution of a war.

Jus ad Bellum — *Why and When Recourse to War Is Morally Permitted*

1. There must be a *just cause* for war. Today the church limits the just cause for war to self-defense or to protect the life and basic human rights of innocents (#86). The bishops include a criterion called "comparative justice," which is meant to emphasize the presumption against war, to relativize absolute claims, and to restrain the use of force even in a justified war (#92–94).

2. The war must be *declared by competent authority* (#87–91). War is a public affair, connected to the common good, not a private responsibility.

3. War must be a *last resort* (#96–97). Again the presumption is for peace and against war. Every diplomatic and nonmilitary option should be exhausted before resorting to force.

4. The war should be waged with a *right intention* (#95). The right intention for war is tied to its cause. War is to restore justice and establish peace and reconciliation. It should not be fought with hatred or an attitude of revenge. The right intention militates against a demand for unconditional surrender and seeks opportunities to end the conflict.

5. There must be a *reasonable hope for success* (#98). The purpose of this criterion is to prevent irrational and disproportionate resort to force or hopeless resistance.

6. The costs and damage incurred by war must be *proportionate* to the benefit expected from taking up arms (#99). For example, many analysts expected that an all-out nuclear war between the United States and the Soviet Union would have resulted in a "nuclear winter" that may have extinguished all human life on earth. No benefit could justify that cost. This principle applies throughout the conflict. A war can become disproportionate.

Jus in Bello — *Restraints on How the War Is Fought, the Conduct during the War*

1. The adversaries must *discriminate* between combatants and noncombatants. It is wrong to intentionally kill or harm noncombatants.

2. Although the principle of indirect effect may allow the destruction of military targets even though some innocents may be killed, collateral damage is limited by the principle of *proportionality.*

The application of each of the criteria to a particular situation of conflict can be complex, ambiguous, and subject to interpretation. For example, should the United Nations be considered an agent to authorize war today? When have we reached last resort? Nevertheless, the just war theory offers a reasonable framework for moral analysis.

Although just war is the prevailing model in both Catholic and Protestant traditions, nonviolence is a minor theme throughout Christian history. It can be found, for example, in the witness of Francis of Assisi (1182–1226), in the thought of Erasmus (1466–1536) and the Renaissance humanists, and in the commitment of the peace churches that evolved out of the radical Reformation — the Mennonites (sixteenth century), the Quakers (seventeenth century), and the Brethren (eighteenth century).[9] Nonviolence continues, for example, in the contemporary witness of Dorothy Day and the Catholic Worker movement, of Martin Luther King Jr. and the civil rights movement, and of organizations such as the Fellowship of Reconciliation and Pax Christi. As we will see in detail later in this chapter, while the contemporary Catholic Church in the United States applauds the nonviolent commitment of individuals, it has not committed the church itself to nonviolence.

Crusade/Holy War

In 1071 Muslims conquered Jerusalem, profaning its holy places and persecuting Christian pilgrims. In 1095, at the Council of Clermont in France, Pope Urban II (1040–99, pope from 1088 to 1099) called for a crusade to reclaim the Holy Land. In the period from 1095 to 1291 eight major crusades and numerous minor ones were launched. Nearly all of the crusades against Islam in Palestine were military failures, but they were quite successful in political, ecclesial, and economic terms. They unified Europe against a common enemy, increased the power of the pope in civil affairs, and opened new trade routes to the East.[10] Theologically, the crusades were clearly a decisive turn away from the message of the gospel.

The medieval church justified the crusades as a preemptive defense of Europe, that is, a just war. The crusade idea, rooted in the "holy warrior" of the Hebrew scriptures, however, goes well beyond just war theory. A just war is fought reluctantly and for a just cause; it is a last resort legitimized by proper civil authority. It is fought discriminately and proportionately in order to restore peace. A crusade is fought under God, for a holy cause. Crusaders are perceived to be good and godly, and their enemies are evil personified. There are no limits on the conduct of a crusade.[11] The logic of a crusade is the logic of genocide.

I am aware of no mainstream Christian theologian or church leader who would justify a crusade today. Along with the Inquisition (a crusade against infidels and heretics *within* the church),[12] crusades are recognized today as a tragic and sinful chapter in Christian history. Yet the twentieth century has been characterized by "total wars," and the "war on terrorism" has some of the characteristics of a crusade. It has been said that it is difficult to move the United States to enter a war, but once at war, Americans tend to fight a crusade. The medieval temptation that the just war theory will degenerate into a crusade will always be with us. Vigilance is the price of morality and integrity.

Catholic Social Teaching on War and Peace during the World Wars

Even though two world wars were fought, there is no papal encyclical on war and peace during the Reform period (1878–1958) that merits inclusion in the canon of modern Catholic social teaching. This does not mean, however, that the popes of this period were indifferent to the search for peace.

Leo XIII (pope, 1878–1903) articulated the themes that would guide the Catholic peace movement in the twentieth century: that peace is founded on a new international order based on justice, that the cost of military defense is a crushing burden on the peoples of the world, and that the justification of even defensive wars in a technological age needs to be reevaluated.[13]

Benedict XV and World War I

During the First World War (1914–18), Benedict XV (pope, 1914–22) emptied the Vatican treasury and dipped into his personal family fortune to minister to the victims of the war, and he worked indefatigably for peace and reconciliation, earning his title the "Pontiff of Peace." His efforts, however, were often misunderstood by the combatants and bore little lasting fruit.[14]

Benedict XV was misshapen in appearance due to an injury at birth. He was temperamentally gentle, approachable, and sympathetic. A former papal diplomat, he was well-suited for the challenges of his time, and he set out to reconcile the major conflicts of his day, beginning with his own house. His predecessor, Pius X (pope, 1903–14), had incited the Modernist crisis in the church by condemning certain modern ideas, silencing and excluding theologians and scholars who proposed them, and imposing an oath against Modernism of all clerics. Benedict ended this repression of new thought and scholarship.

Benedict was opposed to war and considered the just war theory outmoded and theologically inadequate. His ideas on peace were indebted to Erasmus and the Humanist tradition. He rejected the Machiavellian distinction between private and public morality, arguing that the law of charity applied both to individuals and to nations. He remained strictly neutral during the war, with the unfortunate result that both sides accused him of partiality. Trench warfare, the use of chemical weapons, and the beginning of aerial bombing made World War I especially horrific, and Benedict persistently condemned its barbarity and futility. He called for a peace

Trench Warfare

Many expected World War I to be brief, but from the autumn of 1914 until the spring of 1918 the two sides were mostly at a standstill, literally dug in. The trenches stretched from the North Sea to France's border with Switzerland. Opposing forces were only seventy, fifty, or even thirty yards from each other, separated by a "no man's land" of barbed wire, shell holes, and decomposing corpses.

Over two hundred thousand soldiers died in the trenches. Death was a constant companion, whether from the constant shellfire, a sniper's bullet, or disease. Both sides used poison gas (mostly chlorine, phosgene, or mustard gas), and the effect was so unsettling that the use of chemical weapons in warfare was banned in 1925.

Life in the trenches was a mixture of boredom, risk, and endurance. The occupants were often standing in mud and water, soaked through from the rain that flooded the trench. Millions of rats invaded the trenches and fed on the decomposing bodies. Since one pair of rats can produce nine hundred offspring a year, they were impossible to eradicate. Lice caused unceasing itching and sometimes trench fever, a painful illness that requires a three-month recovery period. Clouds of gnats hung over the trenches. Visitors were first struck by the appalling stench from decomposing bodies, overflowing latrines, rotting sandbags, stagnant muck, and unwashed men, but the occupants got used to the smell. And of course a war was being fought with attacks and counter-attacks and random bombardment.[15]

without victory and offered various peace plans to both sides. During the war years, Benedict issued over one hundred encyclicals and letters of instruction and exhortation, consistently advocating noncombatant immunity, relief efforts, truces, the reduction of violence, and the rights of prisoners of war. During and after the war, Benedict actively sought to relieve the suffering of refugees, the wounded, and the grieving.

At the war's end, Benedict called for a fair and just peace treaty that would accomplish reconciliation rather than revenge. He proposed a series of "Points" for a just and lasting peace, including reciprocal disarmament, arbitration under international law, and the rejection of compulsory military service. Unfortunately, his peacemaking efforts offering relief aid for both sides and his neutrality were resented by both sides, and he was specifically excluded from the Versailles Peace Conference (1945), which established the conditions for peace. Benedict XV promoted principles that may have prevented World War II, but the world was in no mood to listen to this peacemaking pope.

Pius XI and the Rise of Totalitarianism[16]

During the papacy of Pius XI (1922–39), totalitarian dictators came to dominate most of Europe with the rise to power of communism in Russia (Stalin), Nazism in Germany (Hitler), and fascism in Italy (Mussolini) and Spain (Franco). The church was already on record as critical of socialism and opposed to atheistic communism. Pius XI, however, tried to accommodate Nazi Germany and fascist Italy at first, and he never opposed Franco in Spain. Not only were these fascist governments anticommunist, but they seemed willing to recognize the autonomy of the church to fulfill its mission.

In his first encyclical *Where Is the Hidden Plan of God?* (*Ubi Arcano Dei Consilio*), Pius reiterated the principle that peace is founded on justice; he also criticized the militarization of nations and called for Catholic lay action. At this point, Pius XI naively seemed to think that such rhetoric would be sufficient to point dictators in the right direction.

Pius XI had an elitist, hierarchical view of society that stressed order; this corresponded to the nature and some of the aims of a totalitarian government. Pius seemed primarily concerned with protecting the freedom and privilege of the church. Thus he entered into the Lateran Treaty (1929) with Mussolini, a treaty that recognized the Italian state, established Catholicism as its official religion, and constituted Vatican City as an independent political entity. In 1933, Pius XI also entered into a concordat with Hitler's Nazi government in Germany that seemed to protect the rights of the church in the religious sphere and the autonomy of the government in the political sphere. Pius XI's actions indicated that he valued order and the institutional church over justice.

In the end Pius discovered that totalitarian governments take over the whole of society, including the church, and that concordats and treaties offered only a false peace. This was especially evident in the church's relationship with Nazi Germany. Hitler's government continually violated the autonomy of the church and responded to church resistance with smear campaigns and persecution. After addressing thirty-four unanswered notes of protest to the Nazi government regarding infractions of the concordat, Pius XI finally responded with an encyclical, *With Burning Sorrow* (in German *Mit Brennender Sorge,* March 1937), which was a scorching indictment of Nazism. The document was smuggled into Germany and continued to be circulated even after the surprised government suppressed it. Pius, now convinced that he must speak out, continued to denounce communism, Nazism, and fascism, their persecution of the church, and their racist policies. It was, however, too late.

Pius XII and World War II

When the college of cardinals convened in March 1939 to elect a new pope, the cardinals naturally turned to the Vatican secretary of state,

Eugenio Pacelli, a skilled diplomat, accomplished linguist, and world traveler. Although seemingly well prepared to bring the faith to bear on a world that would soon be at war, Pius XII's response was tepid and has become controversial.

The Holocaust

The Holocaust (a Greek word for a sacrifice consumed by fire) refers to the systematic, state-sponsored slaughter of Jews by the Nazi regime and its collaborators. The Nazis built dozens of concentration camps — some used as transit sites for deporting Jews and other prisoners, some for forced labor, and others for extermination, i.e., efficient mass murder by gassing the victims and then cremating them. This planned genocide resulted in the deaths of six million Jews, or two of every three European Jews alive at the time.

The racist philosophy of the Nazis extended beyond anti-Semitism to include the Roma (Gypsies) and some Slavic peoples. Two hundred thousand Roma died in the concentration camps and a similar number of disabled people were killed under a Nazi euthanasia program. Some of the concentration camps featured gruesome and deadly medical experimentation. Over two million Soviet prisoners of war perished in the camps, and the Nazis also persecuted people on ideological and behavioral grounds, such as communists, socialists, Jehovah's Witnesses, and homosexuals.[17]

During the war, Rome was eventually occupied by the Nazis and then liberated by the Allies. Pius oversaw a relief effort estimated to have saved eight hundred thousand Jews as well as other displaced and persecuted peoples.[18] Nevertheless, he never publicly condemned the Holocaust, and he maintained a kind of neutrality, or at least balance, throughout the war. Pius XII has been criticized for not being more prophetic during this time of crisis. His defenders argue that if Pius had spoken out, the slaughter would have been intensified, and he would not have been able to save and help so many.

Pius XII chose to address the world through a series of Christmas messages in order to take advantage of the new medium of radio, which was accessible to greater numbers of people, more flexible, and less easy to control than an encyclical. Jesuit theologian John Langan concludes his analysis of Pius XII's Christmas messages during World War II this way:

> What Pius XII was able to articulate in his Christmas messages during this time of grave crisis was a constrained and restricted repetition of some central values of the Catholic tradition of social thought, values

such as the importance of maintaining the moral character of the state. But these values could easily be seen as tautologies or platitudes, since they were not joined with a perceptive and forthright statement of the actual political and moral situation of Europe in this gravely disturbed time or with a prophetic willingness to denounce evil. Generality and neutrality prevailed over courageous commitment and principled resistance to evil. The sound the trumpet gave in the heat of battle and agony was muted and ambiguous.[19]

It may be unrealistic to require the pope to be a prophet, and Pius XII was surely not temperamentally suited to that role. Although it is reasonable to expect moral leadership from the spokesperson for the Catholic Church, Pius XII produced instead abstract generalities and moral bromides. Pius XII can be commended for his service on behalf of persecuted peoples, but he failed the test of moral leadership in a time of war.

At the beginning of the war, Pius XII considered communism a greater threat than Nazism, so it was no stretch for him to stand against communism during the Cold War (1945–91). Based on his personal devotion to the Blessed Virgin Mary, Pius pointed to Mary as the spiritual bulwark against atheistic communism.[20]

In light of the horrific destruction caused by World War II, Pius XII eventually articulated two basic convictions regarding war: "that all wars of aggression were to be prohibited and that defensive war to repel aggression was reluctantly necessary."[21] Pius narrowed the three traditional just causes for war (defense, avenging evil, and restoring violated rights) to one — defense of one's nation or of others being unjustly attacked. He insisted that even a war of self-defense must be proportionate, given the destructive power of modern weapons. A nation may have to endure a measure of injustice, if war would be a greater evil. Pius hoped that the creation of a more adequate political and legal international structure, such as the United Nations, could resolve conflicts and obviate the need for war. Still, a nation has a right to defend itself, a right so strong that Pius thought that a Catholic could not in good conscience refuse to participate in a war declared by a legitimate authority. Thus Pius XII narrowed the principle of just cause for a war, but he also rejected pacifism and conscientious objection.[22]

Catholic Social Thought on War and Peace in the First Half of the Twentieth Century

It is possible to point to Christian and Catholic groups and individuals who worked for peace before and during the world wars, but in general the church in the West was absorbed by the nationalism of the period. After World War I, several concerned Germans, including the Dominican theologian Franziskus Stratmann, founded the German Catholic Peace Union. At

Raining Death from the Skies

On September 7, 1940, Hitler began the Blitz. For fifty-seven straight days London was bombed. Over a dozen other cities in Great Britain were also bombed. During this intensive campaign to break their morale, the British people, and especially the long-suffering Londoners, won the respect of the world for their courage and pluck by carrying on their everyday lives as best they could. Forty-three thousand civilians died as a result of the Blitz. The intensive bombing ended on May 11, 1941, when Hitler decided to move many of his bombers east for the attack on Russia, but intermittent bombing of British cities continued throughout World War II. After 1944 the Germans used rockets for this purpose. Nearly another 9,000 Londoners perished in this onslaught.

The Allies returned the favor near the end of the war by firebombing German and Japanese cities, most famously Dresden and Tokyo. Dresden, the baroque capital of Saxony, was a cultural landmark of little military significance when it was intensively bombed from February 13 to 15, 1945. Thirteen square miles of the city center were destroyed, killing over 25,000 civilians. Tokyo, the Japanese capital, was bombed throughout the war, but very intensively on March 9 and 10, 1945, destroying sixteen square miles of the city center and killing 100,000 civilians over all.

Sixty-seven Japanese cities were firebombed during the war. Hiroshima and Nagasaki were not among them. They were chosen to be the first (and, thus far, only) victims of the atomic bomb precisely because these cities were pristine targets. When "Little Man" (the nickname given to the first atomic bomb) was exploded over Hiroshima on August 6, 1945, two-thirds of the city was instantly destroyed and 70,000 civilians killed. Another 70,000 died within five years from radiation exposure or other wounds, out of a population of 350,000. Humanity had acquired the ability to destroy itself.[23]

---

its peak, it numbered about forty thousand members, including several bishops, and it advocated eloquently for disarmament. When the Nazis came into power in 1933, they targeted the German Catholic Peace Union and effectively squashed it. Many of its original supporters, including some of the bishops, publicly supported the Nazi war campaign.[24]

Almost the only resistance to the Nazis in Germany came from the churches — the Catholic Church and the "Confessing Church" (Protestants, mostly Lutherans, who resisted the Nazis), but such resistance was extremely limited. There are at least three reasons why the church did not courageously oppose an ideology that is so contrary to the values of Christianity. First, the Nazis brooked no dissent; critics were quickly silenced. Second, most

German Catholics were actually rather secular, relegating their faith to a private realm that had little effect on their whole life. Third and most important, the church was infected with nationalism and patriotism. The sentiment was that "good Catholics were good Germans."

Indeed Catholics were somewhat suspect in regard to their patriotism and thus defensively tried to prove themselves good Germans. Thus, most Catholics interpreted the just war theory with an emphasis on the requirement that war be declared by legitimate authority. They gave the benefit of any doubt to the state, assuming that government knew more than private citizens. The church, not just in Germany but throughout the West, was swept up in a tide of nationalism.[25] The Nazis, of course, fanned the flames of German nationalism at every opportunity. The perception in Germany that the Peace of Versailles at the end of the First World War imposed unfair conditions on the nation facilitated this exaggerated nationalism. In general, Christians in the West put the nation before their faith.

Catholics in Holland, Belgium, and France — led by some courageous bishops — did offer significant resistance to the Nazi occupation. There is the amazing story of the Reformed Christian community at Le Chambon, a farming village in south-central France, that provided a haven and safe passage for at least twenty-five thousand refugees, mostly Jewish children, during the Nazi occupation. Under the leadership of their pastors, André Trocmé and Edouard Theis, both of whom suffered imprisonment and exile, this Christian community courageously and creatively put faith before fear of the authorities and practiced hospitality.[26]

World War II also produced a number of martyrs who were executed or perished in concentration camps for their faithful resistance.[27] Among them were Fr. Franz Josef Metzger, who was beheaded in 1944 for trying to organize a peaceful settlement to the war (treason),[28] and Fr. Franz Reinisch, who was beheaded for refusing to take the military oath of unconditional obedience to Adolf Hitler.[29] The most famous Protestant resister was the Lutheran theologian Dietrich Bonhoeffer, who was imprisoned for two years and hanged shortly before the end of the war for his participation in a plot to assassinate Hitler.[30] Fr. Maximillian Kolbe was a Franciscan priest imprisoned in Auschwitz after the Nazis overran Poland. When the Nazis decided to starve to death ten inmates in retaliation for a prison escape, Fr. Kolbe volunteered to take the place of Francis Gajowniczek, a husband and father. Fr. Kolbe was canonized by John Paul II in 1982, with Mr. Gajowniczek present.[31]

There were not many conscientious objectors to World War II on either side. Among very few Germans who objected to Hitler's aggressive war machine was an obscure Austrian farmer named Franz Jägerstätter.[32] Raised in the village of St. Radegund, near the border between Austria and Germany, Franz was a wild youth, known for carousing and fighting. He seems to have undergone a religious conversion around 1936, and the former ruffian became a daily communicant. He married a similarly devout Catholic shortly thereafter, and Franz and Franziska honeymooned in Rome.

Jägerstätter's newly found religious conviction was accompanied by a clear political opposition to the Nazis. Indeed, he was the only person in St. Radegund to vote against the German annexation in 1938, and he refused to accept the benefits of the Nazi government or to cooperate with it in any way. Jägerstätter had a dream about a shining train that everyone was rushing to board, but the conductor said, "This train is going to hell." Franz identified this train with the Nazi regime, and this dream took on the nature of revelation for him.

When he was called to active duty in the Nazi army, Jägerstätter, now the father of three young girls, refused to participate in what he saw as an unjust war. No one supported him in his refusal.[33] Fr. Karobath, his exiled pastor, who had himself served time in prison for speaking out against the Nazis, argued that he should capitulate in light of his family responsibilities. His neighbors, convinced that the German cause, a defense of the fatherland and the faith from the Communists was just, thought that Franz was simply wrong. The bishop of Linz agreed, and visited Franz in prison to tell him so. His wife supported him in following his conscience, but also let him know that his children needed a father. Jägerstätter was unbending in his conviction that he could not kill in an unjust cause. He was beheaded on August 9, 1943.

Jägerstätter's witness would have gone nearly unnoticed except that Gordon Zahn, an American Catholic conscientious objector to World War II,[34] stumbled across his story while researching his sociological study, *German Catholics and Hitler's Wars*,[35] and brought it to light. On October 26, 2007, Franz Jägerstätter was beatified as a martyr in a ceremony in Linz, Austria, that was attended by his ninety-four-year-old widow, Franziska.[36] Although at the time of his execution the bishop of Linz hardly thought Franz exemplary, Jägerstätter is now one step away from being proclaimed a saint, a model of how to live Christian faith fully and radically in extreme circumstances. Jägerstätter witnesses to the integrity of conscience in the face of evil. Unfortunately such vision and integrity were extremely rare in Germany during World War II.

Catholic Social Teaching on War and Peace during the Cold War (1945–90)

War itself changed during World War II. The use of modern technology in warfare resulted in widespread destruction and the death of at least forty million human beings, more civilians than combatants. Aerial bombing, primitive missiles, and nuclear weapons destroyed whole cities and changed the very nature of war.

Berlin as a Symbol of the C~~~

At the end of World War II in 1945, the victorious Allies ~
UK, United States, and USSR) divided Germany among themselves ...
four zones; they also divided the capital, Berlin, into four sectors. Thus
Berlin became a divided city located deep inside the Soviet zone of the
country, which became East Germany.

First, Stalin, the Soviet leader, tried to drive the Western allies out
of Berlin by cutting off all land connections to West Berlin. The United
States airlifted supplies to West Berlin for eleven months in 1948, until
Stalin gave up the effort.

By 1961 West Germany had become more prosperous than East
Germany, and over three million East Germans had crossed the border in
Berlin into the West, seeking a better life. On August 13 the Communist
authorities decisively closed the border by building a wall along the East
Berlin border. In 1980, my wife and I traveled with West German friends
to West Berlin. We were allowed to cross into East Berlin, but East
Germans were not allowed to cross to the West. When we crossed the
border, however, we were surprised to find a long line of East Berliners
doing just that — crossing the border. All of them, we discovered, were
pensioners. Once workers retired, the Communist government did not
care if they left East Germany. These East Berliners would cross to the
West for shopping and return to the East where their housing and cost
of living were subsidized and cheaper.

West Berlin was like any other Western European city. East Berlin was
like stepping into the 1950s. The architecture was dull and the housing
shabby. Unrepaired ruins from the war still dotted the city. Department
stores had a limited range of goods and limited supplies. Bookstores
carried only Marxist philosophy, although our German friends were
interested in some of the literature on sports and training. We were
able to ride a bus around the city center for only a few cents, but we
were happy to return to the West at the end of the day, passing the
pensioners crossing back with consumer goods unavailable in the East.

The Berlin Wall fell on November 9, 1989, symbolizing the collapse
of Communism in Eastern Europe. By 1991 the Soviet Union itself
had broken up into fifteen different republics. Basically Russia had been
exposed as a developing country with a large army and nuclear weapons.
The people demanded a better life.[37]

hnology also changed politics. Advances in communication turned the
h and its disparate peoples into a global village. In the post-war period,
early all of the colonies in Asia and Africa fought for and won their political independence from European control. Global politics was dominated
by the conflict between the West and the East — the United States and
the North Atlantic Treaty Organization (NATO) versus the Soviet Union
and the Warsaw Pact. These blocs of nations represented different ideolo-
gies (democratic capitalism versus socialist communism), and they competed
with each other for political control and influence. This competition resulted
in an arms race for both conventional armaments and nuclear weapons and
their delivery systems. It also resulted in proxy wars and civil conflicts with
a communist/anticommunist tinge (for example in Korea, Cuba, Vietnam,
Nicaragua, and El Salvador). This new situation of total war and global
ideological competition put the question of the morality of war in a new
context and required a creative response.

The church's response to this new situation was understandably complex.
The horror of modern war sparked a renewed peace movement, which in
turn generated a debate between pacifism and just war. This raised questions
about individual conscience and conscientious objection, and it resulted in
the further development of the just war tradition as it struggled to respond
to revolutions and to nuclear ethics. These themes will be the plot of the
story of Catholic social teaching during the Cold War period.

The Catholic Peace Movement

There has been a reciprocal influence between the Catholic peace movement
and the official teaching of the Catholic Church since the end of the Second
World War. Catholic peacemakers influenced church teaching on peace and
were in turn encouraged by that teaching.

The horror of World War II resurrected a dormant peace movement in
Europe. Most of the nations of Europe gradually enacted legislation that
allowed the conscientious refusal of military service, and the numbers of
conscientious objectors (COs) increased dramatically. For example, within
months of the liberalization of West German law in 1977, forty to fifty thousand Germans applied for CO status. Similar movements were underway
elsewhere in Europe. Two women, Mairead Corrigan and Betty Williams,
received the Nobel Peace Prize in 1976 for their courageous efforts to
bring the "Troubles" in Northern Ireland to a peaceful resolution. Lech
Walesa also received the Nobel Peace Prize (1983) for his leadership of the
nonviolent Solidarity movement in Poland, which resulted in the "Velvet
Revolution" against communism in Eastern Europe.[38] Despite the allure of
these stories, we will concentrate our attention on the United States, where
the reciprocal influence between peacemakers and Catholic social teaching
is perhaps even clearer.

Dorothy Day and the Catholic Worker Movement

It would not be too much of an exaggeration to say that Dorothy Day (1897–80), who co-founded the Catholic Worker with Peter Maurin, singlehandedly created the Catholic peace movement in the United States.[39] Dorothy Day is now being considered for canonization, but her life before her conversion to Catholicism at age thirty made this surprising. Day advocated for marginalized people and the cause of social justice all her life, but her bohemian lifestyle was not very saintly. It included an abortion, suicide attempts, divorce, and an out-of-wedlock child. The birth of her daughter, Tamar, prompted her to convert to Catholicism, even though she knew it would mean the end of her relationship with her lover. Dorothy was baptized in December of 1927.[40]

Day was a journalist and writer. She had worked for socialist publications and now also wrote for Catholic periodicals. She was searching for a way to combine her faith with her passion for justice when she met Peter Maurin (1877–1949) in December of 1932. Maurin was an itinerant lay preacher of French background. He was a visionary who combined personalism, anarchism, and Christianity into a dream of building a new civilization in the shell of the old.[41] Maurin was committed to a three-point program of action: education and consciousness-raising through roundtable discussions, houses of hospitality where the works of mercy could be practiced and the poor cared for, and self-sufficient communal farms. Dorothy Day had the skills to implement these ideas and develop a program for change. On May 1, 1933, they launched their movement by distributing twenty-five hundred copies of a periodical called the *Catholic Worker,* charging a penny a copy. Dorothy Day's flat became the first house of hospitality.

By 1940 there were over 185,000 readers of the *Catholic Worker,* and thirty-two houses of hospitality in twenty-seven cities, where Catholic Worker communities cared for the poor and lived in voluntary poverty with the poor. Europe was already at war. In August 1940, Dorothy Day sent an open letter to the Catholic Worker houses insisting that pacifism was central and essential to the movement. When the *Catholic Worker* held to this pacifist stand after the attack on Pearl Harbor (December 7, 1941), two-thirds of the houses closed, and the circulation of the paper dropped to 85,000.[42] Peacemaking and nonviolent resistance, rooted in the life of Jesus and the teaching of the gospel, would complement the works of mercy and simple communal living as the dominant characteristics of the Catholic Worker movement.

The antiwar stand of the Catholic Worker led to a focus on the draft and support for conscientious objectors during and after the war. In World War I, only 4 of 3,989 COs were Catholic. In World War II, 135 of the 11,877 men who refused to participate in the war were Catholic, although there may have been others who accepted noncombatant military service. "Neither the Catholic hierarchy nor Catholic intellectuals denied the right of an individual

"Slowly I began to understand what Peter Maurin wanted: We were to reach the people by practicing the works of mercy, which meant feeding the hungry, clothing the naked, visiting the prisoner, sheltering the harborless, and so on. We were to do this by being poor ourselves, giving everything we had; then others would give too. Voluntary poverty and the works of mercy were the things he stressed above all. This was the core of his message. It had such appeal that it inspired us to action — action which certainly kept us busy and got us into all kinds of trouble besides. . . . I am so convinced of the rightness of his proposals that I have walked in this way now for over thirty years."

— Dorothy Day

A CASE FOR UTOPIA

The world would be better off
if people tried to become better,
and people would become better
if they stopped trying to be better off.
For when everyone tries to become better off
nobody is better off.
Everyone would be rich
if nobody tried to become richer,
And nobody would be poor
if everybody tried to be the poorest.
And everybody would be what they ought to be
if everybody tried to be
what they want the other person to be.

Peter Maurin[43]

to be a conscientious objector after World War II was declared, but they did nothing to support such individuals."[44] The Catholic Worker established a work camp for Catholic COs, but ultimately it could not adequately fund the camp.

The Catholic Worker was battered but still standing after the war. It provided the seed of a Catholic peace movement in the United States that would influence the church's social teaching and have an impact on American society. The story of the silencing of Thomas Merton on the topic of peace provides an entrée into a discussion of the reciprocal influence between the Catholic peace movement and the institutional church.

Conscientious Objection

The U.S. government's Selective Service System (draft) allows a person who is opposed to all war on moral or religious grounds to be recognized as a Conscientious Objector (CO). If the draft system is operational, COs would either do alternate service or serve in the military in a noncombatant role, depending on their beliefs. The government does not allow people to refuse to participate in a particular war that they deem to be unjust and immoral — Selective Conscientious Objection (SCO). Since this is the logic of the just war tradition, the church recognizes both CO and SCO and has unsuccessfully lobbied the government to do so as well.[45]

Thomas Merton — A Voice for Peace

Thomas Merton, a Trappist monk at the Abbey of Gethsemani in rural Kentucky, was deeply influenced by the Catholic Worker movement and became a prominent voice for peace in his own right. In 1948, Merton had published his autobiography, *The Seven Storey Mountain*. Merton's spiritual journey from a free-living agnostic to a committed Catholic monk became a best-seller and turned the thirty-three-year-old monk of six years into a famous writer.

In April of 1962, Merton hurriedly completed a manuscript titled *Peace in the Post-Christian Era* about the immorality of war in the nuclear age. Merton had published on this topic in the previous year. Days after Merton completed the book-length manuscript, he received a letter from the abbot general of the Cistercians forbidding him to publish on the topic of war and peace. The abbot general thought it an inappropriate topic for a monk. Although Merton thought this silencing was wrong-headed, he obeyed the abbot's order — more or less. The abbot of Gethsemani, Merton's local superior, allowed several hundred mimeographed copies to be circulated (rather like the works of unauthorized Russian writers of the time), and the core of Merton's thought on the topic did manage to get published during his life in other works.[46] It is likely that Merton's unpublished manuscript indirectly influenced what Vatican II said about the morality of war.[47]

A year later, Pope John XXIII published his encyclical *Peace on Earth* (*Pacem in Terris*). Merton wrote the abbot general to say that it was a good thing Pope John didn't have to get his encyclical through Cistercian censors. He asked if he could now start up again. The abbot general was unmoved and renewed the prohibition.

Merton's complicated, even paradoxical, thought on war and peace developed from 1960 until his accidental death in 1968. Merton may have personally been a pacifist when he entered the Abbey of Gethsemani in

Merton's Eye-Opening Experience

"In Louisville, at the corner of Fourth and Walnut, in the center of the shopping district, I was suddenly overwhelmed with the realization that I loved all those people, that they were mine and I theirs, that we could not be alien to one another even though we were total strangers. It was like waking from a dream of separateness, of spurious self-isolation in a special world, the world of renunciation and supposed holiness. The whole illusion of a separate holy existence is a dream.... This sense of liberation from an illusory difference was such a relief and such a joy to me that I almost laughed out loud.

"I have the immense joy of being a *man*, a member of a race in which God Himself became incarnate. As if the sorrows and stupidities of the human condition could overwhelm me, now I realize what we all are. And if only everybody could realize this! But it cannot be explained. There is no way of telling people that they are all walking around shining like the sun....

"Then it was as if I suddenly saw the secret beauty of their hearts, the depths of their hearts where neither sin nor desire nor self-knowledge can reach, the core of their reality, the person that each one is in God's eyes. If only they could all see themselves as they really *are*. If only we could see each other that way all the time. There would be no more war, no more hatred, no more cruelty, no more greed.... It is like a pure diamond, blazing with the invisible light of heaven.... I have no program for this seeing. It is only given. But the gate of heaven is everywhere."

— Thomas Merton, *Conjectures of a Guilty Bystander*
(New York: Doubleday, 1966), 156–58

the midst of World War II. His early writings on the topic in the early 1960s, however, argue for a nuclear pacifism in the just war terms of the church's teaching. His thought evolved toward melding Gandhi's active nonviolence with Christian ethics and eschatology, resulting in a call for individual Christian witness through active nonviolence — a revolution through personal conversion. Merton's stance was not far from that of Dorothy Day and Peter Maurin. It would influence the witness of Frs. Philip and Daniel Berrigan and other Catholic peace activists against the Vietnam War and against nuclear weapons, as well as the positions of Vatican II and the U.S. bishops on war and peace.[48]

John XXIII and *Peace on Earth*

John XXIII's *Peace on Earth* (1963) is the fullest general treatment of political morality and of the topic of war and peace among the major social encyclicals, and the first one to be addressed to all people of good will. It marks a turning point in the church's social teaching and its teaching on peace. Published only a few months after Pope John served as a mediator in the Cuban missile crisis of 1962,[49] *Peace on Earth* barely touches on Cold War issues such as nuclear deterrence. Instead, Pope John argues that the positive basis for peace consists in political systems that protect human rights. Catholic social teaching had long held that peace is not the mere absence of war, but the presence of justice. This is the first time, however, that human rights were highlighted as central to justice. John XXIII's treatise on human rights would be developed by Vatican II and his successors, and it would become the backbone of the church's teaching on politics and of its commitment to peacemaking in the contemporary world. It would spark Catholic lay action comparable to the labor movement initiated by Leo XIII's *The Condition of Labor.*[50]

After noting the destructive force of modern weapons, John XXIII says, "Therefore, in an age such as ours, which prides itself on its atomic energy, it is contrary to reason to hold that war is now a suitable way to restore rights which have been violated."   — *Peace on Earth*, #127

There are four themes directly related to war and peace that are worthy of note in *Peace on Earth:*[51]

- human rights as the basis of just government and of peace (#60),

- the primacy of individual conscience and human rights in regard to state authority and sovereignty (#51, 61),

- the irrationality of war in the modern age and the demand for disarmament (#109–19, 126–29), and

- the need to develop a universal political authority to promote the universal common good in an interdependent world community (#137, 142–45).

These themes gave direction to further church teaching on war and peace.

John XXIII was an optimist. *Peace on Earth* has been criticized for being naïve regarding the real tensions and deep conflicts of the Cold War period, and for deemphasizing sin and its consequences. Nevertheless, Pope John's farsighted vision of peace based on human rights continues to offer wisdom and guidance to today's world.[52]

Vatican II and *The Pastoral Constitution on the Church in the Modern World*

John XXIII died in early June 1963, less than two months after publication of *Peace on Earth,* and in between the first and second session of the Second Vatican Council (1962–65). There was considerable debate at the Council about what should be said about modern war, nuclear weapons, and conscientious objection. In the fall of 1965, the Council entered its final session and focused its discussion on *The Pastoral Constitution on the Church in the Modern World* (*Gaudium et Spes*). Representatives of the peace communities in Europe and the United States converged on Rome to lobby the bishops to condemn total war and nuclear weapons and to affirm Catholic conscientious objection.

Dorothy Day and Eileen Egan of the Catholic Worker joined activist theologian James Douglass, peace activist and Latinist Richard Carbray, and Gordon Zahn in Rome. A special edition of the *Catholic Worker* on "The Council and the Bomb" that had been sent to all the bishops of the world became a lobbying tool at the Council. Thomas Merton sent an "open letter" to the Council calling for a condemnation of nuclear war and for clear provisions for conscientious objection.[53] Dorothy Day joined nineteen women from a dozen countries in a ten-day public fast to highlight the message of gospel nonviolence. Meanwhile, Egan, Douglass, Carbray, and Zahn engaged in tireless lobbying of the bishops.[54]

The Pastoral Constitution on the Church in the Modern World (promulgated on December 7, 1965, the last day of the Council), while not entirely satisfying, was cause for celebration in the peace community. It affirmed all four of the points highlighted above in *Peace on Earth* but went beyond John XXIII in its specificity regarding the morality of war in the modern age and its support for conscientious objection.

The Council explicitly said that "peace is not merely the absence of war," nor a balance of power, but the presence of justice, and also "the fruit of love, which goes beyond what justice can provide" (#78). Those who practice nonviolence were conditionally commended (#78), and the document explicitly requested that nations make legal provision for conscientious objectors who accept an alternate form of service (#79), a *reversal* of the teaching of Pius XII noted above. A soldier must disobey commands to do something contrary to the universal natural law, such as genocide or ethnic cleansing, and conventions that restrain the horror of war should be strengthened (#79).

What the Council calls "scientific weapons" led the bishops to reiterate the papal condemnation of total war and to issue the following declaration, "Any act of war aimed indiscriminately at the destruction of entire cities or of extensive areas along with their population is a crime against God and man himself. It merits unequivocal and unhesitating condemnation" (#80). This seems a clear and logical conclusion based on the just war theory's principle of discrimination or noncombatant immunity, but the firmness and force of this statement was welcome, given the church's silence about obliteration bombing and the use of nuclear weapons on civilian targets during World War II.[55] The calamities made possible by scientific weapons moved the Council to say that, "the arms race is an utterly treacherous trap for humanity, and one which injures the poor to an intolerable degree" (#81). The bishops called for a multilateral, negotiated, verified process of disarmament (#82), and for humanity to "find a means for resolving our disputes in a manner more worthy of humanity" (#81). The Council acknowledged that deterrence might yield a "peace of a sort" (#81), and it affirmed a government's right of legitimate defense as a last resort (#79).[56]

Finally, noting that peace must be born of mutual trust, rather than fear, the *Pastoral Constitution* called for leaders to "put aside national selfishness and ambition to dominate," and to work simultaneously for the good of their own people and for the universal common good. It encouraged educated and converted citizens to turn from enmity and hatred and to support and build mutual trust, cooperation, and peace (#82).

Paul VI and the Question of Just Revolution

Paul VI (1963–78) brought Vatican II to a successful conclusion and tirelessly implemented the reforms the Council initiated. He gave an impassioned call for peace before the United Nations in October 1965. Paul began the practice of giving annual World Day of Peace messages (beginning January 1, 1968), which has been continued by his successors. His statements on peace continue the spirit and substance of John XXIII and Vatican II.

"No more war! Never again war! Peace, it is peace that must guide the destinies of people and of all humanity.
— Paul VI, "Address to the United Nations," October 4, 1965

In his encyclical *On the Development of Peoples (Populorum Progressio)*, Paul VI argues that when people are hungry, destitute, uneducated, sick, and homeless, an "exhausting armaments race," as well as any other waste of wealth, is "an intolerable scandal" (#53). Near the end of the encyclical the pope titles a section "Development Is the New Name for Peace" (#76–80). He asserts that the daily struggle against misery and injustice builds the basis for peace (#76).[57] Economic development, human rights, and human flourishing are the foundations for peace.

In this encyclical that focuses on redressing the crippling poverty felt by two-thirds of humankind, Paul VI also addresses the issue of just revolution. Pope Paul acknowledges that in situations of destitution and dependency, when injustice cries to heaven, "recourse to violence, as a means to right

"Individualism causes selfishness, the root of all evil.... Poverty makes people subhuman. Excess of wealth makes people inhuman.

"War is daily becoming more absurd. It is literally true that it could be the collective suicide of humankind. But as well as nuclear warfare and biological warfare we also have poverty, the most bloody, evil and shameful war of them all....

"We must put an end to violence. To do this we must have the courage to recognize the source of all violence and put an end to injustice everywhere. Poor countries suffer from internal colonialism and neocolonialism; rich countries allow groups of poor people to remain within them and the rich have become inhuman through an excess of comfort and luxury. It is easy to show that the wealth of the rich countries is sustained by the misery of the poor countries. We must end all this injustice. The scandal of this century is marginalization, which deprives two-thirds of humanity of progress, the power to create wealth or make their own decisions."   —Dom Helder Camara[58]

these wrongs to human dignity, is a grave temptation" (#30). "We know, however, that a revolutionary uprising—save where there is manifest, long-standing tyranny which would do great damage to fundamental personal rights and dangerous harm to the common good of the country—produces new injustices, throws more elements out of balance and brings on new disasters. A real evil should not be fought against at the cost of greater misery" (#31). Paul makes it clear that he is not counseling passivity; injustice must be courageously fought and overcome (#32). While the pope does not rule out a just revolution, he thinks it is rarely successful or proportionate. He does not directly address other just war criteria regarding the morality of revolution, such as legitimate authority, last resort, and noncombatant immunity.

The Latin American Bishops' Conference (CELAM) echoed Pope Paul's words about just revolution at their meeting at Medellín, Colombia, in 1968 (#19). At Medellín, the Latin American bishops, encouraged by Vatican II to respond to the signs of the times, began to move the church from the side of the rich to solidarity with the poor. CELAM confirmed the preferential option for the poor and the liberation theology developed by Gustavo Gutiérrez and others.

One of their number, Dom (bishop) Helder Camara (1909–99), archbishop of Recife and Olinda in northeast Brazil, is a fitting case study regarding the struggle of the church with the question of violence in the global South. Dom Helder was instrumental in establishing CELAM in the years before Vatican II, and he was an important behind-the-scenes player at the Council. A diminutive man, possessed with a deep mystical spirituality, he became the voice for the poor. Dom Helder symbolized the church's turn to the poor by giving up the trappings of wealth and power associated with the "princes of the church" in Latin America. For example, he turned his bishop's mansion into offices and a community center and lived in a simple apartment at the back of an urban church.

In Dom Helder's analysis, the primary violence in Latin America was the overwhelming reality of abject poverty, which was sustained by repressive violence in the name of "national security," by states controlled by wealthy elites. Systemic, institutional violence was Latin America's primary problem, and repressive violence was its second problem. Dom Helder refused to condemn those who responded to oppression and repression with revolutionary violence. He understood the possibility of just revolution that Pope Paul had kept open. Nevertheless, all his activity was focused on nonviolent resistance to the violence of poverty. He did not think that revolutionary violence was likely to interrupt effectively the spiral of violence and counterviolence that he observed.[59] In response to his efforts to organize the poor to nonviolent resistance against their plight, the Brazilian government declared Dom Helder a nonperson who could not be mentioned by the media. The National Security State in Brazil tried to silence the voice of the poor.[60]

This ambiguity regarding revolutionary violence characterized the liberation struggles in the southern hemisphere during the Cold War. The Colombian priest Camilo Torres embraced guerilla warfare as an act of Christian love, and the Sandinistas in Nicaragua actually overthrew the government in 1979. Archbishop Oscar Romero in El Salvador counseled nonviolence to the army and to the peasants who were victims of the army. Romero suffered martyrdom in 1980, the same fate as four American churchwomen, six Jesuits, and over sixty thousand of those whose cause he had nonviolently championed. Filipinos nonviolently ousted the Marcos dictatorship in the "People Power" revolution in 1986. The black majority in South Africa won their freedom in a fundamentally nonviolent uprising against the oppressive system of apartheid. Both Anglican Archbishop Desmond Tutu (1984) and former prisoner Nelson Mandela (1993) received the Nobel Peace Prize for their roles in the struggle for justice in South Africa. Mandela was elected the first black president of South Africa in 1994.[61]

The United States Conference of Catholic Bishops

The United States participated in its own discussion of violence in the cause of liberation during the civil rights movement in the 1960s. The civil rights movement, sparked by the Montgomery bus boycott in 1955 and 1956, was essentially nonviolent under the leadership of Rev. Dr. Martin Luther King Jr. (1929–68, Nobel Peace Prize, 1964). The movement for freedom and equality for America's black citizens, however, also triggered urban riots, and it was tempted to a philosophy of revolutionary violence by the rise of the Black Power movement in 1966.[62]

"The ultimate weakness of violence is that it is a descending spiral, begetting the very thing it seeks to destroy. Instead of diminishing evil, it multiplies it. Through violence you may murder the liar, but you cannot murder the lie, nor establish the truth. Through violence you may murder the hater, but you do not murder hate. In fact, violence merely increases hate. So it goes. Returning violence for violence multiplies violence, adding deeper darkness to a night already devoid of stars. Darkness cannot drive out darkness: only light can do that. Hate cannot drive out hate: only love can do that."   — Martin Luther King Jr.[63]

From 1962 through 1975 the American Catholic peace movement was preoccupied with the war in Vietnam. As early as November 1962, Tom Cornell, a Catholic Worker, burned his draft card at an anti–Vietnam War protest. In November 1964 the Catholic Peace Fellowship (CPF), an affiliate of the pacifist organization the Fellowship of Reconciliation (FOR), was formed after a retreat of Christian peace activists directed by Thomas Merton at the Abbey of Gethsemani. The CPF organized protest against the war and counseled Catholic conscientious objectors.

In May 1968, a group of nine Catholic activists, including Frs. Daniel and Philip Berrigan, entered the Selective Service headquarters in Catonsville, Maryland (just outside Baltimore), took draft files outside, and burned them with homemade napalm. They prayed while waiting to be arrested. The "Catonsville Nine" kindled other acts of civil disobedience and fueled a debate about the tactic of destroying government property. Dan Berrigan pointed out that napalm was being used in Vietnam to burn people, not paper.[64] By 1970, mass peace rallies, escalating U.S. casualties, and questions about the justness of the cause turned public opinion in a deeply divided nation against the war in Vietnam.

The attitude of the U.S. Conference of Catholic Bishops followed the lead of Catholic opinion during the war. In November 1966 the U.S. bishops thought that it was reasonable to argue that the U.S. presence in Vietnam was justified. In a 1968 pastoral letter titled *Human Life in Our Day*, the bishops raised serious questions about the justification of the Vietnam War, and they affirmed that Catholics could not only be conscientious objectors to all war, but, following the logic of the just war theory, a selective conscientious objector to a particular war. They called for a modification of the draft law to allow selective conscientious objection. In October 1971 the U.S. bishops issued their *Declaration on Conscientious Objection and Selective Conscientious Objection*, and in November they finally condemned the Vietnam War as unjust.[65] The United States did not leave Vietnam until 1975.

In 1980, the Berrigan brothers and small communities of Christian activists turned their attention to nuclear weapons and the arms race.

The War in Vietnam

Vietnam was a French colony in Southeast Asia. For nearly a decade after World War II, the Vietnamese waged a war of independence against the French under the leadership of Ho Chi Minh, finally defeating the French in 1954. At a peace conference, Vietnam was temporarily divided into North and South, with the promise of elections in 1956. South Vietnam, with American backing, refused to hold the reunification elections.

There are at least two perspectives on the complicated situation in Vietnam. The first is a Cold War perspective. In this view, the United States intervened in support of South Vietnam to keep countries in Asia from falling like dominoes to communism (China, North Korea, etc.). The second perspective sees Ho Chi Minh as a nationalist rather than primarily as a communist. In this view, the United States took the place of the French in delaying the independence of Vietnam.

There are over 58,000 Americans whose names are inscribed on the Vietnam Memorial in the Mall in Washington, D.C., and there were 350,000 casualties in America's longest war and only defeat. It is estimated that between 1 and 2 million Vietnamese were killed.

The Vietnam War caused a deep political divide in the United States (in part precipitated by the draft) that was punctuated by campus protests and mass marches in the nation's capital, and tumultuous election campaigns in 1968 and 1972.[66]

Following the call of the prophets Isaiah and Micah, "They shall beat their swords into plowshares, and their spears into pruning hooks" (Isa 2:4; Mic 4:3), they initiated a series of "plowshare" acts of civil disobedience. These peace activists symbolically attacked nuclear warheads in Pennsylvania and Trident submarines in Connecticut.[67] The U.S. bishops were also turning their attention to the ethics of nuclear weapons.

The U.S. Conference of Catholic Bishops (USCCB) issued a pastoral letter titled *The Challenge of Peace: God's Promise and Our Response* in 1983.[68] Although other Catholic bishops' conferences and other church bodies (such as the U.S. Methodist bishops) addressed nuclear ethics at about the same time, *The Challenge of Peace* is remarkable both for the process that produced it and for its content.

In early 1981, a committee of five bishops, chaired by Cardinal Joseph Bernardin of Chicago, was appointed to draft a document on nuclear ethics for the approval of the USCCB. The committee held hearings around the country, listening to thirty-six formal witnesses, who ranged from three past or present secretaries of defense to peace activists, such as Gordon Zahn and Tom Cornell. The committee and its consultants produced three drafts of the document and each time invited a public response.[69] This transparent and consultative process generated considerable public discussion about the morality of modern war. It also produced a clear, accessible, substantive church document.

The Challenge of Peace articulated theological principles related to the morality of war, applied those principles to the questions surrounding nuclear war, and called for peacemaking on both national and personal levels. It was a complex and careful document that generated considerable controversy. Rather than providing a detailed summary of the document,[70] four points will be highlighted with an eye on the bishops' critics: the use of scripture, the relationship of pacifism to just war, the bishops' position on nuclear war, and their call to peacemaking.

1. The Use of Scripture

In the spirit of Vatican II, this document pays significant attention to scripture. The first section of the pastoral letter examines war and peace in the Old Testament and in the New Testament. To the chagrin of pacifist critics, however, the bishops looked to scripture for a general direction regarding peace rather than for specific directives.

Then, in a section titled "Kingdom and History" (#56–65), *The Challenge of Peace* recognizes the eschatological tension wherein the reign of God, taught and initiated by Jesus, is *already* present, but *not yet* fulfilled. "In history, efforts to pursue both peace and justice are at times in tension, and the struggle for justice may threaten certain forms of peace" (#60). Christian pacifists think that disciples should *already* be living according to the values of the reign of God, for example, loving their enemies, as articulated in the Sermon on the Mount (Mt 5–7).[71] Christians who have accepted the just war tradition, including the bishops, think this is unrealistic in sinful historical conditions.

From this point on, the bishops often quote church teaching, but seldom refer to scripture. Still, one could argue that scripture does influence some of the positions the bishops take, such as the strong presumption against war. *The Challenge of Peace* is more biblically informed than most of Catholic social teaching, but the adequacy of its use of scripture is questionable. It fails to integrate the biblical material into the substantive reasoning of the document.[72]

2. The Relationship of Pacifism to Just War

The pastoral letter offers a contemporary explication of the just war criteria (summarized earlier in this chapter) and applies them to questions raised by nuclear war. It is basically a just war document. *The Challenge of Peace* does, however, clarify and elaborate on the affirmation of pacifism and nonviolence stated in *The Pastoral Constitution on the Church in the Modern World* (#78). The U.S. bishops confirm that "refusing to bear arms" and "active nonviolence" are legitimate choices for individuals as ways of securing justice and defending peace (#73). "Catholic teaching sees these two distinct responses [justified warfare and nonviolence] as having a complementary relationship, in the sense that both seek to serve the common good" (#74). The Catholic peace movement in the United States certainly influenced this affirmation of a commitment to nonviolence.

The Church in the Modern World (#78–79) affirmed nonviolence and conscientious objection to war as individual choices rooted in conscience. The U.S. bishops clarify that this personal choice requires a commitment to resist injustice and promote human rights through active nonviolence. "Sectarian withdrawal is not an option for Roman Catholics."[73] Thus *The Challenge of Peace* pastorally affirms a vocational pacifism — the subjective, conscientious choice of an individual to use only nonviolent means to resist injustice.[74] Is it, however, logical and reasonable for the U.S. bishops to contend that pacifism and just war are "complementary?"

In actuality, the pacifist and just war positions are objectively opposed to one another. The bishops rightly emphasize the strong presumption against war that is at the basis of the just war tradition, but pacifism holds that war and violence are absolutely illegitimate. Nonviolent activists and just war adherents can walk together down the road to last resort, but once there, they part company. The morality of war and peace is complex and ambiguous, and there is room for modesty and pluralism within Catholic social teaching on the subject, but "complementary" was probably a poor choice of words.[75]

3. The U.S. Bishops' Position on Nuclear War

The bishops carefully apply just war criteria, in particular the principles of discrimination, proportion, and reasonable hope of victory, to the questions raised by nuclear weapons in the context of the Cold War. They conclude that *counter-population* warfare (#147) and the threat to directly obliterate a civilian center (#149, 178) are categorically wrong. They condemn even the retaliatory use of nuclear weapons targeted on enemy cities after our own country has been struck (#148). The bishops cannot imagine a situation where the deliberate *initiation* of nuclear warfare, no matter how limited, could be morally justified (#150). The bishops are skeptical that any use of nuclear weapons could remain *limited* (#157–61).[76] Basically, then, the U.S. bishops want to draw a thick line between conventional and nuclear warfare, and they want to prohibit the *use* of nuclear weapons. The bishops say "no" to the idea of nuclear war (#188); it is unthinkable. The most reasonable and realistic response to nuclear war is *prevention*.

During the Cold War, the policy of "mutually assured destruction" (MAD) did manage to keep a "peace of a sort." The United States and the Soviet Union threatened to retaliate to a nuclear attack by destroying the attacker with a devastating onslaught of nuclear weapons. The foreign policy of both nations relied on deterrence (MAD) to prevent a nuclear war. If, however, it is impossible to imagine the moral use of a nuclear weapon, is it right to possess them and to threaten to use them? Is such a threat credible? Is nuclear deterrence a morally permissible policy?

After anguished (and tortured) analysis, the U.S. bishops arrived at a provisional "strictly conditioned moral acceptance of nuclear deterrence" (#186). They followed the position of Pope John Paul II, expressed in a message to a United Nations special session on disarmament in 1982: "In current conditions 'deterrence' based on balance, certainly not as an end in itself but as a step on the way toward progressive disarmament, may still be judged morally acceptable" (quoted in #173). To justify this position the bishops have to accept the assurances of the U.S. government that any response to a Soviet nuclear attack would be both discriminate (aimed at military targets) and proportionate (without even unintended massive civilian casualties) (#178–83). This assurance is not credible. Thus, "the bishops' position [on nuclear deterrence] in the final letter is not so ambiguous as it is frankly conflicted."[77]

It is easy, however, to sympathize with the dilemma facing the bishops on the question of nuclear deterrence. Unilateral disarmament is a logical conclusion, given their moral analysis that it would be immoral to ever use a nuclear weapon. If the United States were to unilaterally dismantle its nuclear weapons, Americans would be left in an extremely vulnerable position. It is a complex, morally ambiguous, no-win situation. Perhaps the best response would be for the bishops to say just that, and either prudently argue that deterrence is the lesser evil in this murky situation, or issue a principled call for unilateral disarmament.[78] The bishops do follow their reluctant moral acceptance of deterrence with several specific conditions and limits, including a nuclear freeze, support for negotiated, bilateral deep cuts in the arsenals of both superpowers (#191), and a call for unilateral, independent initiatives aimed at jump-starting the process of disarmament (#205).

4. The U.S. Bishops' Call for Peacemaking

The third section of *The Challenge of Peace* discusses what government and society can do to promote peace, and the final section discusses the role of the church and of individual Christians in making peace. These sections are specific and constructive, but because they are less controversial, there is a danger they might be overlooked. To develop an adequate theology of peace it is essential to highlight the responsibility of individuals, of the Christian community, of nongovernment organizations, and of nations to build and promote peace. It is noteworthy that, in these sections, the bishops call for:

- developing nonviolent means of conflict resolution and even nonviolent civil defense measures (#221–30),
- policies aimed at just international, social, and economic structures based on the unity of humanity and the reality of interdependence (#235–44, #259–73),
- supporting the United Nations (241–42, 267–68), and

 • regarding "even the path of persecution and the possibility of martyrdom" as normal for Christian disciples (#276).

In 1983, *The Challenge of Peace* generated an important conversation in American society about war and nuclear ethics, and it contributed substantially to that discussion. The end of the Cold War, with the fall of the Berlin Wall in 1989 and the dissolution of the Soviet Union by 1991, dissipated the urgency of the pastoral's most controversial sections on nuclear warfare. It did not, however, result in nuclear disarmament. *The Challenge of Peace* has continued to make contributions with its concern about nuclear weapons and disarmament, with its articulation of the just war theory as a way to assess the morality of war, with its affirmation of active nonviolence, and with its call for peacemaking on the part of government, church, and citizens. The bishops continued to insightfully and constructively apply just war criteria to international conflicts and to focus on the moral dimension of foreign policy.

John Paul II and the U.S. Conference of Catholic Bishops in the Post–Cold War World

On the tenth anniversary of *The Challenge of Peace,* in 1993, the USCCB issued *The Harvest of Justice Is Sown in Peace.*[79] Although this document did not receive the media attention that accompanied *The Challenge of Peace,* it seriously and substantially addressed the new situation of the post–Cold War world. We have already seen that the pronouncements of John Paul II (pope, 1978–2005) significantly influenced the U.S. bishops in *The Challenge of Peace.* Both Pope John Paul II and the U.S. bishops emphasize the same two themes regarding peace in the post–Cold War world (1989–2001): the increasing merit of active nonviolence and conflict resolution, and the necessity of recognizing the full spectrum of human rights as the foundation for peace.[80]

John Paul II was the most traveled pope in history, attaining a sort of superstar status. He was certainly one of the most prolific in what became the third longest papacy. He did not publish an encyclical on the topic of peace, but he addressed peace often in his annual World Day of Peace Messages and in less formal talks and statements.[81] He survived an assassination attempt in 1981, then in 2000 met with and forgave the man who shot him, Mehmet Ali Agca. Moreover, John Paul II had a hand, both publicly and behind the scenes, in the basically nonviolent fall of communism in Poland (his homeland) and the rest of Eastern Europe. He is then an important twentieth-century peacemaker, both in deed and word.

The success of active nonviolence in the Philippines (the People Power removal of the Marcos dictatorship in 1986) and Poland (the Solidarity movement) emboldened the pope and the U.S. bishops to recommend nonviolent resistance and conflict resolution even more strongly as an alternative to and a step prior to war. Whereas *The Challenge of Peace* limited nonviolent witness to individuals, *Harvest* wonders, "in light of recent history, whether nonviolence should be restricted to personal commitments or whether it also could have a place in the public order with the tradition of justified and limited war." John Paul II proclaims, "*No to war!* War is not always inevitable. It is always a defeat for humanity. International law, honest dialogue, solidarity between States, the noble exercise of diplomacy: These are methods worthy of individuals and nations in resolving their differences."[82] One effect of this newfound respect for nonviolence and diplomacy is a strengthening of the presumption against war and an emphasis on last resort. Neither the pope nor the bishops became pacifists, but they found war increasingly difficult to justify. They now commended nonviolence to nations as well as individuals, and they emphasized the virtues and vision required for peacemaking.

The other theme stressed by the pope and the U.S. bishops was a focus of John XXIII's *Peace on Earth:* that implementation of the full spectrum of human rights, including political and economic rights, is essential for building the just polity that is the necessary foundation for peace. With Paul VI, they acknowledge that abject poverty is violence and a cause of violence that can be remedied only by economic development and economic justice. They also addressed the rise of ethnic conflict in the post–Cold War world (in Bosnia and Kosovo, Rwanda and Sudan, for example), decried its religious veneer, and commended self-determination, respect for minority rights, a commitment to tolerance and solidarity, and an emphasis on dialogue and reconciliation.[83] Respect for human rights moved both John Paul II and the U.S. bishops to sanction humanitarian intervention in cases of genocide or ethnic cleansing. The pope says that such intervention is obligatory and that indifference is unacceptable, and the bishops point out in *Harvest* that state sovereignty, although important, is not absolute.[84]

Pope Benedict XVI continued this theme of human rights as the basis of peace in his 2007 World Day of Peace Message, "The Human Person, the Heart of Peace." I think it can be said that, while the Catholic Church does not quite become a "peace church" during the papacy of John Paul II, it surely becomes a peacemaking church.[85]

Issues in Catholic Thought on War and Peace after September 11, 2001

In response to the terrorist attacks of September 11, 2001, the United States declared a "war on terror," assisted in overthrowing the Taliban's rule in Afghanistan, and invaded Iraq, overthrowing the regime of Saddam Hussein.

The moral questions accompanying these events also raise theoretical questions regarding how to think about the morality of war and violence. These theoretical questions will be explored first in terms of the just war tradition and then in terms of a new paradigm that is emerging called "just peacemaking."

Controversies and Developments in the Just War Tradition

Terrorism is a complex reality that is difficult to define, but all descriptions of the phenomenon include the central reality of a direct attack on civilians. This is a clear violation of the just war theory's principle of discrimination, and thus, terrorism is always wrong. Indeed, the inhumanity of the attack on the World Trade Center on September 11 was almost unimaginable before it happened. Suicide bombings aimed at civilians are commonplace in some parts of the world (in Iraq and Pakistan in 2010), and such terrorist attacks occur too frequently in other places, such as Bali, Indonesia (October 2002), Madrid (March 2004), London (July 2005), and Mumbai, India (2008).[86] What is a moral response to terrorism?

Obviously it is best to prevent terrorist attacks, and it is necessary to apprehend those responsible and punish them. This response, however, has more in common with law enforcement than with war. The descriptor or metaphor, "war on terror," is morally problematic. Terrorist groups, such as Al Qaeda, are generally diffuse groups of ideological warriors, not nation states. How can a war against such an adversary be won? Furthermore, war often leads to a suspension of civil liberties, and this has occurred in the United States. The war on terror has even been instrumental in the United States succumbing to the temptation to use torture. Such an erosion of human rights seems a victory for the terrorists.[87] War also results in an increase in military spending, which threatens spending on other goods and human needs. Law enforcement seems a more fitting response to terrorism than war.[88]

It is also important to note that sometimes terrorism, like war, is used in a just cause. This does not make terrorism right, but it means that addressing the injustice that gave rise to desperate acts of terrorism can be essential to preventing further acts of terror.[89]

Questioning the Presumption against War

In the wake of the September 11 attacks the United States military assisted Afghan resistance fighters in overthrowing the rule of the Taliban in Afghanistan. As far as I am aware, neither Pope John Paul II nor the U.S. bishops raised serious doubts about the morality of this military involvement in Afghanistan. It was clear that the Taliban sponsored the terrorism of Al Qaeda, and the government established by the Taliban offered little protection of basic human rights for the Afghan people, and especially for women.

The church did, however, raise serious questions about the morality of the U.S. invasion (with a "coalition of the willing") of Iraq in March of 2003, and precisely on just war grounds.[90] This precipitated a debate among theologians about the just war theory itself. The debate centers on the strong presumption against war found in *The Challenge of Peace* and the thought of John Paul II. Catholic neoconservatives George Weigel and Michael Novak have contended that this is a misreading of the classic just war theory, claiming that the just war tradition has a presumption against injustice and in favor of social order, and that the state has the responsibility to use war to establish justice and order if need be. These writers favored the preemptive invasion of Iraq. Their position *permits* war more often. The church's official position is more *restrictive* toward war.[91]

One aspect of this debate is historical. Does the classic just war tradition from Augustine through Aquinas and Grotius contain a presumption against war?[92] This is a matter for historians to wrestle with. It does seem, however, that, in the big picture of church history, the teaching of Jesus and the pacifism of the early church establish a presumption against war. Although historians can discuss this issue, history will not settle it. The just war theory has evolved and developed through history in response to changing circumstances, and such development is surely necessary today, given the changing nature of warfare.

Philosophically, it seems logical that the evil and destructiveness of war would not be one choice among many, but always the last resort, a reluctantly justified lesser evil. Theologically, Jesus' teaching about love of enemies and his offer of salvation through the suffering love of the cross surely predispose Christians to work for justice through nonviolent means. Granted, there is a presumption against injustice and for the full spectrum of human rights, but there is also a presumption against war as a means of establishing justice and resolving conflict.

The Morality of Preemptive War

The permissive interpreters of just war theory are also more open to justifying "preemptive war" in a case like Iraq. The policy of preemption was stated by the Bush administration in the 2002 *National Security Strategy of the United States*.[93] In the context of the nexus between radicalism (extremist groups like Al Qaeda and rogue states) and technology (biological, chemical, and nuclear weapons of mass destruction [WMD]), the United States reserves the right to strike preemptively and unilaterally to forestall or prevent WMD from falling into the hands of radicals committed to the destruction of the United States or its allies. Political analysts dubbed this the "Bush doctrine." The Bush administration argued that Iraq had biological and chemical weapons and sought nuclear weapons, and it implied a connection between Iraq and Al Qaeda (9/11). These were the primary reasons for the invasion of Iraq, which would also liberate the Iraqi people from the tyranny of the regime of Saddam Hussein.[94]

The first problem with the Bush doctrine is its use of the term "preemption." When a nation is threatened by an imminent and grave attack, international law allows a nation to attack preemptively. The *National Security Strategy* recognizes this ordinary definition of preemption, but wants to extend it to preventing the build-up of a serious threat. This is more properly called *preventive war* — an important distinction.

A restrictive interpretation of just war theory does not think preventive war can be justified and thus raises serious questions about the U.S. invasion of Iraq. As we have seen, since Pius XII the church has limited the just cause for war to national self-defense or protection of the rights of the innocent. It is hard to see how a preventive war could be defensive in this sense. As the invasion of Iraq illustrates (in that no weapons of mass destruction were found there), reliable intelligence about a future threat is difficult to gather. It is also hard to imagine how a preventive war could be a last resort. Furthermore, the contention that the United States could unilaterally engage in a preventive intervention exacerbates the problems regarding just cause and last resort, and raises issues with legitimate authority. It should be noted that the United States did not have the sanction of the United Nations Security Council for its invasion of Iraq.[95]

Jus Post Bellum Criteria

There has been considerable theological discussion about expanding the just war tradition to include moral criteria guiding the aftermath of a war — in other words, *jus post bellum*. James Hanigan roots this idea in the work of Thomas Cajetan (1469–1534), the Dominican theologian who influenced Bartolomé de Las Casas (1474–1566) to insist that the invading Spaniards owed restitution to the Indians they had enslaved in the New World. Cajetan based this notion in the traditional obligation to repair injured rights and make restitution for stolen goods. Thus, unjust aggressors owe restitution for an unjust occupation.[96]

Michael Schuck was among the first contemporary moral theologians to point out this lacuna in just war theory.[97] Schuck suggested three principles: repentance, honorable surrender, and restoration. Others have elaborated on these suggested principles.[98]

A consensus seems to be emerging that the termination of a war should be consistent with just cause and just intention, that unjust aggressors should be held accountable and fairly punished, and that there should be efforts at reconciliation, rehabilitation, and restoration. Such nation building can be costly and difficult, but it seems essential for the construction of a just social and political order that respects human rights and works for the common good — the basis for genuine and lasting peace, and the justification for war. This seems to be a goal of the United States in both Iraq and Afghanistan.

At least one theologian, Maureen O'Connell, has suggested a *jus ante bellum* (justice before war) expansion of just war theory.[99] That idea seems to coincide with the trend toward just peacemaking.

Just Peacemaking as a Normative, Supplemental Paradigm

We have seen that the Catholic Church has emphasized the strong presumption against war and the need for active peacemaking efforts during the post–Cold War period. Christian social ethicists have been working hard to develop the positive theology of peace called for by the church. These peace-building efforts have gone under several different titles, but among the most organized and promising is the Just Peacemaking project under the leadership of American Baptist theologian Glen Stassen.

Glen Stassen is a fascinating and talented theological ethicist. He is the son of Harold Stassen, who was the governor of Minnesota from 1939 to 1943, president of the University of Pennsylvania from 1948 to 1953, a cabinet member in the administration of Dwight Eisenhower, president of the American Baptist Convention in 1963–64, and nine-time liberal Republican candidate for U.S. president from 1948 to 1992. As an American Baptist social ethicist, Glen Stassen integrates the faith, politics, and academic interests of his father. Stassen majored in physics at the University of Virginia, studied theology at Union Theological Seminary in New York City and Duke University, and was a post-doctoral scholar in international relations and Christian ethics at Harvard. Perhaps it is his undergraduate science background that gives him an empirical and pragmatic bent, but Stassen, now the Lewis B. Smedes Professor of Christian Ethics at Fuller Theological Seminary in California, is known for being statistically well informed about social issues and for his desire to use ideas and organization to accomplish real political change. He is a creative and constructive thinker and a skilled organizer.

In 1992, Stassen published *Just Peacemaking: Transforming Initiatives for Justice and Peace.*[100] He interprets the teaching of Jesus in the Sermon on the Mount (Mt 5–7, Lk 6:20–49) and of Paul in Romans 12–15 as providing a practical plan for peacemaking, which Stassen translates into seven steps for just peacemaking. Stassen hopes that the just peacemaking paradigm might take Christians beyond the impasse of the just war versus pacifism debate. His model includes the practices of active nonviolent resistance to injustice developed by Gandhi, King, and others, and it makes explicit the steps toward justice that Christians should take before war can be seen as a last resort. Stassen maintains that whether just warriors or pacifists, all Christians should be active peacemakers.

After articulating this just peacemaking model, Stassen became something of an apostle for just peacemaking. Working through the Society of Christian Ethics, he assembled a group of twenty-three scholars and activists who met over a period of five years to hammer out a consensus around ten empirical practices that have been proven to produce justice and to prevent the resort to war. In 1998, this group published *Just Peacemaking: Ten Practices for Abolishing War,*[101] which presented and explained the ten practices:

1. Support nonviolent direct action.

2. Take independent initiatives to reduce threat.

3. Use cooperative conflict resolution.

4. Acknowledge responsibility for conflict and injustice and seek repentance and forgiveness.

5. Advance democracy, human rights, religious liberty, and interdependence.

6. Foster just and sustainable economic development.

7. Work with emerging cooperative forces in the international system.

8. Strengthen the United Nations and international efforts for cooperation and human rights.

9. Reduce offensive weapons and weapons trade.

10. Encourage grassroots peacemaking groups and other voluntary associations.

The just peacemaking paradigm is meant to supplement, not supplant, the just war and nonviolence paradigms. Just peacemaking proponents contend that there is empirical evidence — specific historical examples or political science data analysis — that these practices are often effective, that they work. Thus they claim that this paradigm is realistic, that it is relevant to a postmodern world that stresses community and interactivity, and that it is normative or obligatory, especially for Christians, in that it spells out the other steps that should be taken before any resort to war. Just peacemakers are conscious that they are responding to the call of the churches to develop a positive theology of peace.[102]

Catholic theological ethicist Lisa Sowle Cahill offers a sympathetic critique of the just peacemaking paradigm. She suggests that just peacemaking needs to take sin more seriously and to attend to the need for pressure, even coercion (countervailing force), in enacting justice for the oppressed and in establishing the social basis for genuine peace.[103] Others elaborate on Cahill's critique in a more pointed way, finding just peacemaking's political worldview, which stresses international cooperation, too utopian, and its theological perspective overly optimistic and unrealistic regarding human nature and social systems.[104] While I think Cahill's points can be helpfully integrated into just peacemaking theory, I tend to agree with its hopeful, communitarian perspective.

Finally, a trend that I think may complement just peacemaking can be noted: *just policing*. In response to the preference of many to respond to terrorism, not with war, but with law enforcement, Tobias Winright and Gerald Schlabach have suggested that a model of just policing needs to be articulated, developed, and specified. Schlabach also suggests that just policing may be a way through the just war versus pacifism impasse.[105]

These authors envision an international police force, consonant with the International Criminal Court and employing a community policing model, to enforce international law and prevent crimes, such as terrorism and ethnic cleansing or genocide. While just policing is subject to criteria and principles similar to the just war tradition, it is more restrained in the use of violence and force. This proposal seems parallel to some of the practices of just peacemaking and perhaps supplements them as well.

Just peacemaking seems theologically and ethically sound and potentially effective in enhancing justice and reducing war. It gives particular and pragmatic meaning to the church's strong presumption against war and its understanding of a just social order as the basis of genuine peace. It is an important ecumenical development of the church's tradition regarding war and peace.

Questions for Reflection and Discussion

1. Given the biblical and historical basis for pacifism and the requirement that a just war be a last resort, shouldn't Christians ordinarily be conscientious objectors rather than soldiers? Is the willingness of the church to countenance war an example of the politicization (chap. 2) of the church?

2. Discuss the church's response to World War I, to the rise of totalitarianism between the wars, and to World War II.

3. Franz Jägerstätter's resistance to joining the Nazi army seems admirable, but shouldn't a father of three young girls capitulate in order to avoid execution? What is the responsibility of soldiers, who allow themselves to be put in harm's way, to their families?

4. Discuss the Catholic peace movement during the Cold War period and the Vietnam War. Compare the Catholic peace movement with the official teaching of the church during this period.

5. What is a moral response to terrorism?

6. Can preventive war be morally justified?

7. Is the just peacemaking paradigm a fitting response to the impasse presented by the pacifism versus just war debate? Can just peacemaking work in practice? Can the just war theory work in practice? Can pacifism/nonviolence work in practice?

Chapter 5

A Consistent Ethic of Life
and Care for the Earth

Catholic social thought needs a sound theoretical basis, but it also needs to be lived and practiced. This chapter will explore the "consistent ethic of life" as a framework for the sometimes conflicting principles of Catholic social teaching, and it will examine the environmental ethic being developed by the church. The lived experience of two people who took Catholic social teaching seriously will serve to introduce each of these topics.

On August 31, 1982, John Timothy Leary, age twenty-four, died of cardiac arrest while jogging home from work in Boston. It is hard to imagine a more diverse gathering of people than the mourners at his funeral service. Derelicts rubbed shoulders with distinguished professors. Priests and nuns mingled with Quakers, Jews, and Buddhists. Distinctions of race and ethnicity vanished in the shared grief of this unexpected and incomprehensible loss. It was not just that John was so young when he died, but that he was so good. One of his friends was convinced that he had died from an excess of compassion. The emergency medical technicians who responded after John collapsed on a sidewalk were at first puzzled, not sure he was dead. "He was smiling. You don't often see that."[1]

John Leary was raised in a working-class Irish-Catholic family in Vernon, Connecticut. In high school he turned away from his Catholic upbringing and took advantage of the popularity that flowed from being a handsome, gifted student-athlete. He was precociously involved in politics, managing the local primary campaign of a presidential candidate and working for the environment. A school counselor encouraged him to apply to Harvard University, sensing a promise not evident to John himself.

In his freshman year at Harvard, John made a conscious decision to return to the church. He had decided that if the church had fallen short, it was because ordinary Christians had not really followed the gospel. He decided to do so as best he could. As a result he began volunteering in a prison ministry through the university. Soon he was connected to Haley House, the Catholic Worker community in Boston, and he was feeding the hungry at its soup kitchen, offering hospitality to the homeless, and becoming immersed in the peace movement. By his sophomore year he was so involved in various peace and justice activities that he momentarily decided to drop out of college. He then thought better of turning his back on the opportunity to get a quality education and continued his studies, but he didn't cut back on his service and advocacy. He graduated from Harvard *magna cum laude* and received the prestigious Ames Award for service to the greater community, an honor bestowed by his classmates.

John Leary was one of those activists whose life seems a whirlwind of meetings and commitments but who remain a center of calm, joy, and good will in the midst of chaos. His calendar revealed about twenty scheduled meetings in a typical week over and above his commitments to Haley House and to the Pax Christi USA Center for Conscience and War, where he worked. For a while he and his roommates opened their apartment to the homeless and would have twenty or thirty street people spending the night. When fights started to break out and lice thrived, they rethought the practicality of this arrangement, and their hospitality took a different form, but guests were always welcome.

John helped organize and participated in a weekly protest vigil at Draper Laboratories, a Cambridge-based nuclear weapons research facility. Every Monday a small group of demonstrators would greet the employees with leaflets designed to get them thinking about the morality of the work they were doing. Sometimes one of the demonstrators would engage in civil disobedience by trespassing on the facility's restricted property. John was arrested a couple of times in this peace protest. He was also arrested several times in sit-in demonstrations blocking access to abortion clinics. John insisted that these protests were linked by a respect for life. He saw a connection between the issues of abortion, war, and capital punishment that many of his friends found not just surprising, but shocking.

John Timothy Leary quietly dedicated his life to a Christian witness on behalf of nonviolence, life, and justice. His remarkable story challenges all of us to reflect on the meaning of discipleship and the direction of our lives. It seems to me that he is a model for the "consistent ethic of life" or the "seamless garment of life issues" that was articulated by Cardinal Joseph Bernardin and others. Why is it that the demonstrators at the abortion clinic and those at Draper Laboratories were not the same folks (except for John)? Is there a link between a pro-life position and advocacy for social justice and peace?

Cardinal Bernardin and the Consistent Ethic

Cardinal Joseph Louis Bernardin (1928–96) was one of the most influential American churchmen of the modern era.[2] He was raised in a closely knit family in South Carolina, a state where Catholics are neither numerous nor prominent, the son of immigrants from northern Italy. He began his higher education as a pre-med student at the University of South Carolina but shifted to studying for the priesthood, receiving degrees in theology and education from the Catholic University of America. Nearly all his priestly ministry was as an administrator, but he was able to bring much pastoral sensitivity to administration. Fourteen years after ordination he was appointed auxiliary bishop of Atlanta. He served as archbishop of Cincinnati from 1972 to 1982, and then until his death in 1996 as cardinal archbishop of Chicago, the second largest archdiocese in the United States.

He was respected by his brother bishops and by people of faith, and those of no faith, for his intelligence and wisdom, his leadership and reconciliation skills, and his civility, faith, and courage. He weathered a false accusation of sexual abuse and graciously forgave the troubled accuser who had wounded him deeply and publicly. His journal chronicling the last months of his life when he was dying from cancer, *The Gift of Peace: Personal Reflections* (Loyola Press, 1997), became an inspirational best-seller. He received the Presidential Medal of Freedom for his contributions to American civil life, and his articulation of the consistent ethic of life was a part of those contributions.

Bernardin served as president of the U.S. Conference of Catholic Bishops (USCCB) from 1974 to 1977. In the early 1980s he served as chair of the ad hoc committee of bishops that prepared *The Challenge of Peace,* the pastoral letter on nuclear ethics approved by the USCCB in 1983. This peace pastoral was important for both the consultative process of its development and its content. After shepherding the peace pastoral to completion, Bernardin was appointed the chair of the Committee on Pro-Life Activities, which he led from 1983 to 1989. Immediately Bernardin drew a connection between nuclear ethics and abortion, and, in the well-received Gannon Lecture at Fordham University on December 6, 1983, he articulated this linkage in terms of a consistent ethic of life. For the remainder of his life Bernardin energetically developed this concept of a consistent ethic (CE) in three dozen public lectures, articles, symposia, and in documents of the USCCB. The CE continues to be a helpful framework, both in American Catholic circles and in the wider society.[3]

In his final presentation on the CE at Georgetown University on September 9, 1996, Cardinal Bernardin offered this description of the idea:

> In proposing the "Consistent Ethic" over a decade ago, my purpose was to help create a dialogue about the full range of threats to life which modern society poses. I recognize the difference between the obligation to care for life and the obligation to defend life from attack. I recognize that the moral failure to care for life adequately is different from the moral crime of taking innocent life. But I was convinced — and still am firmly convinced — that the overriding moral need of our society is to cultivate a conviction that we must face *all* the major threats to life, not only one or two. The "Consistent Ethic" precisely seeks to relate our moral analysis about *different* kinds of moral problems. It seeks to provide a framework within which individuals and

"Bernardin Asks Catholics to Fight Both Nuclear Arms and Abortion"

Joseph Cardinal Bernardin, the Archbishop of Chicago, called on Roman Catholics yesterday to open a broad attack on a cluster of issues related to the "sanctity of life," among them nuclear arms, abortion, and capital punishment....

Delivering the Annual Gannon lecture at the Bronx campus of Fordham University, the Cardinal said the various issues made a "seamless garment" that deserved the utmost attention of the American Catholic church.

He said Catholics should build a "constituency" to press all of the church's "pro-life" moral positions rather than treat them as separate causes. Many church leaders have noted tensions and isolation between foes of abortion, on the one hand, and critics of nuclear arms on the other.

While stressing the need for moral "consistency," the Cardinal conceded that sharp divisions existed over these issues among Catholics. He also said concern for the unborn fetus must be accompanied by concern for people living in poverty....

— Kenneth A. Briggs, *New York Times,* December 7, 1983

groups, who begin with a concern for one moral dimension of life, can be brought to see the threat posed by other issues in our societies.[4]

Cardinal Bernardin was trying to connect caring for life and defending it, protecting life and promoting it. He hoped the CE would counter a culture of violence with a culture of respect for life. He recognized the differences and complexities of each issue, but also saw a link between them.

He repeatedly said that he wanted to counter any impression that the church engaged in single-issue politics. Rather the church was an advocate regarding a spectrum of issues linked by the sanctity of human life and the dignity of the human person, created in the image of God.

Those who defend the right to life of the weakest among us must be equally visible in support of the quality of life of the powerless among us: the old and the young, the hungry and the homeless, the undocumented immigrant and the unemployed worker. Such a quality of life posture translates into specific political and economic positions on tax policy, employment generation, welfare policy, nutrition and feeding programs, and health care. Consistency means we cannot have it both ways. We cannot urge a compassionate society and vigorous public policy to protect the rights of the unborn and then argue that compassion and significant public programs on behalf of the needy undermine the moral fiber of society or are beyond the proper scope of government responsibility. Right to life and quality of life complement each other in domestic society.[5]

Given the political realities in the United States, advocacy for a CE means that the church's positions cut across party politics. This should make it easier for the church to avoid partisanship, but it also makes it difficult to build a political constituency.

Bernardin worked to shape a consensus on a consistent ethic of life in the USCCB, among Catholics, and in the wider society. He gave dozens of addresses on the CE and on its constituent moral issues — abortion, deterrence, foreign policy, poverty, the death penalty, euthanasia, health care reform, managed care, genetic research, and the church and politics. He was successful in getting the bishops' conference to adopt the framework of a consistent ethic in its election-year statements about the moral issues facing the nation. There are, however, a variety of interpretations and emphases regarding the CE among U.S. bishops and among U.S. Catholics in general, and there are critics of various stripes as well. Indeed, the Catholic Common Ground Project, spearheaded by Cardinal Bernardin in the last months of his life, was aimed at overcoming the polarity among American Catholics and building a more unified church.[6] Nevertheless, the CE does provide an important framework for bringing Catholic social and moral teaching to the public forum.

Rooted in Initiatives by the Laity

Cardinal Bernardin was an articulate spokesperson for the consistent ethic of life in the American church, but the idea itself was originated by Catholic lay activists.[7] Eileen Egan (1922–2000) was a friend and companion of Dorothy Day, a collaborator with and biographer of Mother Teresa, a minister to refugees during and after World War II, and a lifelong nonviolent activist and co-founder of Pax Christi USA.[8] Egan coined the "seamless garment of life" metaphor in early 1971 in an interview with British journalist Malcolm Muggeridge. When asked her views about abortion, war, and capital punishment, Egan said that the life issues are woven together in a seamless garment, a reference to Jesus' tunic, over which the soldiers cast lots at the crucifixion (Jn 19:23–24).

At about the same time, a young Catholic journalist, Margaret O'Brien Steinfels, was struck by the inconsistency in the moral leadership of her bishop, Cardinal Terrence Cooke of New York. The cardinal was photographed wearing a pilot's helmet in the cockpit of a bomber in Vietnam, giving his implicit blessing to the war, when the previous Sunday a letter from Cardinal Cooke opposing New York's reform legislation permitting abortion had been read from the pulpit. In modern parlance, she apparently thought, "What's wrong with this picture?" Unlike Cardinal Cooke, Steinfels saw a link between abortion and the victims of war.[9] So did one of Cooke's colleagues, Humberto Medeiros, archbishop of Boston, who gave an address in 1971 titled "A Call for a Consistent Ethic of Life and the Law."[10]

I have had similar jarring experiences. While the Vietnam War raged in the early 1970s, I was teaching religion at a Catholic high school. When I invited a local antiabortion activist to address my classes on the morality of abortion, she came wearing a button that proclaimed her support for the U.S. war in Vietnam. In our discussions in response to the speaker, several students pointed to this apparent disparity, which they thought undermined the consistency and credibility of the speaker.

In the mid-1980s I taught college-level theology in Connecticut. A national pro-life conference aimed at youth was held in the area, and I was invited to give a presentation on nuclear ethics. I was delighted to accept because I was convinced that the connection between these life issues should be part of the pro-life agenda. As the conference approached, however, I received a phone call asking me detailed questions about my stance on abortion. Apparently someone had questioned my pro-life credentials. I am normatively opposed to abortion, but I think direct abortion might be objectively morally right in some very limited circumstances, such as the case of an ectopic pregnancy in order to preserve the life and future fertility of a woman. This nuanced position, which is admittedly not shared by the *magisterium* of the church, was not judged sufficiently pro-life, and I was disinvited from speaking. I asked my questioner if the other speakers were being grilled about their views on nuclear weapons, but to no avail.

When Pam Goltz, a member of the Columbus, Ohio, branch of the National Organization of Women (NOW), objected to NOW's decision to promote the legalization of abortion as a central goal of feminism, she was expelled for her pro-life views. Her friend Catherine Callaghan agreed with her that abortion was contrary to and counter-productive for a movement for the equality of women. Together they founded Feminists for Life (FFL) in 1974. As psychologist and ethicist Sidney Callahan, another prominent pro-life feminist, put it, "Women will never climb to equality and social empowerment over mounds of dead foetuses, numbering now in the millions."[11] FFL continues to advocate on behalf of women and against violence and abortion and to publish *The American Feminist*.[12] FFL claims Elizabeth Cady Stanton, who organized one of the first women's rights meetings in 1848, as one of its foremothers because she linked the cause of women with that of children.

A second grassroots movement, Prolifers for Survival, linking opposition to abortion to opposition to nuclear weapons, was started by Juli Loesch in 1979. This organization became the Seamless Garment Network in 1987, broadening its scope of issues beyond abortion and war to include poverty, capital punishment, euthanasia, and racism. Carol Crossed served as its executive director then and remains on the board today. In 2002, it again changed its name to Consistent Life. It remains an international network of over two hundred organizations and of individuals for peace, justice, and life — more of an umbrella or clearing house than an organization itself.[13] It clearly illustrates that the spirit of the consistent ethic is alive and well.

The lay activism of John Timothy Leary and of the women who founded FFL and Prolifers for Survival preceded Cardinal Bernardin in making the link between abortion, war, and human rights. Indeed, nonviolent activists, such as Gordon Zahn, Eileen Egan, and those in the Catholic Worker movement had long nurtured the concept of a consistent ethic, even though their activism might have been centered on opposition to war and the protection of human rights.[14] Mother Teresa, who famously recognized the face of Christ in the distressing disguise of the poor, often spoke out against abortion and other forms of violence as well. The idea even receives ecumenical support among progressive evangelicals such as Jim Wallis and the Sojourners community and pacifist Protestant ethicists such as Stanley Hauerwas. Not all pro-life activists, however, made the connection with other forms of violence, such as war, capital punishment, and poverty, nor did all justice seekers oppose abortion and euthanasia.

The Seamless Garment in Catholic Social Teaching

The "seamless garment" metaphor did not appear until 1971, and the vision of a consistent ethic was not developed until about 1983, but the concept has deep roots in scripture, Christian tradition, and the contemporary social teaching of the church. Indeed the seamless garment is a biblical metaphor. (Since Cardinal Bernardin was convinced that Christians should use language accessible to as many people as possible in our pluralistic public forum, he preferred consistent ethic.) This section will focus on the foundation and the development of the CE in contemporary Catholic teaching.[15]

The Pastoral Constitution on the Church in the Modern World of the Second Vatican Council (1965) ably articulates the vision of a consistent ethic:

> In our times a special obligation binds us to make ourselves the neighbor of absolutely every person, and of actively helping him when he comes across our path, whether he be an old person abandoned by all, a foreign laborer unjustly looked down upon, a refugee, a child born of an unlawful union and wrongly suffering for a sin he did not commit, or a hungry person who disturbs our conscience by recalling the voice of the Lord: "As long as you did it to one of these, the least of my brethren, you did it for me" (Mt. 25:40).

> Furthermore, whatever is opposed to life itself, such as any type of murder, genocide, abortion, euthanasia, or wilful self-destruction, whatever violates the integrity of the human person, such as mutilation, torments inflicted on the body or mind, attempts to coerce the will itself; whatever insults human dignity, such as subhuman living conditions, arbitrary imprisonment, deportation, slavery, prostitution, the selling of women and children; as well as disgraceful working conditions, where men are treated as mere tools for profit, rather than as free and responsible persons; all these things and others of their like are infamies indeed. They poison human society, but they do more harm to those who practice them than those who suffer the injury. Moreover they are a supreme dishonor to the Creator (27).

The Council clearly linked a plethora of issues through the values of the sanctity of life and the dignity of the human person.

The U.S. Catholic bishops picked up the connection between the nuclear question, abortion, and other life issues in their pastoral letter *The Challenge of Peace* (1983), which was produced by an ad hoc committee chaired by Bernardin:

> When we accept violence in any form as commonplace, our sensitivities become dulled. When we accept violence, war itself can be taken for granted. Violence has many faces: oppression of the poor, deprivation of basic human rights, economic exploitation, sexual exploitation and pornography, neglect or abuse of the aged and the helpless, and innumerable other acts of inhumanity. Abortion in particular blunts a sense of the sacredness of human life. In a society where the innocent unborn are killed wantonly, how can we expect people to feel righteous revulsion at the act or threat of killing non-combatants in war (285)?

As Cardinal Bernardin and others developed the consistent ethic, it was consciously incorporated into the guidelines for political responsibility issued by the USCCB in presidential election years, beginning with the 1988 election.[16] In 1994, the USCCB issued a pastoral message titled "Confronting a Culture of Violence," which catalogued the gruesome realities of violence in American life, including the fact that the most violent site is at home, that the United States is flooded with guns and inundated with violence in the media, and the holocaust of abortion occurs daily. The bishops presented the consistent ethic of life as an antidote to this culture of violence.[17]

Although Pope John Paul II did not use the term "consistent" ethic, he certainly preached the concept in season and out. His papacy was dedicated to a defense of humanity wherever it was under threat. One of his clearest articulations of the sanctity of life was his 1995 encyclical *The Gospel of Life* (*Evangelium Vitae*). In the first section of the encyclical the pope decried what he called a "Culture of Death" — a "conspiracy against life" and "a war of the powerful against the weak." After this broad cultural analysis, John Paul II addressed in particular the issues of abortion and euthanasia, and also the death penalty. Based on the principle that prohibits the direct killing of the innocent, Pope John Paul II was absolutely opposed to abortion and euthanasia, feeling this prohibition should be directly enshrined in law.

The church has historically recognized that the state has the right to execute a criminal as justified punishment and to protect the community. Indeed, until 1969 Vatican City allowed capital punishment for attempting to assassinate the pope.[18] John Paul II, however, repudiated the exercise of this right because the community can ordinarily be protected without execution. The pope could not imagine the need to practice the death penalty in the contemporary world, and he famously forgave the man who wounded him in an assassination attempt.

Like the USCCB, John Paul calls for a cultural transformation, the building of a "culture of life" to confront the "culture of death." The pope hopes that consciences formed to respect the inviolable worth of every human life will result in a new lifestyle that values being over having, persons over things. John Paul does not cover the spectrum of issues addressed by the CE in *The Gospel of Life,* but he is clearly in sympathy with its vision:

> Where life is involved, the service of charity must be profoundly consistent. It cannot tolerate bias and discrimination, for human life is sacred and inviolable at every stage and in every situation: it is an indivisible good. We need then to "show care" for all life and for the life of everyone (87).

This encyclical gave an implicit endorsement to the consistent ethic of life movement.

During the July 7, 2009, Vatican press conference that presented Pope Benedict XVI's social encyclical, *Charity in Truth (Caritas in Veritate)*, Archbishop Giampaolo Crepaldi of Trieste, Italy, was asked whether the document contained anything new. Crepaldi pointed to Benedict's insistence that the Catholic Church's pro-life message and its peace and justice concerns belonged together as an original contribution of the encyclical. Crepaldi insisted that Benedict's tying together of anthropology (sanctity of life and human dignity) and sociology (economic, social, and cultural themes) invited a new way of thinking and of living.[19]

Charity in Truth was originally scheduled for release in 2007 to mark the fortieth anniversary of Paul VI's encyclical *On the Development of Peoples (Populorum Progressio)*. In the first chapter of *Charity in Truth* Benedict interprets *The Development of Peoples* in the context of Paul VI's thought. Here he insists that this social encyclical is linked with Paul's 1968 encyclical on birth control, *On Human Life (Humanae Vitae)*, that life ethics and social ethics go together (#15). Benedict makes this connection four more times in *Charity in Truth:*

"This is not a question of purely individual morality. *Humanae Vitae* indicates the *strong links between life ethics and social ethics,* ushering in a new era of magisterial teaching that has gradually been articulated in a series of documents, most recently John Paul II's *Evangelium Vitae.* The Church forcefully maintains this link between life ethics and social ethics, fully aware that 'a society lacks solid foundations when, on the one hand, it asserts values such as the dignity of the person, justice and peace, but then, on the other hand, radically acts to the contrary by allowing or tolerating a variety of ways in which human life is devalued and violated, especially where it is weak or marginalized' (EV, #101)."

— Benedict XVI, *Charity in Truth,* #15

+ he links respect for life with integral development (#28);

+ he calls for respect for life in discounting population growth as a primary cause of poverty (#44 and #28);

+ he connects human ecology (respect for life and human dignity) with environmental ecology (respect for the earth) (#51);

+ he argues that a cultural mindset that denies human dignity results in a materialistic and mechanistic understanding of human life that is open to eugenics and euthanasia and is indifferent toward intolerable injustices (#75).

Like John Paul II, Benedict does not use the term "consistent ethic of life," but the concept is a significant theme in *Charity in Truth.* The thought of both of these popes was also vulnerable to the problems that the consistent ethic of life encountered in the United States.

The Controversy over the Consistent Ethic

When Cardinal Bernardin introduced the consistent ethic as a moral and political framework late in 1983, he invited discussion and dialogue about this vision. He got his wish. Much of the response was positive, but there were critiques from the right and the left, from pro-life conservatives and from justice-oriented progressives. Bernardin was always clear that there were important differences among these complex moral issues, but he insisted that they were also connected, both morally and politically. In general, conservatives emphasize the *differences* among the issues, insisting that the sanctity of life is more important than the quality of life, thus giving ethical and political priority to abortion and the related issues of stem cell research and euthanasia. Progressives are more prone to focus on the *similarities* among the issues, either by resisting all killing through a commitment to nonviolence or by balancing the political weight of social and economic injustice and of other forms of violence with that of abortion. A key to this tension is the question of moral absolutes in ethical theory and, in particular, the absolute moral prohibition of abortion.

The church's absolute prohibition of abortion, as articulated by John Paul II in *The Gospel of Life,* is based in natural law or reason. The pope recognizes that scripture never addresses the question of deliberate abortion (61), but he correctly brings the Bible's deep respect for life to bear on the issue. Still the church's position is rooted in a deduction from the principle that prohibits the direct killing of innocent human life, not a command found in revelation.

John Paul acknowledges that the value of the fetus is central to this discussion, and he restates the church's nuanced theological position that at the moment of conception a human life begins that will become a person. "The mere probability that a human person is involved would suffice to justify an absolutely clear prohibition of any intervention aimed at killing a human embryo" (60). The church does not know for sure that a human person is present in an embryo, but the value at stake is so fundamental that the embryo is given the benefit of any doubt.

Since a direct abortion is the intentional killing of an innocent human being, the pope argues that it always constitutes a grave moral disorder and that it should be prohibited by law in any humane society. "No circumstance, no purpose, no law whatsoever can ever make licit an act which is intrinsically illicit, since it is contrary to the law of God which is written in every human heart, knowable by reason itself and proclaimed by the church" (62). This argument is the official teaching of the Catholic Church. It is accepted and proclaimed by Cardinal Bernardin and the USCCB.[20]

Since this argument is based on reason, it should be obvious to all persons of intelligence and good will. Yet the morality of abortion is one of the most contentious issues of our time. Many of those who are not persuaded by the church's logic also begin with the value of the fetus. Probability is a precarious perch on which to place an absolute prohibition. Many think that the fetus becomes a person at some point in its development, but is not a person at conception. Even if one is willing to value the fetus from conception, are there ever competing values that might justify a direct abortion? Many think that when a pregnancy threatens the life of the woman, as with an ectopic pregnancy (the fertilized egg attaches to the fallopian tube, rather than the uterus), a direct abortion, which can preserve the fallopian tube and the woman's future fertility, can be objectively morally right. Some think that abortion can be morally justified in the case of rape; others in the case of a serious anomaly, such as anencephaly, in the fetus. If the moral prohibition of abortion is not absolute, then what sort of law should a humane society have in regard to abortion? Abortion has been the enduring priority on the official church's political agenda. Should abortion and related issues trump all other issues embraced by a consistent ethic?[21]

Several critics of the CE and of the moral teaching of the Catholic Church point to what appears to be a double standard that operates in regard to social teaching and sexual matters. In regard to war, for example, the direct or intentional targeting of civilians is prohibited by the principle that protects innocent human life, yet indirect effect allows for considerable "collateral damage." Indeed there has been no contemporary war where the number of civilians killed has not totally eclipsed the number of combatants. Modern war mainly kills the innocent. In warfare the church allows considerable prudential judgment to commanders and soldiers in the trenches. Both Bernardin and John Paul II acknowledge the difficulties and complications encountered by a woman facing a problem pregnancy,[22] but a woman's experience is not allowed to affect the absolute norm prohibiting abortion. Women are not allowed prudential judgment in the "reproductive trenches." The bishops tend to approach social issues with quiet ambiguity, but address sexual issues with loud absolutes.[23]

Thus the controversy over the consistent ethic turns in part over ethical methodology and in particular over the question of moral absolutes.[24] There is a moral and legal clarity that flows from moral absolutes, and a certain passion as well. Thus the priority given to abortion by the church since the Supreme Court decided *Roe vs. Wade* in 1973, which had the effect of allowing abortion on demand in the United States until the third trimester. Many who take this pro-life position felt that the CE might compromise their concern for life.[25]

Cardinal Bernardin had no intention of compromising the passion for pro-life. He did, however, want to broaden its scope to include issues such as nuclear weapons, which threaten humanity's very future, and capital punishment, which undermines respect for life. In truth, there are some who are opposed to abortion, but who favor capital punishment and a militaristic foreign policy. Such positions are out of step with the current official teaching of the church, although, admittedly, the church has strengthened the presumption against war and restrained the exercise of the death penalty only in recent times.[26] Many pro-lifers see these moral issues in a different light from abortion. These are complex issues, as Bernardin admitted, but he also insisted that they are life issues. To be pro-life means working against a nuclear holocaust and outlawing the death penalty.

On the other hand, even if there might be some morally justified exceptions to the prohibition against abortion, the norm prohibiting abortion seems reasonable, and the annual average of 1.5 million abortions in the United States is thus a moral outrage. The CE at minimum asks Catholic progressives what they are doing to make abortion rare. What are those who care about the oppressed and powerless doing to protect the unborn? Undoubtedly many Catholic progressives will point to empowering and supporting women as an important component of reducing the number of abortions, a justice issue that has not received focused attention from the USCCB.

This conflict between conservatives and progressives regarding absolutes generated a related controversy over whether bishops should make *specific* public policy proposals. For conservatives, absolute moral prohibitions regarding the sanctity of life logically lead to clear legal restrictions. Affirmations about the quality of life, however, are more politically complex, and bishops have neither the expertise nor the authority to make specific proposals in this realm.[27]

Progressives, on the other hand, tend to see the translation of ethical principles into public policy prescriptions as complex across the board. They recognize that the bishops' teaching about moral *principles* has greater authority than their public policy *proposals*,[28] and that the quality of the argument for specific policies is key to its persuasiveness, but they think it is important for the church to be specific, as well as open to disagreement.

The consistent ethic of life expects society to be responsible for promoting the common good and the state to have an active role on behalf of the public order.[29] Conservatives, however, generally emphasize the principle of subsidiarity in a way that restricts or limits the role of the state. Progressives tend to emphasize the principle of solidarity, which gives more of a role to the state.

There are two other major issues or questions associated with the consistent ethic of life. The first is its *scope*.[30] Cardinal Bernardin explicitly addressed a variety of social and medical issues under the umbrella of the CE, including abortion, war, capital punishment, euthanasia, genetic research, poverty, and health care policy. Feminists For Life include sexism and the rights of women, a troubling and ambiguous justice issue for the church.[31] The consistent ethic network includes racism. Should the CE also embrace heterosexism and address the violence done to gay, lesbian, and trans-gendered people? Should the moral vision of the CE be extended to creation and the biosphere, environmental justice, and the ecological web of life, as Benedict XVI insists (*Charity in Truth*, #51)? Each of these moral issues is different, but is there also a connection among them?

Second, does the consistent ethic of life adequately capture the social and communal dimension of Catholic social teaching? In sketching the theological basis of the CE, Cardinal Bernardin explains:

> Catholic teaching is based on two truths about the human person: human life is both *sacred* and *social*. Because we esteem human life as *sacred*, we have a duty to protect and foster it at all stages of development, from conception to natural death, and in all circumstances. Because we acknowledge that human life is *social*, society must protect and foster it.[32]

The CE has much to say about the sanctity of life and about human dignity, but the communal dimension of Catholic social teaching tends to be reduced to society's responsibility to protect and promote the sanctity of life. Indeed, when Protestant theologian James Gustafson notes that the "life is social" theological proclamation does not seem to yield a strong moral imperative in Bernardin's articulation of the consistent ethic, the cardinal admits that "a priority has been given to the *individual* 'made in the image and likeness of God' '" in Catholic thinking. "In moments of conflict between the individual and the social, the individual must predominate for it is here that the fullest presence of the divine is to be encountered."[33] In effect this would give priority to personal issues, such as abortion, as opposed to social issues, such as poverty.

It seems to me, however, that contemporary Catholic social teaching does proclaim moral imperatives related to the theological truth that human dignity is realized in community, through the principles of the common good, solidarity, human rights, and the option for the poor. This communitarian aspect of Catholic social teaching would add balance to the focus on the individual in the CE, and it would also complicate its moral analysis, as Gustafson contends. Can the common good ever take precedence over the sanctity of life in the analysis of a moral dilemma or a social issue? For example, in the national debate about health insurance reform in 2009, the U.S. Catholic bishops' advocacy of the right to health care seemed to take a back seat to their concern about using federal funds to pay for abortions. Perhaps here the common good should have received greater emphasis.

Further questions could be raised regarding the consistent ethic. How does it relate to the internal practice of the church, and especially the treatment of dissenting theologians?[34] Given the natural law basis of the CE,[35] does it adequately bring the radical challenge of the gospel to bear on issues of public policy?[36] Nevertheless, the consistent ethic offers a framework both for understanding the teaching of the church and for evaluating and influencing public policy. The CE brings the moral dimension to the public forum and challenges society and the state to protect and promote human life and human dignity and the common good. It is an important articulation of the social teaching of the church.

If Christians genuinely integrate the sanctity of human life and human dignity with solidarity and the common good into a lifestyle, Christianity will become significantly countercultural. In a violent world, Christians will choose life by proclaiming that abortion is not a life-giving response to a problem pregnancy, that execution will not combat crime, that more and better guns will not make our homes safe and more and better weapons will not make our homeland secure, that war does not resolve conflict or stop terrorism, that euthanasia is no way to cope with the burdens of aging, illness, and disability. In a greedy world, Christians will express our gratitude to God by an open-handed generosity that is willing to pay more taxes to ensure that every American has access to health care and no child on earth is hungry or malnourished. In a world of exclusion and unjust discrimination, Christians will practice a hospitality that includes women, people of color, homosexuals, and immigrants as full participants in our communities. John Timothy Leary grasped and practiced such a consistent ethic.

An Ecological Theology and Environmental Ethic

In his 2009 social encyclical *Charity in Truth,* Pope Benedict XVI enlarges the consistent ethic of life to include the natural environment.

> *The way humanity treats the environment influences the way it treats itself, and vice versa....* In order to protect nature, *... the decisive issue is the overall moral tenor of society.* If there is a lack of respect for the right to life and to a natural death, if human conception, gestation and birth are made artificial, if human embryos are sacrificed to research, the conscience of society ends up losing the concept of human ecology and, along with it, that of environmental ecology.... The book of nature is indivisible: it takes in not only the environment but also life, sexuality, marriage, the family, social relations: in a word, integral human development. Our duties toward the environment are linked to our duties towards the human person, considered in himself and in relation to others. It would be wrong to uphold one set of duties while trampling on the other. Herein lies a grave contradiction in our mentality and practice today: one which demeans the person, disrupts the environment and damages society. (*Charity in Truth,* #51)[37]

The life of Sister Dorothy Stang is a witness to the connection between integral human development and environmental responsibility.

Dorothy Stang: Martyr of the Amazon

Dorothy Stang grew up in Dayton, Ohio, the fourth of nine children.[38] Her father, Henry, was a chemical engineer who enlisted the whole family in tending a half-acre organic garden, long before organic was fashionable. Her mother, Edna, for years ran the annual St. Joseph's Orphan Home picnic and the parish's fall festival. The devoutly Catholic family was known for its generous hospitality toward struggling relatives as well as strangers. At age seventeen Dorothy and her lifelong friend Joan Krimm joined the Sisters of Notre Dame de Namur. Dorothy's dream was to be a missionary.

After her novitiate, Dorothy was sent to teach elementary school in Illinois. Two years later (1953) she volunteered to teach at a mission school in Arizona that served a diverse parish comprised of Native Americans, Hispanic migrant workers, and middle-class whites. Dorothy loved the children and families she served and found the hard work of establishing a school and pastoral outreach into the community rewarding. She was superior of the local community and principal of the school when, in 1963, Pope John XXIII asked American religious communities to commit 10 percent of their personnel for service in Latin America. Dorothy immediately volunteered and was chosen to be in the second group of Notre Dame de Namur sisters sent to Brazil.

Dorothy arrived in Brazil in 1966, just one year after the completion of the Second Vatican Council (1962–65). The five sisters went to the Center for Intercultural Formation to learn Portuguese (a struggle for Dorothy) and to immerse themselves in the culture. Two of their instructors were Fathers Gustavo Gutiérrez and Jon Sobrino, early proponents of liberation theology. In response to Vatican II the church in Latin America was moving to the side of the poor — sharing their poverty and empowering the poor to claim their human rights.

The sisters' first assignment was working with two Italian priests in the state of Maranhão in northern Brazil. They plunged into pastoral work, visiting all the families in the parish and gradually developing base ecclesial communities (small communities of Christians who meet regularly, under lay leadership, to support one another in responding to the gospel). They found that the impoverished workers were living in a semi-feudal relationship of dominance and subservience with the wealthy landowners. Through education and leadership training the sisters opened up the Bible to the poor, and the people were led by scripture to a sense of their rights as human beings. The sisters consciously cast their lot with the poor, preferring, for example, to stay in the cramped quarters of peasant homes rather than in the luxury of the landowner's houses when they traveled to distant villages. Soon the wealthy landowners became suspicious of the sisters.

Dorothy and her pastoral colleagues shared the deprivations of the poor. Maranhão of Brazil is near the equator, and the weather is hot, humid, and often rainy. Roads are primitive, and the few vehicles available break down often. Diseases (malaria and worms, for example) are common; food is scarce. In the rural areas there is no electricity, clean water, or sanitation.

After many years in Maranhão, Dorothy felt called to follow some of the peasant farmers who were migrating west into the state of Pará. The Trans-Amazon Highway was opening up new areas and the government was offering free land to settlers to develop the area. The problem was that the poor farmers often did not understand the process for getting deeds to the land they settled, the wealthy ranchers and loggers coveted the land, and the government agencies, police, and judges were corrupt. The result was a violent campaign of intimidation and harassment by the ranchers and loggers against the poor farmers and those, like Dorothy, who supported them. Hired thugs would sow weeds among the crops or simply burn the farms to the ground. Sometimes they would murder the peasants. Since 1985 it is estimated that there have been 1500 such murders over land, all but a handful carried out with impunity.[39]

The contemporary environmental movement began to flower in the early 1970s, and by the 1990s there was focused concern on the devastation of the rainforest in the Amazon region of Brazil, which has been called "the lungs of the earth." The forest was being reduced at a rate in excess of 100,000 square kilometers a year, more than the area of Switzerland and the Netherlands combined. It was being clear cut for its valuable wood (cedar and mahogany) or burned to create cropland or fields for grazing cattle. Poor farmers also engaged in "slash and burn" in the forest so they could plant crops, but their impact is insignificant in comparison to that of the agribusiness supported by multinational corporations. Unfortunately, the emerald beauty of the rainforest is only skin deep. The luxuriant vegetation and canopy of two-hundred-feet tall trees are supported by the constant decay of the ground surface. When cleared it quickly degenerates into a desert. Such deforestation is the worst of both worlds: it is economically short-sighted and ecologically devastating.[40] The burning of the forest releases huge amounts of carbon into the atmosphere, accelerating global warming, and, along with the forest, untold species of animals, insects, and plants are destroyed. About 25 percent of all pharmaceutical products used in the world come from Amazon plant species.

It is little wonder then that Sr. Dorothy, having witnessed this environmental catastrophe firsthand, often wore a T-shirt that proclaimed in Portuguese, "The death of the forest is the end of our lives." In 1991, Dorothy spent part of a sabbatical leave from her work in Brazil at the Institute of Culture and Creation Spirituality, founded by the charismatic and controversial Matthew Fox, at Holy Names College in California. Here Dorothy found confirmation of her experiences in Brazil: that creation spirituality and liberation theology were natural allies, and that there was an intrinsic connection between the abuse of women, the exploitation of the poor, and the desecration of the earth.[41]

When she returned to Brazil, Dorothy attended the historic Earth Summit in Rio de Janeiro in June 1992. The goal of the Earth Summit was to find a model of socioeconomic development that would be environmentally sustainable. As Dorothy moved deeper into the forest of the Anapu region, she worked with the government to establish preserves dedicated to sustainable development projects that would keep 80 percent of the land as forest. She persuaded the farmers to plow under the vegetation rather than burn it off, thus preserving its nutrients and creating fertile soil. She also tried to set up a fruit processing plant in an effort to work with the natural produce of the forest. She convinced the farmers to plant tens of thousands of trees in an effort to reforest. All the while she worked to get legal documents for the peasant farmers to protect their land from the corrupt claims of loggers and ranchers, and she reported illegal logging to the authorities, which sometimes resulted in hefty fines for the logging companies. Dorothy was pleased when Luiz Inácio Lula de Silva (called Lula), a worker himself and former union organizer, was elected president of Brazil in 2002. She traveled to the capital, Brasilia, to directly lobby the new government on behalf of poor farmers and sustainable development. She was disappointed when little changed.

In 2004 things were getting increasingly precarious for Dorothy. She was arrested and questioned by the authorities. Death threats against her were becoming more persistent. In the midst of this she was honored with the

Chico Mendes medal by the Brazilian Lawyers Organization for Human Rights. Chico Mendes was a rubber tree tapper who organized his fellow workers to try to stop the destruction of the Amazon forest. At first his concern was for the livelihood of the workers, but soon he joined the cry of the poor with the cry of the earth — just as Dorothy was doing. His voice on behalf of the poor and the forest was internationally recognized, and he became increasingly effective in protecting forest reserves from loggers and ranchers. "The Gandhi of the Amazon" was murdered in 1988.[42]

Dorothy's perseverance and determination and the increasing recognition that her message was receiving sealed her fate. Two ranchers put up $25,000 to have her murdered. Two of the men involved in harassing the peasant farmers were hired by an intermediary to do the job. On the morning of February 12, 2005, in a gentle rain, Dorothy set off for an important meeting with the farmers. Dorothy knew the two men who blocked her way, and she engaged them in conversation, pulling out a map from her ever-present plastic bag to show that the area was a reserve for sustainable development and that logging would be illegal. When one of them asked if she had a weapon, she produced her well-worn Bible from her bag, and proceeded to read to them from the Beatitudes. She invited the men to the community meeting, blessed them, and turned to leave. They called her name and when she turned back they shot her in the abdomen. After she fell face down, she was shot five more times and killed. The voice of this seventy-three-year-old nun was silenced.

Dorothy Stang was known for her joyful smile and her piercing blue eyes. She was a relentless advocate for the human rights of poor farmers and workers and for the preservation of the Amazon forest. There was an almost naïve stubbornness about her — a single-mindedness, combined with a simple belief in the goodness of others — in her work on behalf of justice and the earth in the face of exploitation and destruction.[43] She was well aware of the risks she was taking, of the ruthlessness of her adversaries. There is no denying her faith and her courage. Dorothy once wrote to a friend, "I have learned that faith sustains you, and I have also learned that three things are difficult: as a woman, to be taken seriously in the struggle for land reform; to stay faithful to believing that these small groups of poor farmers will prevail in organizing and carrying their own agenda forward; and to have the courage to give your life in the struggle for change."[44] She thought being an American and an "old woman" would protect her, but she was wrong about that.

Catholic Social Teaching and the Environment

Sister Dorothy Stang was a pastoral worker among the poor in a developing country. She was on the cutting edge of one of the most difficult dilemmas facing the church and the world as the ecological crisis becomes increasingly clear. How do we reconcile the needs of the poor with our concern for the environment? Economic development is in tension with environmental responsibility. In a very practical way Dorothy was fashioning a way to meet the needs of the poor while respecting the earth and the needs of future generations through sustainable development in the forest reserves. She was a martyr for land reform and for the earth.[45] Dorothy was not a theologian or a theorist, yet she put into practice the remarkably consistent environmental ethic that has been unfolding in official church teaching since about 1987.

There is no major church document dedicated to the environment (with the authority of an encyclical or conciliar document or even a substantial pastoral letter from a national conference of bishops), and that in itself is problematic. The environment is, however, explicitly mentioned in papal encyclicals and addressed in papal statements, Vatican documents, and statements by national conferences and regional groups of bishops.[46] These sources have developed a coherent environmental ethic that is helpful and yet perhaps inadequate. This section will first articulate the key interrelated themes in this official Catholic environmental ethic then raise some critical questions about it.

Key Themes in the Church's Teaching on the Environment

The foundation of the church's environmental ethic is that creation is a gift of God entrusted to humanity to take care of and cultivate. "Human beings legitimately exercise a *responsible stewardship over nature,* in order to protect it, to enjoy its fruits and to cultivate it in new ways, with the assistance of advanced technologies, so that it can worthily accommodate and feed the world's population" (*Charity in Truth,* #50). Human beings are seen as co-creators with God and as stewards of earth and its resources.

Church teaching wants to steer a middle course between the extremes of biocentrism or ecocentrism (an earth-centered approach promoted by deep ecologists and others) and total human domination of the earth.

> Nature is not at our disposal as a "heap of scattered refuse," but as a gift of the Creator who has given it an inbuilt order, enabling man to draw from it the principles needed in order to "till it and keep it" (Gen 2:15). But it should also be stressed that it is contrary to authentic development to view nature as something more important than the human person. This position leads to attitudes of neo-paganism or a new pantheism — human salvation cannot come from nature alone, understood in a purely naturalistic sense. This having been said, it is also necessary to reject the opposite position, which aims at total technical domination over nature, because the natural environment is more than raw material to be manipulated at our pleasure; it is a wondrous work of the Creator containing a "grammar" which sets forth ends and criteria for its wise use, not its reckless exploitation. (*Charity in Truth,* #48)

The church's position is clearly anthropocentric, or human-centered. Humans are above nature, but should work with nature in meeting human needs.

Both John Paul II and Benedict XVI work to achieve a balance between the doctrines of creation and redemption in order to correct an overemphasis on salvation that tended to exclude attention to creation. They stress that Christ redeems and transforms not only humanity but all of creation.[47]

The connection between care for creation and the sanctity of life has already been mentioned at the beginning of this section. The church's environmental ethic also draws on three other established and interrelated principles in Catholic social teaching: the universal destiny of created goods, the common good, and the option for the poor.[48]

God gave the earth and its resources to the whole human race for the sustenance of everyone, without favoring or excluding anyone.[49] "On this earth there is room for everyone; here the entire human family must find the resources to live with dignity, through the help of nature itself — God's gift to his children — and through hard work and creativity. At the same time we must recognize our grave duty to hand the earth on to future generations in such a condition that they too can worthily inhabit it and continue to cultivate it" (*Charity in Truth*, #50). The *universal destiny of created goods* is a powerful argument against the greedy consuming and hoarding of the rich and of the developed countries in the face of two-thirds of humanity who do not have their basic needs met (see chapter 3 above). It calls for solidarity and sacrifice on the part of those with more than enough so that the poor can have a life of dignity. It challenges behavior and policies that exhaust the resources of earth or extinguish species of plants and animals, depriving future generations of access to them. To paraphrase Gandhi: the earth has enough for everyone's need, but not for everyone's greed.

The idea of the *common good* — that human flourishing and a good society are interdependent with one another — has been extended globally in contemporary Catholic social teaching. In the church's environmental ethic the common good is further extended to include the planet or the whole of creation. Human ecology is interrelated with natural ecology. Humans cannot flourish on a polluted, depleted earth. This properly extends the scope of the common good from society to the global commons. Environmental issues transcend borders, and some of them, such as global warming and climate change, are truly planetary. Global problems require global solutions.

In Catholic social teaching, the universal common good is often fleshed out in terms of universal human rights. In this case, the right to a safe environment is added to the right to a dignified life where one's basic needs are met, that is, to the right to development.[50] This environmental ethic struggles to hold three potentially conflicting goods in balance: the welfare of the planet as a web of natural systems, justice for the living (especially the poor), and justice for future generations.[51]

The *preferential option for the poor* engages the values of equity and social justice that are already implied by the principles of the universal destiny of created goods and the common good. First, the church points out that, although the poor are not primarily responsible for environmental damage, they are usually its primary victims. Environmental pollution is almost always a matter of injustice toward those on the margins of society. Second, the church engages in the discussion of the ecological crisis in the context of its call for integral or authentic development for the poor. In this context the church decries the greed and selfishness at the root of a consumerist society that exploits workers and ravages the earth and its resources, and it calls for solidarity and sacrifice in the name of justice for the poor and stewardship of the earth. Catholic social teaching supports *sustainable development* that promises justice for the poor, justice for future generations, and the integrity of earth.

Thus the church sees the ecological crisis as a moral problem and calls for an ethic of environmental responsibility and stewardship.[52] This Catholic ethic reminds the Christian community of a sacramental view of creation where we encounter the Creator in the "book of nature." This renewed attitude of respect for nature should bear fruit in a lifestyle characterized by moderation and sacrifice on behalf of the poor and future generations. Since environmental problems are global in nature, they require international cooperation and structural changes that promote justice and the integrity of creation.

"Modern society will find no solution to the ecological problem unless it *takes a serious look at its lifestyle.* In many parts of the world society is given to instant gratification and consumerism while remaining indifferent to the damage which these cause. As I have already stated, the seriousness of the ecological issue lays bare the depth of man's moral crisis. If an appreciation of the value of the human person and of human life is lacking, we will lose interest in others and the earth itself. Simplicity, moderation and discipline, as well as a spirit of sacrifice, must become a part of everyday life, lest all suffer the negative consequences of the careless habits of a few."

—John Paul II, *The Ecological Crisis*, #13

Although the church is sometimes criticized for not practicing what it preaches, in this case its witness is perhaps more powerful than its words — Vatican City has gone green. Through putting solar panels on the roof of the Paul VI Audience Hall, increasing energy efficiency in its buildings, and purchasing carbon-effect credits, the small city-state that is the center of the Roman Catholic Church has become the world's first completely carbon-neutral state. Hopefully this commitment by church leaders at the Vatican will inspire dioceses, parishes, Catholic institutions, and individual

Christians to take practical steps in exercising environmental responsibility. One can see green shoots popping up that have been planted by Christians and church institutions.[53]

Some Questions regarding the Church's Environmental Ethic

Twice in the creation story recounted in Genesis 1, in verses 26 and 28, God gives humankind, created in God's image and likeness, "dominion" over every living thing on earth, which humans are to "fill" and "subdue." In 1967, the historian Lynn White famously argued that Western Christianity "bears a huge burden of guilt" for the current ecological crisis because of its anthropocentric view of nature.[54] He did not think that there would be a solution to our ecological crisis until a radically different view of the relationship between humans and nature took root in human consciousness. He pointed to the alternative vision of St. Francis of Assisi for environmental salvation. In 1979 Pope John Paul II named Francis the patron of those who promote ecology, but the church's environmental ethic has clung to its anthropocentrism rather than adopt a Franciscan kinship or companionship model.

Many contemporary theologians propose a "stewardship" interpretation of the creation stories, and thus criticize Lynn White for misinterpreting Genesis.[55] Contemporary theology is right to rethink the interpretation of Genesis 1 and 2, but White is correct that medieval and modern Christians interpreted dominion as domination. The church's stewardship model may improve on the total domination of nature approach, but it remains clearly and consciously anthropocentric, and that may not be an adequate conceptual or theological response to our ecological crisis. St. Francis of Assisi may indeed show us a way out of our ecological debacle.

In their book *Fullness of Faith: The Public Significance of Theology,* Fathers Michael Himes, a systematic theologian, and Kenneth Himes, a social ethicist (who are brothers) address the topic of "Creation and an Environmental Ethic" (chap. 5). They agree with Lynn White that an anthropocentric approach to nature is inadequate. While the church may claim that it gives intrinsic value to nature, anthropocentrism logically demeans the natural world and treats it as a mere resource for human well-being. Treating nature with "enlightened self-interest" is a fundamentally flawed environmental ethic. In response to this realization, some go to the opposite extreme and propose a biocentric (earth-centered) approach that prioritizes nature and reduces humanity to an instrumental value. The church is right to resist this dehumanizing approach. Both anthropocentrism and biocentrism, however, put humanity at odds with nature.

Michael and Kenneth Himes propose a genuinely theocentric and relational approach. They see nature as "creation," which gives the natural

The Historical Roots of Our Ecological Crisis

What did Christianity tell People about their relations with the environment?... Christianity inherited from Judaism not only a concept of time as nonrepetitive and linear but also a striking story of creation.... Man named all the animals, thus establishing his dominance over them. God planned all of this explicitly for man's benefit and rule; no item in the physical creation had any purpose save to serve man's purposes. And, although man's body is made of clay, he is not simply part of nature: he is made in God's image.

Especially in its Western form, Christianity is the most anthropocentric religion the world has ever seen.... Man shares, in great measure, God's transcendence of nature. Christianity... not only established a dualism of man and nature but also insisted that it is God's will that man exploit nature for his proper ends....

By destroying pagan animism, Christianity made it possible to exploit nature in a mood of indifference to the feelings of natural objects.

I personally doubt that disastrous ecologic backlash can be avoided simply by applying to our problems more science and more technology. Our science and technology have grown out of Christian attitudes toward man's relation to nature which are almost universally held not only by Christians and neo-Christians but also by those who fondly regard themselves as post-Christians. Despite Copernicus, all the cosmos rotates around our little globe. Despite Darwin, we are *not,* in our hearts, part of the natural process. We are superior to nature, contemptuous of it, willing to use it for our slightest whim.... To a Christian a tree can be no more than a physical fact. The whole concept of a sacred grove is alien to Christianity and to the ethos of the West. For nearly two millennia Christian missionaries have been chopping down sacred groves, which are idolatrous because they assume spirit in nature.

What we do about ecology depends on our ideas of the man-nature relationship. More science and more technology are not going to get us out of the present ecologic crisis unless we find a new religion or rethink our old one....

The greatest spiritual revolutionary in Western history, St. Francis, proposed what he thought was an alternative Christian view of nature and man's relation to it: he tried to substitute the idea of equality of all creatures, including man, for the idea of man's limitless rule of creation. He failed.... The profoundly religious, but heretical, sense of the primitive Franciscans for the spiritual autonomy of all parts of nature may point a direction. I propose Francis as the patron saint for ecologists.   — Lynn White world a sacred quality that can be perceived by a "sacramental vision." Their interpretation of the creation stories in Genesis highlights *relationship*. Even in the creation myth the God of the covenant is present, calling humanity into relationship with God, with each other, and with other creatures. To be the image of God means that humans are to be relational, not sovereign. Thus the image for the relationship between humankind and the natural world proposed by the Himes brothers is *companionship*, which implies mutuality.[56] Using the biblically infused categories of Martin Buber,[57] they propose an I-Thou relationship between humanity and creation rather than an instrumental I-It relationship.

Drawing on the Noahic covenant in Genesis 9:10, the mystical vision of Augustine of Hippo, and especially the kinship with nature expressed by Francis of Assisi,[58] the Himes brothers root the companionship model in the equal poverty of all creatures before God and in the sacramental vision of Catholicism that sees every creature as a revelation of the love of God. All creatures are united by the fact of being creatures, by their absolute dependence on God for existence. A sacramental vision allows Christians to reverence every creature as a "Thou," a companion. Thus Francis could sing of Brother Sun and Sister Moon, Brother Wind and Sister Water, Brother Fire and Sister Earth in his "Canticle of the Sun."[59]

The companionship model enlarges the common good to include all of creation. It can recognize a special role for humanity, but it gives the natural world a genuinely intrinsic value. Humans are part of the great community of creation, evolving within and along with all of creation. Humankind and the natural world are in a mutually interdependent relationship; indeed, humanity is more dependent on nature than nature is on us.[60] "Companionship strips us of the belief that the world is just *there*. We are in relation to a 'thou' that is not of our making, nor simply for us. Such an attitude serves to check the instrumental rationality that has fostered an abuse of the environment."[61]

The church's move from a domination model to a stewardship model, then, may be a mere half step in the right direction. To adequately address the ecological crisis it may well be necessary for the church to make the more radical move from anthropocentrism to a relational companionship attitude toward creation.

Even the stewardship model could allow the church to acknowledge the "huge burden of guilt" that Western Christianity bears for environmental destruction and the ecological crisis that is present today. A companionship model would make repentance and a firm resolution to mend our ways clearer and nearly unavoidable. It seems essential for the church to name this assault on creation as "sinful and contrary to the teachings of our faith," as did the Catholic bishops of the Philippines. An acknowledgement that Christian domination of the earth has played a large part in causing an environmental catastrophe could be the first step toward adopting the companionship model.

A sacramental vision of our kinship and companionship with the earth and all its creatures does not easily resolve the tension between poverty and ecology, between economic development and environmental responsibility. Humans are in relationship with one another and especially with the poor as well as with creation. We have a responsibility to create a world where each and every person can flourish and to repair the damage we have done to the earth and its various habitats. Perhaps it is important to acknowledge more forthrightly the conflict between the economic growth that development often requires and the consumption of resources and environmental damages that such growth often causes.[62]

Sustainable development is the correct principle, but it is also something of an oxymoron. It is important to note that integral human development does not necessarily mean increased consumption, that developed countries have a greater responsibility to sacrifice in order to reduce pollution and to overcome poverty, and that raising the standard of living of the poor will have some long-term positive effects on the environment.[63] Nevertheless the demands of the option for the poor and of environmental responsibility are in tension. We need the tenacious commitment to the poor and the ecological sensitivity of a Dorothy Stang (who once asked a group of state legislators if they knew "what a sobbing monkey sounds like") to creatively imagine and practically implement sustainable development.

In conclusion then, the church has moved from a human domination of the earth model to a stewardship approach that sees humanity as the responsible caretaker of the natural world. The stewardship model, however, remains clearly and consciously anthropocentric; it still views the earth and its resources in service of human needs and recognizes only the instrumental value of creation. Some theologians are proposing a Franciscan companionship model rooted in a biblically based and scientifically sound kinship understanding of the human-nature relationship. Given the current ecological crisis raised by global warming and climate change, it seems that the church needs to address environmental issues more often and with more authoritative documents, and that it may need to adopt a more radical rethinking of the Christian tradition regarding the natural world.

Questions for Reflection and Discussion

1. John Timothy Leary was drawn back to the church by the realization that we, the people of God, *are* the church. If the church is to be a credible witness to the teachings of Jesus, it is up to us. If you were put on trial for being a Christian, would there be enough evidence to convict you?

2. Do you see a link between issues such as abortion, euthanasia, nuclear weapons, capital punishment, and human rights? Can a consistent

ethic of life overcome the political polarization within church and society?

3. Discuss the question of moral absolutes in regard to abortion and nuclear weapons.

4. The consistent ethic of life results in the church taking moral positions on issues of public policy that cut across the political spectrum. Is this a good thing? Are there specific issues or situations that would justify "single-issue" politics or that would justify church endorsement of a particular candidate or party?

5. In her ministry in the Amazon region of Brazil, Sister Dorothy Stang managed to reconcile the needs of the poor and concern for the environment. Nevertheless, the option for the poor often conflicts with responsibility for the environment. Discuss this tension and strategies for its resolution. Is "sustainable development" a realistic and practical option?

6. What is the difference between an anthropocentric environmental ethic and an ecological theology rooted in the relationship or kinship or companionship between humanity and the natural world? Do these different visions of the relationship between humanity and creation make any practical difference on issues such as recycling or reducing our carbon footprint?

Chapter 6

Conclusion

This brief conclusion offers a critical appraisal of Catholic social teaching, noting first some problems and weaknesses and then some contributions and strengths.[1] It is the job of Catholic social *thought* to interpret and critique Catholic social *teaching* so that the church can more adequately bring Christian faith to bear on social questions and issues.

Problems and Weaknesses of Catholic Social Teaching

While Catholic social teaching has made remarkable contributions toward social justice and peace, some methodological and practical problems are associated with it.

As we have seen, there has been significant development in Catholic social teaching. To cite just one example, prior to Vatican II the church taught that Catholicism, considered to be the one true faith, should ideally be the established religion in every state. At Vatican II, however, the church embraced religious freedom and its implication that church and state should be separate (see chapter 2 above).[2] Such development in response to changing times and challenges is essential for the enterprise of Catholic social teaching.[3] The problem is that the *magisterium* of the church (the pope and bishops) has a *difficult time acknowledging any development* in what it often refers to as Catholic social *doctrine*. John Paul II and Benedict XVI, for example, emphasize the consistency of Catholic social teaching, rather than its development, even as they offer innovations themselves.

This trend can be seen in the references cited in most Vatican documents. There are, for example, 159 endnotes in Benedict XVI's *Charity in Truth* (*Caritas in Veritate,* 2009), referring to 25 sources. All but three of the sources are Vatican documents; there is one reference each to St. Augustine, St. Thomas Aquinas, and Heraclitus of Ephesus. The overwhelming majority of the references are to previous social encyclicals. This defensive and institutionally self-centered posture inhibits the development of Catholic social teaching and the church's responsiveness to the signs of the time.

It is not the role of the church to offer technical solutions or public policy prescriptions, but the church's moral guidance should be based on *sound social analysis,* and this is often absent or obscured in Vatican documents. *Charity in Truth,* for example, was supposedly delayed by the global economic recession of 2008. There is no analysis, however, of the economic causes of that recession, nor of globalization, which is a major theme of the encyclical, nor of climate change in the section on the environment (#48–51). In a document that primarily addresses global poverty and authentic human development, there is no reference to social scientists or theologians. Benedict XVI calls for new commercial entities that tie profit to the common good, and he mentions the "economy of communion," an oblique reference to the Focolare movement (*Charity in Truth,* #48). There is no reference, however, to the Italian economist Stefano Zamagni, the only layperson present at the press conference announcing the encyclical, who has been a significant influence on the creation of such business enterprises. This obscurity makes it difficult to understand, interpret, and critique Vatican documents; it gives the impression of an insular institution; and it fails to provide a firm foundation for the church's moral positions.

Underlying many of the changes in Catholic social teaching has been a development in the church's approach to social questions, its *methodology.* Beginning with Pope John XXIII the church moved from a classical, deductive, and abstract approach toward one that is based in experience and that is aware of context, history, and change. This important development is also largely unacknowledged by the Vatican, and it is inconsistently applied. The church's social teaching is now more historically conscious, while its sexual ethics tends to reflect a classical approach that yields absolute moral principles. If the church is to offer coherent moral guidance in a changing world, it will need to consistently use a historically conscious methodology.

There are also some practical problems regarding Catholic social teaching. The first relates to the *relevance* of the church's social teaching. *Charity in Truth* (2009) was the first social encyclical in eighteen years. Much has happened since 1991, including globalization, an increasing awareness of potentially catastrophic climate change, and the rise of terrorism. Although the popes and bishops have addressed these issues in various statements, the encyclical tradition has not. It is not necessary for the church to speak to every social trend, but society needs the church's moral guidance in response to major historical events and social change. The church is sometimes too slow in finding its voice.

This results in some *omissions and inadequacies* in the church's social teaching. Perhaps the two most glaring of these are the lack of an encyclical on ecology and the church's inadequate response to the issue of justice for women. The magnitude of the issue of climate change makes it deserving of the church's most authoritative moral guidance and of a response that probes the Christian tradition in a way that goes beyond the church's current anthropocentric environmental ethic (see chapter 5 above).

The Vatican's insistence on using exclusive language in its teaching signals that it is deaf and blind on the issue of justice for women. Thus in *Charity in Truth,* Benedict XVI shows no evidence of sensitivity to the particular suffering of women as a result of poverty and globalization, nor to the crucial role of women in integral human development. It is not surprising then that the Vatican has not seriously or satisfactorily addressed justice for women in its teaching. The U.S. Catholic bishops tried to produce a pastoral letter on the subject in the period from 1988 to 1992, but the process was aborted after four drafts when they sensed that they lacked credibility on the issue.

Finally, the church is too often guilty of *hypocrisy* in regard to its social teaching: it does not practice what it preaches. For example, the church has been a stalwart advocate of worker's rights, including the right to organize into unions. Yet American dioceses, Catholic universities, and Catholic hospitals have often resisted the formation of unions on behalf of Catholic teachers, professors, and health care workers. One of the principles of Catholic social teaching is participation, which implies shared or democratic decision making. There is, however, nearly no lay participation in decision making in the hierarchical Catholic Church and very little transparency.

The synod document *Justice in the World* (1971) is correct when it says, "While the Church is bound to give witness to justice, she recognizes that everyone who ventures to speak to people about justice must first be just in their eyes." Catholic social *teaching* is important, but Catholic social *witness* by every Catholic from the pope, to politicians, to priests, to peasants, to professors, is even more important. The fact that Vatican City is the world's first carbon-neutral state speaks volumes about environmental responsibility. Catholics at all levels have endless opportunities to witness to justice and peace.

Contributions and Strengths of Catholic Social Teaching

Neither the church nor its social teaching is perfect. Catholic social teaching (CST), however, is a respectable body of work, and the church has an honorable track record regarding justice and peace. There are three strengths of the corpus of Catholic social teaching worth noting.

Through the *content or substance* of its social teaching, the church has become a significant moral voice in the contemporary world. The foundational values of Catholic social teaching — human dignity, realized in community — challenge the individualism and self-centeredness that too often characterize modern culture. So do the key principles of Catholic social teaching: human rights, the sanctity of life, solidarity and subsidiarity on behalf of the common good, participation, the option for the poor, the dignity of work and the rights of workers, peacemaking, and care for creation. The church is aware that sin infests social structures and that therefore social change or the transformation of social systems is required to create a just society and a peaceful world. Thus the church calls all its members to direct service to those in need, to be responsible and active citizens, and to transform the world toward the kingdom of God. Christians have leavened the world.

Second, the foundational values of Catholic social teaching give it a remarkable *balance* that enhances its effectiveness. CST affirms the dignity of the individual and the necessity of community, thus avoiding both individualism and collectivism. Thus CST has critiqued both capitalism and socialism. CST has affirmed both subsidiarity, a de-centralizing principle, and solidarity: that we are all in this together, a global village, a human family that sometimes needs competent government action and effective global institutions. The Catholic principle of the common good links human flourishing with the health of the community in a way that mutually reinforces both. The tone of Catholic social teaching is "both...and" rather than "either...or." This balance gives CST a realism and pragmatism that yields it a hearing in society and amplifies its effectiveness.[4]

Third, Catholic social teaching has a *humanistic basis in natural law* that allows it to be addressed to all people of good will, and it is now *biblically based* in a way that facilitates ecumenical dialogue within the Christian community. The pastoral letters of the U.S. bishops on peace (1983) and economic justice (1986) are especially good examples of these two points. They explore the biblical basis of the church's teaching on peace and on justice, yet their positions are also argued on the basis of reason. Thus CST allows the church to engage in fruitful conversation with the whole of society and with all Christians.

Given these characteristics of the body of work that is Catholic social teaching, there is no reason for it to remain "the church's best kept secret." CST should be proclaimed from pulpits and taught from podiums. It should become part of the vocabulary of Catholics as they work to transform the world. And perhaps it is.

The church, however, has not only taught about justice and peace; it has a reputable track record in working for justice and peace. As an institution the church has stood for human rights, insisted on hospitality for immigrants, lobbied on behalf of the poor and for peace, and shared in the persecution of the oppressed. Throughout this text we have heard the stories of witnesses who have put their faith into action — people and organizations who have worked for justice for the oppressed, bread for the hungry, community for the alienated, righteousness for society, and peace on earth. The real challenge of Catholic social teaching is for each of us to become one of those stories.

Notes

Introduction

1. John A. Coleman, "Introduction: A Tradition Celebrated, Reevaluated, and Applied," in *One Hundred Years of Catholic Social Thought: Celebration and Challenge,* ed. John A. Coleman (Maryknoll, N.Y.: Orbis Books, 1991), 2.

Chapter 1: The Development of Catholic Social Thought

1. Paul Misner, *Social Catholicism in Europe: From the Onset of Industrialization to the First World War* (New York: Crossroad, 1991), 27–28; and Thomas A. Shannon, "Commentary on *Rerum Novarum* (*The Condition of Labor*)," in *Modern Catholic Social Teaching: Commentaries and Interpretation,* ed. Kenneth R. Himes et al. (Washington, D.C.: Georgetown University Press, 2005), 128–29.

2. *Rerum Novarum* means "Of new things," and like most of these Latin titles tells us little about the topic of the document. For this reason and because most contemporary Catholics are unfamiliar with Latin, I will generally use the official English title of the document. Most of the scholarly literature in the field, however, uses the Latin titles.

3. Edward P. DeBerri and James E. Hug, with Peter J. Henriot and Michael Schultheis, *Catholic Social Teaching: Our Best Kept Secret,* 4th rev. ed. (Maryknoll, N.Y.: Orbis Books, 2003).

4. Richard R. Gaillardetz, "The Ecclesiological Foundations of Modern Catholic Social Teaching," in *Modern Catholic Social Teaching: Commentaries and Interpretation,* ed. Kenneth R. Himes et al. (Washington, D.C.: Georgetown University Press, 2005), 86–90.

5. Pontifical Council for Justice and Peace, *Compendium of the Social Doctrine of the Church* (Washington, D.C.: United States Conference of Catholic Bishops, 2004).

6. Kenneth Himes suggests that Pope John Paul II consciously used the term "social doctrine" in order to salvage it from the pejorative use by French theologian Marie-Dominique Chenu. Chenu argued that there was an important discontinuity in Catholic social teaching when it moved from a deductive method to a more inductive approach. John Paul II wanted to stress the continuity of the teaching. See Kenneth R. Himes, "Introduction," in his *Modern Catholic Social Teaching,* 4. Michael Schuck wants to use "social doctrine" to refer to the principles enunciated in Catholic social teaching, as opposed to the application of those principles. This seems too fine a distinction to me. See his "Modern Catholic Social Thought," in *The New Dictionary*

of Catholic Social Thought, ed. Judith A. Dwyer (Collegeville, Minn.: Liturgical Press, 1994), 614.

7. Schuck, "Modern Catholic Social Thought," 612–14; Michael P. Hornsby-Smith, *An Introduction to Catholic Social Thought* (Cambridge and New York: Cambridge University Press, 2006), 87 and 330.

8. See Marvin L. Krier Mich, *Catholic Social Teaching and Movements* (Mystic, Conn.: Twenty-Third Publications, 1998), chap. 1; Misner, *Social Catholicism in Europe;* Shannon, "Commentary on *Rerum Novarum,*" 131–32; and Normand Paulhus, "Fribourg Union," in *The New Dictionary of Catholic Social Thought,* ed. Judith A. Dwyer (Collegeville, Minn.: Liturgical Press, 1994), 404–5.

9. Judith A. Merkle, *From the Heart of the Church: The Catholic Social Tradition* (Collegeville, Minn.: Liturgical Press, 2004).

10. Schuck, "Modern Catholic Social Thought," 614.

11. David J. O'Brien and Thomas A. Shannon, eds., *Catholic Social Thought: The Documentary Heritage* (Maryknoll, N.Y.: Orbis Books, 1992).

12. See, for example, Hornsby-Smith, *Introduction to Catholic Social Thought.*

13. Most of these documents are found in O'Brien and Shannon, eds., *Catholic Social Thought.* The "Declaration on Religious Freedom" can be found in *The Documents of Vatican II,* ed. Walter M. Abbott (New York: America Press, 1966), 675–96. The documents by the Latin American Bishops Conference (CELAM) can be found in Alfred T. Hennelly, *Liberation Theology: A Documentary History* (Maryknoll, N.Y.: Orbis Books, 1990). Pope Benedict XVI's two encyclicals (and most of the Vatican documents) can be found at *www.vatican.va.* Kenneth R. Himes has established a web page with both the Latin and English versions of the papal and Vatican social documents at *www2.bc.edu/~khimes/publications/mcst/.*

14. See, for example, Hornsby-Smith, *Introduction to Catholic Social Thought,* chap. 7, and Marvin L. Krier Mich, *The Challenge and Spirituality of Catholic Social Teaching* (Louisville: JustFaith, 2005), chaps. 3 and 4.

15. A Catholic theologian who has addressed both the family and bioethics from a social and a feminist perspective is Lisa Sowle Cahill. See her "Commentary on *Familiaris consortio* (Apostolic Exhortation on the Family)," in *Modern Catholic Social Teaching: Commentaries and Interpretation,* ed. Kenneth R. Himes et al. (Washington, D.C.: Georgetown University Press, 2005), 363–88, and *Theological Bioethics: Participation, Justice, and Change* (Washington, D.C.: Georgetown University Press, 2005).

16. These documents are generally available from the U.S. Conference of Catholic Bishops in Washington, D.C., *www.usccb.org.* Thomas J. Massaro and Thomas A. Shannon, eds., *American Catholic Social Teaching* (Collegeville, Minn.: Liturgical Press, 2002) comes with a CD that has twenty-three statements of the U.S. Catholic bishops from 1792 through 1999. The USCCB's 2008 election guide, *Forming Consciences for Faithful Citizenship* (2007) has an extensive list of the statements of the USCCB grouped under four headings: Protecting Human Life, Promoting Family Life, Pursuing Social Justice, and Practicing Global Solidarity.

17. John R. Donahue, "Biblical Perspectives on Justice," in *The Faith That Does Justice,* ed. John C. Haughey (New York: Paulist Press, 1977), 69, 73–74.

18. See Ronald J. Sider, *Rich Christians in an Age of Hunger: Moving from Affluence to Generosity* (Dallas: Word, 1997), 69–75 and part 2 regarding a biblical perspective on the poor and possessions.

19. See Fred Kammer, *Doing Faithjustice: An Introduction to Catholic Social Thought* (New York: Paulist Press, 1991), chap. 1, esp. 29–40.

20. Donahue, "Biblical Perspectives on Justice," 69, 77. See also John R. Donahue, "The Bible and Catholic Social Teaching: Will This Engagement Lead to Marriage?" in *Modern Catholic Social Teaching: Commentaries and Interpretation,* ed. Kenneth R. Himes et al. (Washington, D.C.: Georgetown University Press, 2005), 14: "In general terms the biblical idea of justice can be described as *fidelity to the demands of a relationship.*" Donahue's essay outlines biblical themes relevant to social teaching.

21. Hornsby-Smith, *Introduction to Catholic Social Thought,* chap. 3.

22. This account of the life and thought of Clarence Jordan depends on Joyce Hollyday, "Clarence Jordan: Theologian in Overalls," in *Cloud of Witnesses,* ed. Jim Wallis and Joyce Hollyday (Maryknoll, N.Y.: Orbis Books, 1991, rev. 2005), 60–65; James Wm. McClendon Jr., *Biography as Theology: How Life Stories Can Remake Today's Theology* (Philadelphia: Trinity Press International, 1974, 1990), chap. 5; and Douglas M. Strong, *They Walked in the Spirit: Personal Faith and Social Action in America* (Louisville: Westminster John Knox Press, 1997), chap. 7.

23. *Koinonia* means fellowship or community. It is the Greek word used by Luke in Acts to describe the early Christian community.

24. Terrence W. Tilley, *Story Theology* (Wilmington, Del.: Michael Glazier, 1985), 46–50.

25. McClendon, *Biography as Theology,* 103. I have quoted the dialogue directly from McClendon. Robert Jordan supported segregation throughout his public career.

26. Sider, *Rich Christians in an Age of Hunger,* 77–89.

27. See Glen H. Stassen, *Just Peacemaking: Transforming Initiatives for Justice and Peace* (Louisville: Westminster John Knox Press, 1992), chap. 3, esp. 55–58.

28. Peter C. Phan, *Social Thought: Message of the Fathers of the Church,* vol. 20 (Wilmington, Del.: Michael Glazier, 1984), 21; and William J. Walsh and John P. Langan, "Patristic Social Consciousness — The Church and the Poor," in *The Faith That Does Justice,* ed. John C. Haughey (New York: Paulist Press, 1977), 113.

29. Phan, *Social Thought,* 26.

30. Walsh and Langan, "Patristic Social Consciousness," passim.

31. Ibid., and Peter C. Phan, "Fathers of the Church, Influence of," in *The New Dictionary of Catholic Social Thought,* ed. Judith A. Dwyer (Collegeville, Minn.: Liturgical Press, 1994), 388–91, 393.

32. Walsh and Langan, "Patristic Social Consciousness," 136, quoting *Quis Dives Salvetur?* trans. R. B. Tollinton, *Clement of Alexandria* (London: n.p., 1914), 318.

33. Ibid., 141, quoting *On Matthew: Homily 35.5.*

34. This is how Trappist monk Thomas Merton describes his mind-changing, life-altering epiphany on March 18, 1958, on a trip to the dentist: "In Louisville, at the corner of Fourth and Walnut [now Muhammad Ali Blvd.], in the center of the shopping district, I was suddenly overwhelmed with the realization that I loved all those people, that they were mine and I theirs, that we could not be alien to one another even though we were total strangers.... There is no way of telling people that they are all walking around shining like the sun" (*Conjectures of a Guilty Bystander* [New York: Doubleday, 1966], 156–58).

35. Phan, *Social Thought,* 25.

36. Ibid., 32.

37. See Roland H. Bainton, *Christian Attitudes toward War and Peace: A Historical Survey and Critical Re-evaluation* (Nashville: Abingdon Press, 1960), chap. 5; and Ronald G. Musto, *The Catholic Peace Tradition* (Maryknoll, N.Y.: Orbis Books, 1986), chap. 3.

38. Richard P. McBrien, *The Lives of the Popes: The Pontiffs from St. Peter to John Paul II* (San Francisco: HarperSanFrancisco, 1997), 77, 431.

39. Robert Ellsberg, *All Saints: Daily Reflections on Saints, Prophets, and Witnesses for Our Time* (New York: Crossroad, 1997), 164.

40. My account of the story of Gregory the Great is based on ibid., 379–81; McBrien, *Lives of the Popes,* 96–98; and Phan, *Social Thought,* 260–67.

41. Phan, *Social Thought,* 261, quoting *The Pastoral Rule* (also called *Pastoral Care*), III, 21. This book by Gregory the Great was a practical guide for pastoral ministry adapted to the needs of the people. It was influential in his own time and throughout the Middle Ages.

42. This section on St. Francis of Assisi is based on Leonardo Boff, *Saint Francis: A Model for Human Liberation* (New York: Crossroad, 1982), esp. 59–71; Ellsberg, *All Saints,* 432–33; Adolf Holl, *The Last Christian: A Biography of Francis of Assisi,* trans. Peter Heinegg (Garden City, N.Y.: Doubleday, 1980), esp. 38–39; and Jim Wallis, "St. Francis of Assisi: Consumed with the Gospel," in *Cloud of Witnesses,* ed. Jim Wallis and Joyce Hollyday (Maryknoll, N.Y.: Orbis Books, 1991, rev. 2005), 3–8.

43. On St. Clare see Ellsberg, *All Saints,* 345–47.

44. Boff, *Saint Francis,* 39.

45. Ellsberg, *All Saints,* 433; Holl, *The Last Christian,* chap. 10; and Musto, *The Catholic Peace Tradition,* 83.

46. Wallis, "St. Francis of Assisi," 4. This brief essay, originally in the December 1981 issue of *Sojourners,* is a powerful reflection on how the story of Francis has challenged Wallis to live according to the gospel. It is a good example of the meaning of a "saint," which G. K. Chesterton described as "a medicine because he is an antidote.... He will generally be found restoring the world to sanity by exaggerating whatever the world neglects" (Ellsberg, *All Saints,* 237).

47. The life of Thomas Aquinas depends on Ellsberg, *All Saints,* 49–50; James Martin, *My Life with the Saints* (Chicago: Loyola Press, 2006), chap. 12; and a public lecture on St. Thomas Aquinas by Dr. Thomas Maloney, professor of philosophy at the University of Louisville, February 5, 2009.

48. This brief exposition of the influence of Aquinas on modern Catholic social teaching depends primarily on Robert Barry, "Thomas Aquinas, Contribution of," in *The New Dictionary of Catholic Social Thought,* ed. Judith A. Dwyer (Collegeville, Minn.: Liturgical Press, 1994), 940–51. See also Merkle, *From the Heart of the Church,* 53–55.

49. Charles E. Curran, *Catholic Social Teaching, 1891–Present: A Historical, Theological, and Ethical Analysis* (Washington, D.C.: Georgetown University Press, 2002), 21–22. This "both/and" balance means that Catholic social teaching is usually prudent, but it is seldom prophetic.

50. Barry, "Thomas Aquinas," 949. Schuck, *That They Be One: The Social Teaching of the Papal Encyclicals, 1740–1989* (Washington, D.C.: Georgetown University Press, 1991), 178–80. Misner (*Social Catholicism in Europe,* 323–24), however, says that the dignity of the human person, rooted in neo-Thomism, anchored papal teaching from Leo XIII on.

51. McBrien, *Lives of the Popes,* 275.

52. See Ellsberg, *All Saints,* 269–70, for a brief synopsis of the story of Thomas More, and the film *A Man for All Seasons* (1966), directed by Fred Zinnemann, which dramatically portrays the conflict between Henry VIII and his Lord Chancellor, Thomas More, that resulted in More's beheading for treason.

53. Ellsberg, *All Saints,* 467–69.

54. See Fred Dallmayr, *Peace Talks — Who Will Listen?* (Notre Dame, Ind.: University of Notre Dame Press, 2004), esp. chap. 1; and Musto, *Catholic Peace Tradition,* chap. 9, esp. 122–35.

55. McBrien, *Lives of the Popes,* 276.

56. Joseph J. Fahey, *War and Christian Conscience: Where Do You Stand?* (Maryknoll, N.Y.: Orbis Books, 2005), 135. Fahey explains that a series of eight major crusades and several minor ones were fought against Islam from 1095 to 1291; while nearly all of them were military failures, they were successful economically (wider trade) and politically (unified Europe with a common enemy). The church called, preached, and supported these "holy wars" against the infidels. And it was a small step from fighting the infidels abroad to rooting out heretics and dissidents at home. Thus was born the Inquisition, which took place in three major stages: the Medieval Inquisition of 1233; the Spanish Inquisition of 1478, which eventually spread to Mexico and Peru; and the Roman Inquisition in 1542, aimed primarily at Protestants and Catholic dissidents (see 121–36).

57. It is estimated that from 1532 (after the Caribbean population had already been nearly wiped out) the Amerindian population dropped from nearly 17 million to just over 1 million — almost certainly the worst genocide in history. Those who survived were culturally and economically destitute. See Musto, *The Catholic Peace Tradition,* 138.

58. The film *Black Robe* (1991), directed by Bruce Beresford and set in French Canada, addresses this well. It contains some violent scenes.

59. On Las Casas see Ellsberg, *All Saints,* 306–7; Musto, *Catholic Peace Tradition,* 140–44; Juan Friede and Benjamin Keen, eds., *Bartolomé de Las Casas in History* (DeKalb: Northern Illinois University Press, 1971); and Gustavo Gutiérrez, *Las Casas: In Search of the Poor of Jesus Christ* (Maryknoll, N.Y.: Orbis Books, 1993).

60. See Michael J. Schuck, *That They Be One,* and "Modern Catholic Social Thought," 611–32; also his "Early Modern Catholic Social Thought, 1740–1890," in *Modern Catholic Social Teaching,* ed. Kenneth R. Himes et al. (Washington, D.C.: Georgetown University Press, 2005), 99–124; and Joe Holland, *Modern Catholic Social Teaching: The Popes Confront the Industrial Age 1740–1958* (New York: Paulist Press, 2003).

61. Schuck, *That They Be One,* calls the periods "Pre-Leonine, Leonine, and Post-Leonine." This is good except that the "Leonine" period includes four popes besides Leo XIII, none of whom are named Leo. In addition, Schuck's designation does not tell us much about the nature of the period itself. Holland uses "Anti-Modern, Modern, and Postmodern." Holland's project in *Modern Catholic Social Teaching* is to align the church's teaching with developments in capitalism (see his chart on p. 17). His designations are also acceptable, but it seems to me that "postmodern" has ambiguous and unwelcome connotations.

62. Schuck, "Modern Catholic Social Thought," 617.

63. John A. Coleman, "A Tradition Celebrated, Reevaluated, and Applied," in *One Hundred Years of Catholic Social Thought: Celebration and Challenge,* ed. John A. Coleman (Maryknoll, N.Y.: Orbis Books, 1991), 3.

64. See Michael J. Schuck, "Early Roman Catholic Social Thought, 1740–1890"; Misner, *Social Catholicism in Europe,* chaps. 3, 4, 5, 7–10; and Mich, *Catholic Social Teaching and Movements,* chap. 1.

65. John A. Coleman, "Neither Liberal nor Socialist: The Originality of Catholic Social Teaching," in *One Hundred Years of Catholic Social Thought,* ed. John A. Coleman (Maryknoll, N.Y.: Orbis Books, 1991), 30–31; and Ellsberg, *All Saints,* 390–91.

66. Joan L. Coffey, *Leon Harmel: Entrepreneur as Catholic Social Reformer* (Notre Dame, Ind.: University of Notre Dame Press, 2003); and Misner, *Social Catholicism in Europe,* 111 and passim.

67. David J. O'Brien, "A Century of Catholic Social Teaching: Contexts and Comments," in *One Hundred Years of Catholic Social Thought,* ed. John A. Coleman (Maryknoll, N.Y.: Orbis Books, 1991), 14–15.

68. Ibid., 16–18.

69. McBrien, *Lives of the Popes,* 349–50.

70. O'Brien, "A Century of Catholic Social Teaching," 18–21.

71. McBrien, *Lives of the Popes,* 346, 353–54.

72. R. Scott Appleby, "American Idol: Rome vs. the 'Modernists,'" *Commonweal* 134 (September 14, 2007): 12–20.

73. McBrien, *Lives of the Popes,* 365.

74. Ibid., 450.

75. This section on John XXIII depends upon Ellsberg, *All Saints,* 243–44; Peter Hebblethwaite, *Pope John XXIII: Shepherd of the Modern World* (Garden City, N.Y.: Doubleday, 1985), esp. chaps. 13 and 16; Martin, *My Life with the Saints,* chap. 9; and McBrien, *Lives of the Popes,* 369–75.

76. Apparently it was the custom for the pope to dine alone. John XXIII said he had thoroughly vetted scripture regarding this practice and could not find any corroboration for it. So he happily shared his meals with friends and colleagues.

77. McBrien, *Lives of the Popes,* 430, 440–41.

78. In Peter Hebblethwaite, *Paul VI: The First Modern Pope* (New York: Paulist Press, 1993), 13, quoting Eugene Kennedy, *The Now and Future Church: The Psychology of Being an American Catholic* (1984), 105. Hebblethwaite argues that Paul VI is the first modern pope and "the most naturally talented man to become pope in this century" (9).

79. Ibid., 6–7; Mich, *Catholic Social Teaching and Movements,* 154–65, 177–96.

80. The Medellín Documents, which can be found in Hennelly, *Liberation Theology: A Documentary History,* affirm this theological and pastoral move to the side of the poor. The history of the Catholic Church in Latin America since then is the struggle to accomplish this move toward the poor.

81. The literature of and on liberation theology is vast. See, for example, Gustavo Gutiérrez, *A Theology of Liberation: History, Politics, and Salvation,* rev. ed. (Maryknoll, N.Y.: Orbis Books, 1988); Ignacio Ellacuría and Jon Sobrino, eds., *Mysterium Liberationis: Fundamental Concepts of Liberation Theology* (Maryknoll, N.Y.: Orbis Books, 1993); Leonardo Boff and Clodovis Boff, *Introducing Liberation Theology* (Maryknoll, N.Y.: Orbis Books, 1986, 1987); and Alfred T. Hennelly,

Liberation Theologies: The Global Pursuit of Justice (Mystic, Conn.: Twenty-Third Publications, 1995).

82. The papacy of John Paul I was so brief that it did not allow him to have much effect, although it is interesting to speculate what he might have done. He was the first pope in a millennium to dispense with being crowned with the triple tiara, being invested instead with a simple woolen pallium (McBrien, *Lives of the Popes,* 368).

83. Ibid., 384–92.

84. Stephen J. Pope, "Natural Law in Catholic Social Teachings," in *Modern Catholic Social Teaching,* ed. Kenneth R. Himes et al. (Washington, D.C.: Georgetown University Press, 2005), 41–48.

85. John Paul II's *The Splendor of Truth* (*Veritatis Splendor*), 1993, focuses on ethical theory, and his *The Gospel of Life* (*Evangelium Vitae*), 1995, addresses issues of a more personal nature, especially abortion, euthanasia, and capital punishment. In these encyclicals John Paul II takes a more deductive approach and arrives at positions that are often absolute, based on natural law. These encyclicals can be found at *www.vatican.va.*

86. Pope, "Natural Law in Catholic Social Teaching," 52.

87. Curran, *Catholic Social Teaching,* 54–55; Pope, "Natural Law in Catholic Social Teaching," 54; Hornsby-Smith, *Introduction to Catholic Social Thought,* 87–91.

88. Pope, "Natural Law in Catholic Social Teaching," 54.

89. Curran, *Catholic Social Teaching,* 67; Pope, "Natural Law in Catholic Social Teaching," 54–55.

90. Gaillardetz, "The Ecclesiological Foundations of Modern Catholic Social Teaching," 72–98, at 72–74; Schuck, "Modern Catholic Social Thought," 624; and Curran, *Catholic Social Teaching,* chap. 3, at 103–4. These are significant sources for this section on ecclesiology.

91. Gaillardetz, "The Ecclesiological Foundations of Modern Catholic Social Teaching," 74–75.

92. Mich, *Catholic Social Teaching and Movements,* 179–89; Gaillardetz, "The Ecclesiological Foundations of Modern Catholic Social Teaching," 75–76.

Chapter 2: Faithful Citizenship

1. United States Conference of Catholic Bishops (USCCB), *Forming Consciences for Faithful Citizenship: A Call to Political Responsibility from the Catholic Bishops of the United States* (Washington, D.C.: USCCB, 2007). Available from *www.usccb.org.* Further references to church documents will use their paragraph numbers in parentheses, directly in the text.

2. For a sampling of the many articles on this topic in the secular and religious press, see Karen Tumulty, "Battling the Bishops," *Time* (June 21, 2004): 34–37; articles by Amy Sullivan, Sidney Callahan, and Franz Jozef van Beeck, in *Commonweal* 131 (June 4, 2004): 13–20; and Cardinal Theodore McCarrick, "The Call to Serve in a Divided Society," *Origins* 34 (March 24, 2005): 638. There was a similar controversy in the spring of 2009 when President Obama accepted an invitation from the University of Notre Dame to give its commencement address and receive

an honorary degree. The local bishop refused to attend commencement and share the platform with a pro-choice president.

3. The communitarian nature of the Catholic tradition is a central theme of John E. Tropman, *The Catholic Ethic in American Society* (San Francisco: Jossey Bass, 1995).

4. See Michael J. Himes and Kenneth R. Himes, "A Public Faith: Christian Witness in Society," in *The Catholic Church, Morality, and Politics: Readings in Moral Theology No. 12,* ed. Charles E. Curran and Leslie Griffin (New York: Paulist Press, 2001), 100–102; and Francis Campbell, "No Future in the Ghetto," *The Tablet* 262 (February 2, 2008): 12–13, which discusses the roots and effects of secularization.

5. See Charles E. Curran, *American Catholic Social Ethics: Twentieth Century Approaches* (Notre Dame, Ind.: University of Notre Dame Press, 1982), 5–13.

6. Marvin L. Mich, "Commentary on *Mater et Magistra* (*Christianity and Social Progress*)," in *Modern Catholic Social Teaching: Commentaries and Interpretations,* ed. Kenneth R. Himes et al. (Washington, D.C.: Georgetown University Press, 2005), 204. Mich goes on to make the point that John XXIII replaced this spirituality of detachment with a spirituality of engagement.

7. Arthur Simon, *Christian Faith and Public Policy: No Grounds for Divorce* (Grand Rapids, Mich.: William B. Eerdmans, 1987), 12.

8. This story is in all three of the synoptic gospels: Mark 12:13–17, Matthew 22:15–22, and Luke 20:20–26. See Pontifical Council for Justice and Peace, *Compendium of the Social Doctrine of the Church* (Washington, D.C.: United States Conference of Catholic Bishops, 2004), #378–83. Also available at *www.vatican.va.*

9. This document is available at the Vatican website, *www.vatican.va.*

10. The Second Vatican Council, *The Pastoral Constitution on the Church in the Modern World,* in *Catholic Social Thought: The Documentary Heritage,* ed. David J. O'Brien and Thomas A. Shannon (Maryknoll, N.Y.: Orbis Books, 1992). See also Charles E. Curran, *The Church and Morality: An Ecumenical and Catholic Approach* (Minneapolis: Fortress Press, 1993), 67.

11. "Principalities and powers" is a translation of a complex New Testament term that refers to rulers and authorities in both an earthly and a spiritual sense (see Eph 6:10–17). Protestant scripture scholar Walter Wink has written a three-volume series centered on the "Powers": *Naming the Powers* (1984), *Unmasking the Powers* (1986), and *Engaging the Powers* (1992) published by Fortress Press. He followed up the series with *The Powers That Be* (Doubleday, 1998).

12. Richard McBrien, *Lives of the Popes* (San Francisco: HarperSanFrancisco, 1997), 434–38 at 435. McBrien lists in chronological order the "worst of the worst" popes. I chose Innocent IV out of the list of twenty-four because he lived in the same historical period as St. Francis.

13. Donald E. Pelotte, *John Courtney Murray: Theologian in Conflict* (New York: Paulist Press, 1975), 1–9. An academic life is often uneventful. Much has been written about Murray's thought. Pelotte's book uses Murray's correspondence and his published articles to sketch his life and his thought, but even here there is little comment on Murray's personality.

14. Curran, *American Catholic Social Ethics,* 18–92; and Curran, *Catholic Social Teaching 1891–Present: A Historical, Theological, and Ethical Analysis* (Washington, D.C.: Georgetown University Press, 2002), 222–35.

15. In December 1964 Murray published a significant recapitulation of his position ("The Problem of Religious Freedom," *Theological Studies* 25 [December 1964]:

503–75), which was also published under the same title as a book, *The Problem of Religious Freedom* (Westminster, Md.: Newman Press, 1965). This book serves as an important source of Murray's thought. See pp. 7–17 for Murray's summary of the thought of his opponents. See also Curran, *American Catholic Social Ethics,* 192–93; J. Leon Hooper, "Dignitatis Humanae," in *The New Dictionary of Catholic Social Thought,* ed. Judith A. Dwyer (Collegeville, Minn.: Liturgical Press, 1994), 285–86, where Hooper contrasts Pius IX's *Syllabus of Errors* (1864), which declared the separation of church and state anathema and denied non-Catholics in Catholic countries the right to worship, with Vatican II's *Declaration on Religious Freedom,* which says the opposite; and Leslie Griffin, "Commentary on *Dignitatis Humanae (Declaration on Religious Freedom)*," in *Modern Catholic Social Teaching: Commentaries and Interpretations,* ed. Kenneth R. Himes et al. (Washington, D.C.: Georgetown University Press, 2005), 245–46.

16. The first amendment to the United States Constitution states, "Congress shall make no law respecting an establishment of religion, or prohibiting the free exercise thereof; or abridging the freedom of speech, or of the press; or the right of the people peaceably to assemble, and to petition the Government for a redress of grievances."

17. Murray, *The Problem of Religious Freedom,* 17–45, esp. 28–31, and 93. See also Curran's synthesis of Murray's position in *American Catholic Social Ethics,* 193–210, and in *Catholic Social Teaching 1891–Present,* 227–29; John Coleman, "Vision and Praxis in American Theology: Orestes Brownson, John A. Ryan, and John Courtney Murray," *Theological Studies* 37 (March 1976): 34–38; Pelotte, *John Courtney Murray,* chap. 4; Thomas T. Love, *John Courtney Murray: Contemporary Church-State Theory* (Garden City, N.Y.: Doubleday, 1965); and Thomas P. Ferguson, *Catholic and American: The Political Theology of John Courtney Murray* (Kansas City, Mo.: Sheed & Ward, 1993).

18. Coleman, "Vision and Praxis in American Theology," 37.

19. Ferguson, *Catholic and American,* ix, xii, and passim. This is the central thesis of Ferguson's book. See also Murray, *The Problem of Religious Freedom,* 47–84, 88–89, 98–104, and passim.

20. Gerard J. Hughes sums up the constant principles in Christian tradition this way: "The constant principles have been comparatively general: the authority of the state derives from God as a consequence of the nature of human beings and not from any arbitrary human decision; its proper exercise is therefore limited by the demands of the common good; the church has an important role to play in promoting the values of the gospel in society and has the right to do so freely" ("Authority, Political," in *The New Dictionary of Catholic Social Thought,* ed. Judith A Dwyer [Collegeville, Minn.: Liturgical Press, 1994], 67).

21. John Courtney Murray, *We Hold These Truths: Catholic Reflections on the American Proposition* (New York: Sheed & Ward, 1960).

22. Leslie Griffin, "Commentary on *Dignitatis Humanae,*" 249. Griffin emphasizes the coauthorship of Fr. Pietro Pavan, who had also drafted *Peace on Earth* by John XXIII, and he tells the story of the controversy at the Council over the *Declaration on Religious Freedom.*

23. Curran, *American Catholic Social Ethics,* 207–13, at 207: "Perhaps the primary concern in the whole discussion of religious liberty at the Second Vatican Council was this question of the development of doctrine." See also Griffin, "Commentary on *Dignitatis Humanae,*" 253–54.

24. Murray, *The Problem of Religious Freedom,* 102.

25. Murray makes these points most persuasively and fully in the collected essays in *We Hold These Truths.*

26. Curran, *American Catholic Social Ethics,* 178–85.

27. See "Theology and Philosophy in Public: A Symposium on John Courtney Murray's Unfinished Agenda," ed. David Hollenbach, and including John A. Coleman, Robin Lovin, and J. Bryan Hehir, *Theological Studies* 40 (December 1979): 700–715.

28. Robert W. McElroy, "Murray, John Courtney," in *The New Dictionary of Catholic Social Thought,* ed. Judith A Dwyer (Collegeville, Minn.: Liturgical Press, 1994), 652.

29. See J. Leon Hooper, "Religious Freedom," in ibid., 822–26.

30. See, for example, Curran, *American Catholic Social Ethics,* 223–32; and Ferguson, *Catholic and American,* Appendix A, "An Analysis of Some Interpretations of Murray's Political Theology," 131–48.

31. This account is based on Mich, "Commentary on *Mater et Magistra,*" 192–93.

32. Peter Hebblethwaite, *Pope John XXIII: Shepherd of the Modern World* (Garden City, N.Y.: Doubleday, 1985), 292.

33. Ibid., 194–95. See also Drew Christiansen, "Commentary on *Pacem in Terris* (*Peace on Earth*)," in *Modern Catholic Social Teaching: Commentaries and Interpretations,* ed. Kenneth R. Himes et al. (Washington, D.C.: Georgetown University Press, 2005), 219.

34. Mich, "Commentary on *Mater et Magistra,*" 196–98, 209.

35. Vivian Boland, "*Mater et Magistra,*" in *The New Dictionary of Catholic Social Thought,* ed. Judith A. Dwyer (Collegeville, Minn.: Liturgical Press, 1994), 580–81.

36. This section depends on Mich, "Commentary on *Mater et Magistra,*" 203–5.

37. Mich, "Commentary on *Mater et Magistra,*" 203. This should boost service learning programs at Catholic schools and universities. It also hints at the importance of stories (saints) and models in teaching a public faith. Pope John practiced what he preached.

38. This section depends on Kenneth P. J. Hallahan, "*Pacem in Terris,*" in *The New Dictionary of Catholic Social Thought,* ed. Judith A. Dwyer (Collegeville, Minn.: Liturgical Press, 1994), 698–99, 704, and Christiansen, "Commentary on *Pacem in Terris,*" 217–28.

39. Christiansen, "Commentary on *Pacem in Terris,*" 217 and 238, regarding Nobel laureates.

40. Hollenbach, "Commentary on *Gaudium et Spes,*" 271–77.

41. Ibid., 275. The paragraph refers to H. Richard Niebuhr's classic work *Christ and Culture* (New York: Harper & Row, 1951).

42. Ironically, Cardinal Roy may have produced the first of several drafts of this apostolic letter. *A Call to Action* can be found in *Catholic Social Thought: The Documentary Heritage,* ed. David O'Brien and Thomas Shannon (Maryknoll, N.Y.: Orbis Books, 1992), 265–86.

43. This section depends on Christine E. Gudorf, "Commentary on *Octogesima Adveniens* (*A Call to Action on the Eightieth Anniversary of Rerum Novarum*)," in *Modern Catholic Social Teaching: Commentaries and Interpretations,* ed. Kenneth R. Himes et al. (Washington, D.C.: Georgetown University Press, 2005), 319–30, and Bernard F. Evans, "*Octogesima Adveniens,*" in *The New Dictionary of Catholic*

Social Thought, ed. Judith A. Dwyer (Collegeville, Minn.: Liturgical Press, 1994), 686–90.

44. Gudorf, "Commentary on *Octogesima Adveniens,*" 330.

45. Neither John XXIII nor Paul VI censured any theologian or bishop (save Archbishop Lefebvre, who rejected Vatican II and separated himself from the church). John Paul II reprimanded Bishop Hunthausen of Seattle among others, and the list of censured theologians is long and still growing under Benedict XVI, who, as Cardinal Ratzinger, was head of the Congregation for the Doctrine of the Faith.

46. See Kenneth R. Himes, "Introduction," in *Modern Catholic Social Teaching: Commentaries and Interpretations,* ed. Kenneth R. Himes et al. (Washington, D.C.: Georgetown University Press, 2005), 4.

47. Mary Elsbernd, "Whatever Happened to *Octogesima Adveniens?*" *Theological Studies* 56 (March 1995): 39–60, at 40.

48. Ibid., 51, 59, and passim.

49. Ibid., 60. See also David Hollenbach, who decries the centralization of the church and the move away from collegiality ("Joy and Hope, Grief and Anguish," *America* 193 [December 5, 2005]: 12–15).

50. Regarding John Paul II's discomfort with democracy see Julie Clague, "*The Gospel of Life:* John Paul II on Spiritual Malaise and Its Social Aftermath," in *The New Politics: Catholic Social Teaching for the Twenty-First Century,* ed. Paul Vallely (London: SCM Press, 1998), 114–31, at 126–27; and Paul Vallely, "Into the Twenty-First Century: John Paul II and the New Millennium," ibid., 132–47, at 137–41.

51. Gudorf, "Commentary on *Octogesima Adveniens,*" 327.

52. Ibid., 328.

53. Griffin, "Commentary on *Dignitatis Humanae,*" 257–60. It seems to me that it is not truth or freedom, but freedom and truth. Certainly freedom is for seeking the truth, but historical contingency makes it more difficult to discover truth absolutely.

54. Gudorf, "Commentary on *Octogesima Adveniens,*" 328.

55. Ibid., 328–29.

56. Pope Paul VI began the practice of calling synods of bishops at the beginning of the final session of the Second Vatican Council. Such synods are expressions of the episcopal collegiality articulated by Vatican II, but they are advisory to the pope. They are usually convened for a period of about a month. The 1971 synod was the last to publish a document in its own name, perhaps because of the difficulty of producing a text and a consensus in so short a period. Often the pope will publish a document in response to a synod. Paul VI allowed *Justice in the World* to be published, but he did not explicitly approve it. For a description of the workings of a synod and the process of this synod see Kenneth R. Himes, "Commentary on *Justitia in Mundo (Justice in the World),*" in *Modern Catholic Social Teaching: Commentaries and Interpretations,* ed. Kenneth R. Himes et al. (Washington, D.C.: Georgetown University Press, 2005), 333–62, at 335–38, 354, 356.

57. Ron Hamel, "Justice in the World," in *The New Dictionary of Catholic Social Thought,* ed. Judith A. Dwyer (Collegeville, Minn.: Liturgical Press, 1994), 495–501, at 495; and John F. X. Harriott, "The Difficulty of Justice," *Month* 5 (January 1972): 9.

58. *Justice in the World* can be found in *Catholic Social Thought: The Documentary Heritage,* ed. David O'Brien and Thomas Shannon (Maryknoll, N.Y.: Orbis Books, 1992), 288–300. Unlike papal and conciliar documents, the official version

of the synod statement does not number its paragraphs. This text will refer to the page numbers in O'Brien and Shannon.

59. See Charles Murphy, "Action for Justice as Constitutive of the Preaching of the Gospel: What Did the 1971 Synod Mean?" in *Readings in Moral Theology, #5,* ed. Charles E. Curran and Richard A. McCormick (New York: Paulist Press, 1986), 150–66; and Himes, "Commentary on *Justitia in Mundo,*" 352–55. Those who drafted the text disagreed with how to interpret "constitutive," with one arguing it meant integral, and three contending it meant essential.

60. This section depends on Hamel, "Justice in the World," 496–500; and Himes, "Commentary on *Justitia in Mundo,*" 345–54.

61. Hamel, "Justice in the World," 497.

62. Ibid., 497–99; and David Hollenbach, *Claims in Conflict: Retrieving and Renewing the Catholic Human Rights Tradition* (New York: Paulist Press, 1979), 85–89.

63. Paulo Freire, *Pedagogy of the Oppressed* (New York: Herder & Herder, 1970).

64. Himes, "Commentary on *Justitia in Mundo,*" 352.

65. Arthur McCormack, "The Synod and World Justice," *The Tablet* 225 (November 20, 1971): 1115.

66. Robert Schreiter, "*Evangelii Nuntiandi,*" in *The New Dictionary of Catholic Social Thought,* ed. Judith A. Dwyer (Collegeville, Minn.: Liturgical Press, 1994), 353–63, at 353.

67. See Richard A. McCormick, "Notes on Moral Theology: April–September, 1975 — Human Rights and the Mission of the Church," *Theological Studies* 37 (March 1976): 107–19, at 108. McCormick discusses the issue as raised at the 1974 Synod of Bishops. Paul VI's *On Evangelization in the Modern World* appeared shortly after McCormick wrote his essay. I think McCormick would have been pleased with Pope Paul's discussion of the issue.

68. Pope Paul VI had attended the Medellín meeting of the Conference of Latin American Bishops in 1968, and Gustavo Gutiérrez had published his groundbreaking *A Theology of Liberation* in 1971 (it was translated into English in 1973 [Maryknoll, N.Y.: Orbis Books]). McCormick, "Notes on Moral Theology," says that the literature on liberation theology is "already out of control" by late 1975 (112).

69. Schreiter, "*Evangelii Nuntiandi,*" 357–58, 362.

70. McCormick, "Notes on Moral Theology," 117–18.

71. Charles M. Murphy, "Charity, Not Justice, as Constitutive of the Church's Mission," *Theological Studies* 68 (June 2007): 274–86, at 275 and passim. Murphy's essay is a key source for this section, but it must be said that he is more tactful than I am about the change in church teaching signaled by Pope Benedict XVI. He concludes his article this nuanced way: "Achieving the proper balance, however, between the Church as a political force and one that is merely the religious expression of individuals practicing their faith in private is difficult to accomplish. 'Laicity,' the stepchild of the old anticlericalism that would be pleased to see the Church as an organization having no public role whatsoever and the fatalism that can beset faithful Christians about their earthly existences are dangers still to be avoided" (286). See also William Collinge, "A Contemporary Augustinian Approach to Love and Politics — Pope Benedict XVI's *Deus Caritas Est,*" in *The Heart of Catholic Social Teaching: Its Origins and Contemporary Significance,* ed. David Matzko McCarthy (Grand Rapids, Mich.: Brazos Press, 2009), 85–94; and John Sniegocki, "The Social

Teaching of Pope Benedict XVI: Clergy, Laity, and the Church's Mission for Justice," in *Catholic Identity and the Laity,* ed. Tim Muldoon, *The Annual Publication of the College Theology Society* 54 (2008) (Maryknoll, N.Y.: Orbis Books, 2009), 120–33.

72. Benedict does not return to this issue in *Charity in Truth* (*Caritas in Veritate,* 2009). While "charity" is in the title of this encyclical, Benedict connects charity with justice in an integral way: "justice is inseparable from charity, and intrinsic to it" (#6). See Vincent Miller, "Encyclical Signals Church Not Pulling Out of Politics," *National Catholic Reporter* 45 (July 24, 2009): 8: "Fears and hopes that Benedict would subordinate justice to charity in a manner that signaled a withdrawal of the church from politics were not realized. On the contrary, Benedict offers a complex account of the interplay of justice and charity."

73. The first two chapters of part 1 of *The Pastoral Constitution on the Church in the Modern World,* titled "The Dignity of the Human Person" and "The Community of Mankind," address these fundamental themes.

74. John C. Dwyer, "Person, Dignity of," in *The New Dictionary of Catholic Social Thought,* ed. Judith A. Dwyer (Collegeville, Minn.: Liturgical Press, 1994), 724–37, at 724. Dwyer emphasizes the theological basis of human dignity articulated by Vatican II (734–36).

75. Vatican II, *The Pastoral Constitution on the Church in the Modern World,* #32.

76. John XXIII, *Christianity and Social Progress,* #65. See *The Pastoral Constitution on the Church in the Modern World,* #26.

77. John XXIII, *Peace on Earth,* #60.

78. David Hollenbach, "Common Good," in *The New Dictionary of Catholic Social Thought,* ed. Judith A. Dwyer (Collegeville, Minn.: Liturgical Press, 1994), 192–97, at 192.

79. Catholic Bishops' Conference of England and Wales, *The Common Good and the Catholic Church's Social Teaching* (1996); #48, *www.catholicchurch.org.uk.*

80. Hollenbach, "Common Good," 192–93.

81. David Hollenbach, *The Common Good and Christian Ethics* (Cambridge: Cambridge University Press, 2002), 3, 7–8. Hollenbach argues in this study that a recovery of the concept of the common good, which has been preserved in Catholic social teaching, is important for the success of democracy and can provide a framework for a public policy responsive to contemporary American social problems such as urban poverty (chap. 7). In chap. 8 he extends the concept of the common good to global issues as well.

82. This account is based on Jimmy Carter, "A Village Woman's Legacy," *Time* (March 31, 2008): 62. President Jimmy Carter is himself a wonderful example of a faithful Christian (Baptist) who works to transform public policy and puts these principles into action.

83. Dwyer, "Person, Dignity of," 734.

84. Martin Luther King Jr., "Beyond Vietnam," in *A Testament of Hope: The Essential Writings of Martin Luther King, Jr.,* ed. James M. Washington (San Francisco: Harper & Row, 1986), 254.

85. John Paul II reflects on solidarity in his 1987 encyclical *On Social Concern* (*Sollicitudo Rei Socialis*), #38–40. See also Hollenbach, "Common Good," 195; and Matthew Lamb, "Solidarity," *The New Dictionary of Catholic Social Thought,* ed. Judith A. Dwyer (Collegeville, Minn.: Liturgical Press, 1994), 908–12.

86. See Michael E. Allsopp, "Subsidiarity, Principle of," in *The New Dictionary of Catholic Social Thought,* ed. Judith A. Dwyer (Collegeville, Minn.: Liturgical Press, 1994), 927–29, at 928.

87. John XXIII, *Christianity and Social Progress (Mater et Magistra,* 1961), #51–67. See also Eustas O. Heideain, "Socialization," in *The New Dictionary of Catholic Social Thought,* ed. Judith A. Dwyer (Collegeville, Minn.: Liturgical Press, 1994), 891–94.

88. See the excellent overview by Judith A. Merkle, "Sin," in *The New Dictionary of Catholic Social Thought,* ed. Judith A. Dwyer (Collegeville, Minn.: Liturgical Press, 1994), 883–88, which includes a good bibliography up to 1994; and James T. Cross, "Communal Penance and Public Life: On the Church's Becoming a Sign of Conversion from Social Sin," in *Faith in Public Life,* ed. William J. Collinge, *The Annual Publication of the College Theology Society* 53 (2007) (Maryknoll, N.Y.: Orbis Books, 2008), 284–97.

89. *The Pastoral Constitution on the Church in the Modern World,* #25. See also John XXIII, *Christianity and Social Progress,* #59–67.

90. Merkle, "Sin," 885–87.

91. Shirley Erena Murray, "God in Your Grace," for the 9th World Council of Churches Assembly.

92. USCCB, *Economic Justice for All: Pastoral Letter on Catholic Social Teaching and the U.S. Economy,* in *Catholic Social Thought: The Documentary Heritage,* ed. David O'Brien and Thomas Shannon (Maryknoll, N.Y.: Orbis Books, 1992), #24. On the option for the poor see also Daniel G. Groody, ed., *The Option for the Poor in Christian Theology* (Notre Dame, Ind.: University of Notre Dame Press, 2007).

93. The emergence of a Catholic vision of human rights is traced in David Hollenbach, *Claims in Conflict: Retrieving and Renewing the Catholic Human Rights Tradition* (New York: Paulist Press, 1979), chap. 2, 41–106; Curran, *Catholic Social Teaching 1891–Present,* 215–21; and Michael P. Hornsby-Smith, *An Introduction to Catholic Social Thought* (Cambridge: Cambridge University Press, 2006), 118–20. Although Hollenbach recognizes the development in Catholic thought on human rights, he stresses the continuity in Catholic social teaching from Leo XIII through Paul VI and the 1971 Synod of Bishops in *Claims in Conflict.* Hollenbach seems more straightforward about the discontinuity in the tradition, the Catholic human rights revolution introduced by John XXIII, in some of his more recent writings on human rights. See his "A Communitarian Reconstruction of Human Rights: Contributions from Catholic Tradition," in *Catholicism and Liberalism: Contributions to American Public Philosophy,* ed. R. Bruce Douglass and David Hollenbach (Cambridge: Cambridge University Press, 1994), 127–50, at 127.

94. David Hollenbach, "Global Human Rights: An Interpretation of the Contemporary Catholic Understanding," in his *Justice, Peace, and Human Rights: American Catholic Social Ethics in a Pluralistic World* (New York: Crossroad, 1988), 91; and Michael J. Himes and Kenneth R. Himes, *Fullness of Faith: The Public Significance of Theology* (New York: Paulist Press, 1993), 63.

95. See Table 4.1 "Internationally Recognized Human Rights," in J. Milburn Thompson, *Justice and Peace: A Christian Primer* (Maryknoll, N.Y.: Orbis Books, 2003), 95, where I cross-reference the "International Bill of Human Rights" developed by Jack Donnelly in *International Human Rights* (Boulder, Colo.: Westview Press, 1993), 9, with John XXIII's *Peace on Earth.* Hornsby-Smith (*Introduction to*

Catholic Social Thought, 121–46) also elaborates on the specific rights embraced by the church.

96. See Hollenbach, *Claims in Conflict,* 13–27; Frank Brennan, "Rights and Duties," in *The New Dictionary of Catholic Social Thought,* ed. Judith A. Dwyer (Collegeville, Minn.: Liturgical Press, 1994), 849–51, at 850. Because the Universal Declaration of Human Rights did not have the binding force of a treaty two international covenants were developed in 1953, one on civil and political rights and one on economic, social, and cultural rights. The United States insisted on two different covenants and they were finally issued in 1966. The United States ratified the International Covenant on Civil and Political Rights in 1992; it has never ratified the International Covenant on Social, Economic, and Cultural Rights. See Donnelly, *International Human Rights,* 10, 100–103, 182.

97. This paragraph is based on "The Trinity and Human Rights," chap. 3, 55–73 in Himes and Himes, *Fullness of Faith.* The quotation is on p. 59. The genius of the Himes brothers in this chapter is rooting human dignity in creation in the image of a trinitarian God. The idea that the Catholic vision of human rights integrates civil and political and social and economic rights and thus resists both individualism and collectivism is widely available in the literature on a Christian perspective on human rights. See, for example, Hollenbach, *Claims in Conflict,* and "A Communitarian Reconstruction of Human Rights"; Brennan, "Rights and Duties"; and Thomas Hoppe, "Human Rights," in *The New Dictionary of Catholic Social Thought,* ed. Judith A. Dwyer (Collegeville, Minn.: Liturgical Press, 1994), 455–70.

98. For an overview of the Christian ethics and torture see John Perry, *Torture: Religious Ethics and National Security* (Maryknoll, N.Y.: Orbis Books, 2005); and J. Milburn Thompson, "Catholic Social Teaching and the Ethics of Torture," *Journal of Peace and Justice Studies* 17, no. 2 (Autumn 2008): 22–42.

99. Hollenbach, "A Communitarian Reconstruction of Human Rights," 144–45.

100. Scott Shane, David Johnston, and James Risen, "Secret U.S. Endorsement of Severe Interrogations," *New York Times* (October 4, 2007): A1, A22–23. See also David Johnston and Scott Shane, "Memo Sheds New Light on Torture Issue," ibid. (April 3, 2008), A15; Mark Mazzetti and Scott Shane, "Debate over Interrogation Methods Sharply Divided the Bush White House," ibid. (May 4, 2009), A13; and Mark Danner, "US Torture: Voices from the Black Sites," *New York Review of Books* 56 (April 9, 2009).

101. Tom Carney, "Americans, Especially Catholics, Approve of Torture," *National Catholic Reporter* 42 (March 24, 2006), 5; and Peter Smith, "Tolerance of Torture in Terror Cases Studied," *Louisville Courier-Journal* (May 9, 2009), B3. See also the website of the Pew Research Center.

102. Donnelly, *International Human Rights,* 150; and David P. Gushee, "Against Torture: An Evangelical Perspective," *Theology Today* 63 (2006): 252–60. This issue of *Theology Today* is devoted to a Christian perspective on torture.

103. Mark Bowden, "The Dark Art of Interrogation," *Atlantic Monthly* 292 (October 2003): 51–76 at 53.

104. See Bowden, "The Dark Art of Interrogation," 57–70, for a discussion of the effectiveness of torture and coercion; and Jane Mayer, "Outsourcing Torture," *New Yorker* 81 (February 14, 2005): 106–23, at 108, regarding prosecution and torture. On the whole story of the United States and torture in the Bush years, see

Jane Mayer, *The Dark Side: The Inside Story of How the War on Terror Turned into a War on American Ideals* (New York: Anchor, 2009).

105. Stephen Budiansky, "Truth Extraction," *Atlantic Monthly* 295 (June 2005): 32–35. Scott Shane and Mark Mazzetti, "Advisers Fault Harsh Methods in Interrogation," *New York Times* (May 30, 2007), A1, A12, report that a group of expert advisers to the Intelligence Science Board "argue that the harsh techniques used since the 2001 terrorist attacks are outmoded, amateurish and unreliable."

106. Frank Rich, "The Banality of Bush White House Evil," *New York Times* (April 26, 2009), 14, argues that the primary purpose for torture was not a ticking bomb sort of scenario, but the desire to connect Iraq with Al Qaeda in justifying the invasion of Iraq.

107. *Forming Consciences for Faithful Citizenship*, issued on November 14, 2007, by the USCCB, absolutely condemns torture in a list of intrinsically evil acts three times (#23, 64, 88), but torture is not highlighted among the ten goals the bishops lift up as special concerns for political candidates in the 2008 election (#90). The United States Conference of Catholic Bishops should have issued a statement similar to that of the Presbyterians to help form the conscience of Catholics on torture in a time of terrorism. Any statement from the church should counter the climate of impunity that surrounds the U.S. policy regarding torture and its practice throughout the world. Some of the bishops in Chile eventually issued orders of excommunication for torturers and those who ordered torture. The American context is different from that of Chile, but this precedent is worth critical discussion.

108. Besides the documents of the USCCB listed below, Cardinal Roger Mahony, archbishop of Los Angeles, publicly declared that he would instruct priests to disobey a proposed law that would make it a criminal offense to assist an undocumented immigrant in February 2006. See Roger Mahony, "Called by God to Help," *New York Times* (March 22, 2006), op-ed page. For a critique of Mahony on this issue see Richard John Neuhaus, "Who Speaks for the Church?" *First Things* (August/September 2007): 65–66. The Catholic Church in America is an immigrant church, and many of today's immigrants happen to be Catholic.

109. The right to immigrate is at least implied in *On the Condition of Labor* by Pope Leo XIII, and Pius XII wrote an apostolic constitution titled *On the Spiritual Care of Migrants* (*Exsul Familia*) in 1952. Pope John Paul II released *The Church in America* (*Ecclesia in America*) in January 1999 at the Basilica of Our Lady of Guadalupe in Mexico, a response to the 1997 Vatican Synod of Bishops on evangelization in the Americas. Paragraph 65 explicitly addresses immigration. *Strangers No Longer* was published on the fourth anniversary of Pope John Paul II's document. Prior to this joint pastoral letter, the USCCB published a statement titled *Welcoming the Stranger among Us: Unity in Diversity* (2000). Both are available at *www.usccb.org*.

110. Thus when human rights are in conflict, basic rights have priority and the other key principles of Catholic social teaching, including the option for the poor, can guide further prioritization. See Hollenbach, *Claims in Conflict,* chap. 5, esp. 203–7 for further reflection on this question.

111. There seems to be some false information about immigrants (and perhaps some racism) that fuels the animosity of some people. Some assume that immigrant workers are getting a free ride in the United States by using services developed for (needy) citizens although they do not pay taxes. In fact the majority of undocumented workers pay federal, state, local, and sales taxes, and if they don't, they

are likely being exploited through low wages and unsafe working conditions. The majority also pay into Social Security and Medicare. They do not, however, receive many benefits. Documented immigrants (except refugees) in the country for less than five years and all undocumented immigrants are not eligible for most public benefits including Social Security, Supplemental Security Income (SSI), Temporary Assistance for Needy Families (Welfare), Medicaid, Medicare, housing assistance, and food stamps. See Gabriela Alcalde, "Myths about Immigration," *Louisville Courier-Journal* (October 31, 2007), A7. Thus the huddled masses are actually giving Americans a free ride.

112. While respect for law is an important value, with Jesus we can say that humanity is more important than law. Immigration law has changed throughout American history, and one can question the fairness of current law. Moreover, crossing a border without permission with the intention of working is a violation of administrative law; it is more like a traffic violation than a serious criminal offense. See the "Immigration Issue Paper," under "Election 2008: Voting the Common Good," on the Center of Concern website, *www.coc.org,* accessed June 6, 2009.

113. A website sponsored by a number of Catholic organizations, including the USCCB, has been established to educate and advocate regarding justice for immigrants: *www.justiceforimmigrants.org.*

114. Mich, *Catholic Social Teaching and Movements,* addresses Catholic participation in opposition to racism (133–53) and regarding justice for women in chap. 12 (347–84).

115. Readers may not be familiar with the remarkable story of Mother Antonia. See Mary Jordan and Kevin Sullivan, *The Prison Angel: Mother Antonia's Life of Service in a Mexican Jail* (New York: Penguin Press, 2006). Always involved in direct service, this twice-divorced Californian in her forties could not find a religious order that would accept her. After being introduced to the notorious La Mesa state penitentiary in Tijuana, Mexico, she began visiting there and then in 1978 she moved into a small cell to minister to the inmates, who lived in deplorable conditions. Every local church provides opportunities for the ministry of direct service, whether it is serving a meal at a soup kitchen, bereavement ministry, or the Christmas giving tree. My brother, Kevin, a dentist, has gone on several dental missions to Kenya, and his daughter, Kara Beth, a physician, has made a commitment of at least two years on a medical mission in Cameroon. We all know of such service by our neighbors and friends.

116. The USCCB has its roots in the National Catholic Welfare Council (NCWC). In 1966, responding to the spirit and directives of the Second Vatican Council, the bishops organized the National Conference of Catholic Bishops (NCCB) to attend to ecclesial matters, and the United States Catholic Conference (USCC) to address public policy matters. In July 2001 the NCCB and the USCC were combined to form the USCCB, which continued all the work previously done and with basically the same staff of more than 350 laypersons, priests, and religious with particular expertise. See Kristin E. Heyer, *Prophetic and Public: The Social Witness of U.S. Catholicism* (Washington, D.C.: Georgetown University Press, 2006), 136–57, at 139. Heyer is a basic source for this section on the USCCB.

117. See Mich, *Catholic Social Teaching and Movements,* 198–200; Thompson, *Justice and Peace,* 216–17; and the Center of Concern website at *www.coc.org.*

118. This quote is from the NETWORK website, *www.networklobby.org*. On NETWORK see Heyer, *Prophetic and Public*, 120–28; and Mich, *Catholic Social Teaching and Movements*, 200–03.

119. Heyer, *Prophetic and Public*, 124.

120. See the Bread for the World website at *www.bread.org*.

121. Mich, *Catholic Social Teaching and Movements*, 203–7, at 207.

122. Ibid. The website of the ICCR can be found at *www.iccr.org*.

123. See Heyer, *Prophetic and Public*, 128–36; Mary Evelyn Jegen, "Peace and Pluralism: Church and Churches," in *One Hundred Years of Catholic Social Thought*, ed. John A. Coleman (Maryknoll, N.Y.: Orbis Books, 1991), 293–94; and Mich, *Catholic Social Teaching and Movements*, 299–301. The Pax Christi USA website can be found at *www.paxchristiusa.org*. Pax Christi is a Latin term meaning Peace of Christ.

124. Paul VI, "World Day of Peace Message" (January 1, 1972), available at *www.vatican.va*.

125. Quote taken from the Pax Christi website, April 9, 2008.

126. *Living the Catholic Social Tradition: Cases and Commentary,* ed. Kathleen Maas Weigert and Alexis K. Kelly (Lanham, Md.: Rowman & Littlefield, 2005), presents nine cases of local faith-based community action.

127. "A Call to 'Catch a Falling Child,'" Letter to the Editor from Rev. Louis Meiman and Bishop Walter Jones, Co-Presidents of CLOUT, *Louisville Courier-Journal* (March 26, 2008), A8; and Charlie White, "Leveraging CLOUT," *Courier-Journal* (April 1, 2008), B3. CLOUT's website is at *www.cloutky.org*.

Chapter 3: Economic Justice

1. There are over a dozen biographies of César Chávez and several studies of *la causa*. This section will rely primarily on Frederick John Dalton, *The Moral Vision of César Chávez* (Maryknoll, N.Y.: Orbis Books, 2003); and Marjorie Hope and James Young, *The Struggle for Humanity: Agents of Nonviolent Change in a Violent World* (Maryknoll, N.Y.: Orbis Books, 1977), chap. 5. There is a PBS documentary film titled *The Fight in the Fields: Cesar Chavez and the Farmworkers Movement* (New York: Cinema Guild, 2003), produced and directed by Ray Telles and Rick Tejada-Flores, and an accompanying book of the same title, written by Susan Ferriss and Ricardo Sandoval, ed. Diana Hembree (New York: Harcourt Brace & Company, 1997).

2. Saul Alinsky virtually created community organizing as a way to empower the poor in Chicago. Cardinal Montini of Milan, the future Pope Paul VI, invited Alinsky to consult with the church about better serving workers in his diocese. Alinsky is the author of *Reveille for Radicals* (Chicago: University of Chicago Press, 1946), which was updated in 1969 and reprinted by Vintage Press in 1989.

3. Dolores Huerta, the mother of eleven children, worked with César throughout his life on behalf of *la causa*. She became the chief negotiator for the United Farm Workers and was key in developing the boycott strategy of the UFW. See Michael True, "Dolores Huerta and Cesar Chavez," *To Construct Peace: 30 More Justice Seekers, Peace Makers* (Mystic, Conn.: Twenty-Third Publications, 1992), 68–73.

4. Accurate information on migrant farm workers is difficult to collect. I have relied on "Facts about Farmworkers," on the website of the National Center for

Farmworker Health, *www.ncfh.org*, accessed on May 2, 2008. See also the National Agricultural Workers Survey by the U.S. Department of Labor Employment and Training Agency at *www.doleta.gov*. Note that this survey is not limited to migrant farm workers, but includes all agricultural workers.

5. Dalton, *The Moral Vision of César Chávez*, 82–85, 100–105.

6. Fittingly César Chávez received the Bishop Donnelly Memorial Award for an individual who has made significant contributions to the achievement of the Catholic vision of social justice from the Archdiocese of Hartford in 1987. See the articles by David Fortier and Daria Keyes in the *Catholic Transcript* 90 (October 23, 1987): 1.

7. Dalton, *The Moral Vision of César Chávez*, 46–58.

8. Patricia A. Lamoureux, "Commentary on *Laborem exercens (On Human Work)*," in *Modern Catholic Social Teaching: Commentaries and Interpretations*, ed. Kenneth R. Himes (Washington, D.C.: Georgetown University Press, 2005), 389–414, at 389. This essay is an important source for this section on John Paul's *On Human Work*. See also Pontifical Council for Justice and Peace, *Compendium of the Social Doctrine of the Church* (Washington, D.C.: United States Conference of Catholic Bishops, 2004), chap. 6, "Human work" (#255–322).

9. Richard A. McCormick, "Laborem Exercens and Social Morality," in *Readings in Moral Theology, No. 5: Official Catholic Social Teaching*, ed. Charles E. Curran and Richard A. McCormick (New York: Paulist Press, 1986), 219–32, at 220–21; William Werpehowski, "Labor and Capital in Catholic Social Thought," in *The New Dictionary of Catholic Social Thought*, ed. Judith A. Dyer (Collegeville, Minn.: Liturgical Press, 1994), 516–27, at 526.

10. The "race to the bottom" dynamic is a result of free trade and ruthless competition. Powerful corporations can move their production facilities from Ohio to Mexico to China in search of cheap labor and lax restrictions on production. Thus there is tremendous pressure on nations to lower minimum wage and worker safety standards, environmental restrictions, and product safety regulations. This race to the bottom benefits corporations but not workers, consumers, or citizens. See Chuck Collins and Mary Wright, *The Moral Measure of the Economy* (Maryknoll, N.Y.: Orbis Books, 2007), chap. 6, at 109–10.

11. On the rights of workers see also Benedict XVI, *Charity in Truth*, #25, 63–64.

12. See Christine Firer Hinze, "Commentary on *Quadragesimo anno (After Forty Years)*," in *Modern Catholic Social Teaching*, ed. Kenneth R. Himes (Washington, D.C.: Georgetown University Press, 2005), 151–74, at 159; Marvin L. Mich, "Commentary on *Mater et magistra (Christianity and Social Progress)*," ibid., 191–216, at 199; and Frank D. Almade, "Just Wage," in *The New Dictionary of Catholic Social Thought*, ed. Judith A. Dyer (Collegeville, Minn.: Liturgical Press, 1994), 491–95.

13. On the struggle for wage justice in the U.S. context see Elizabeth Hinson-Hasty, "For Workers," in *To Do Justice: Engaging Progressive Christians in Social Action*, ed. Rebecca Todd Peters and Elizabeth Hinson-Hasty (Louisville: Westminster John Knox Press, 2008), chap. 1.

14. Collins and Wright, *The Moral Measure of the Economy*, 60–62; Justin Fox, "How the Next President Should Fix the Economy," *Time* (May 26, 2008): 38–39.

15. Collins and Wright, *The Moral Measure of the Economy*, 67–72.

16. See Lamoureux, "Commentary on *Laborem exercens*," 401; Andrea Lee and Amata Miller, "Feminist Themes and Laborem Exercens," in *Readings in Moral Theology, No. 5: Official Catholic Social Teaching,* ed. Charles E. Curran and Richard A. McCormick (New York: Paulist Press, 1986), 411–41; and Carol Coston, "Women's Ways of Working," in *One Hundred Years of Catholic Social Thought: Celebration and Challenge,* ed. John A. Coleman (Maryknoll, N.Y.: Orbis Books, 1991), 256–69.

17. Gregory Baum, "Laborem Exercens," in *The New Dictionary of Catholic Social Thought,* ed. Judith A. Dyer (Collegeville, Minn.: Liturgical Press, 1994), 527–35, at 534. For a theology of work see William E. May, "Work, Theology of," ibid., 991–1002.

18. See Charles E. Curran, *Catholic Social Teaching, 1892–Present: A Historical, Theological, and Ethical Analysis* (Washington, D.C.: Georgetown University Press, 2002), 173–83; Thomas A. Shannon, "Commentary on *Rerum novarum (The Condition of Labor)*" in *Modern Catholic Social Teaching,* ed. Kenneth R. Himes (Washington, D.C.: Georgetown University Press, 2005), 127–50, at 135–36 and 141–43; and Daniel Finn, "Commentary on *Centesimus annus (On the Hundredth Anniversary of* Rerum Novarum)," ibid., 436–66. at 444–48. These theologians suggest that Leo XIII misinterpreted Thomas Aquinas on private property and socialism.

19. Pius XI, *After Forty Years,* #44–46; John XXIII, *Christianity and Social Progress,* #43; Vatican II, *The Pastoral Constitution on the Church in the Modern World,* #69, 71; Paul VI, *On the Development of Peoples,* #22–24; John Paul II, *On Human Work,* #14; *On Social Concern,* #42; *On the Hundredth Anniversary,* #30–32; USCCB, *Economic Justice for All,* #115.

20. Evangelical theologian Ronald Sider uses the parable as a metaphor for the contemporary gap between the rich and the poor in his popular book *Rich Christians in an Age of Hunger: Moving from Affluence to Generosity,* rev. ed. (Dallas: Word Publishing, 1997). This principle is at the heart of his thesis.

21. Charles Curran makes the point that solidarity is a sounder basis for the social purpose of the works of human hands and human ingenuity than the doctrine of creation, which seems more appropriate for land and natural resources and an agricultural economy, in *Catholic Social Teaching, 1892–Present,* 181–83.

22. A central source for this section is Gerald S. Twomey, *The "Preferential Option for the Poor" in Catholic Social Thought from John XXIII to John Paul II* (Lewiston, N.Y.: Edwin Mellen Press, 2005). Twomey's book is very thorough and relatively recent. Donal Dorr has written perceptively about the option for the poor in several places. See his *Option for the Poor: A Hundred Years of Catholic Social Teaching,* rev. ed. (Maryknoll, N.Y.: Orbis Books, 1992), esp. 357–64. This is a fine introduction to Catholic social teaching with a focus on the option for the poor. See also Donal Dorr, "Poor, Preferential Option for," in *The New Dictionary of Catholic Social Thought,* ed. Judith A. Dyer (Collegeville, Minn.: Liturgical Press, 1994), 755–59; and "Option for the Poor Revisited," in *Catholic Social Thought: Twilight or Renaissance,* ed. J. S. Boswell, F. P. McHugh, and J. Verstraeten (Leuven: Leuven University Press, 2000), 248–62. See also Marvin L. Krier Mich, *The Challenge and Spirituality of Catholic Social Teaching* (Louisville: JustFaith, Inc., 2005), chap. 5; Peter J. Henriot, *Opting for the Poor: A Challenge for North Americans,* rev. ed. (Washington, D.C.: Center for Concern, 2004); and Curran, *Catholic Social Teaching, 1892–Present,* 183–88. These are the principal sources for this section.

23. Dorr, "Option for the Poor Revisited," 251; Mich, *The Challenge and Spirituality of Catholic Social Teaching*, 95–97; and Sider, *Rich Christians in an Age of Hunger*, 50–52.

24. David J. O'Brien and Thomas A. Shannon, eds., *Renewing the Earth: Catholic Documents on Peace, Justice and Liberation* (Garden City, N.Y.: Image Books, Doubleday, 1977), "The Medellín Conference Documents," 541–80. The documents of the Medellín Conference are also in Alfred T. Hennelly, ed., *Liberation Theology: A Documentary History* (Maryknoll, N.Y.: Orbis Books, 1990).

25. On the development of the option for the poor in Catholic social teaching see Henriot, *Opting for the Poor*, 18–21; and Twomey, *The "Preferential Option for the Poor,"* throughout, but summarized in chap. 1.

26. Twomey, *The "Preferential Option for the Poor,"* 15.

27. Allan Figueroa Deck, "Commentary on *Populorum Progressio* (*On the Development of Peoples*)," in *Modern Catholic Social Teaching*, ed. Kenneth R. Himes (Washington, D.C.: Georgetown University Press, 2005), 292–314, at 298; and Christine E. Gudorf, "Commentary on *Octogesima Adveniens* (*A Call to Action on the Eightieth Anniversary of* Rerum Novarum)," ibid., 315–32, at 323.

28. Virgilio Elizondo, "Collaborative Theology: Latin American Bishops, the Pope and the Poor," *Commonweal* (January 31, 2008): 8–9.

29. On the definition of the preferential option for the poor see Henriot, *Opting for the Poor*, 23–25; and Twomey, *The "Preferential Option for the Poor,"* 26–35.

30. Sider, *Rich Christians in an Age of Hunger*, 49–50, 63–66.

31. Curran, *Catholic Social Teaching, 1892–Present*, 85–91; and Deck, "Commentary on *Populorum Progressio*," 306–7.

32. Brief accounts of all these saints and witnesses can be found in Robert Ellsberg, *All Saints: Daily Reflections on Saints, Prophets, and Witnesses for Our Time* (New York: Crossroad, 1997).

33. John Dear, *Jean Donovan: The Call to Discipleship*, Pax Christi USA Peacemakers Pamphlet Series (Erie, Pa.: Pax Christi USA, 1980); and John Dear, *Oscar Romero and the Nonviolent Struggle for Justice*, rev. ed., Pax Christi USA Peacemakers Pamphlet Series (Erie, Pa.: Pax Christi USA, 2004).

34. Helen Prejean, *Dead Man Walking: An Eyewitness Account of the Death Penalty in the United States* (New York: Vintage Books, Random House, 1993), 3–11. Helen Prejean is not included in Ellsberg's *All Saints*.

35. Deck, "Commentary on *Populorum Progressio*," 305–8; and Mary Hembrow Snyder, "Development," in *The New Dictionary of Catholic Social Thought*, ed. Judith A. Dwyer (Collegeville, Minn.: Liturgical Press, 1994), 278–82 for a discussion of the concept of development. Both of these essays have influenced this section.

36. Clifford Longley, "Fraternity and the Modern Age," *The Tablet* 263 (July 11, 2009), 4–5.

37. David Nirenberg, "Love and Capitalism," *New Republic* 240 (September 23, 2009): 39–42 at 41. See also "New Sins, New Virtues; Faith, Economics and Ecology," *The Economist* 392 (July 11, 2009), 59. These ideas are expressed in *Charity in Truth*, #34–37.

38. Longley, "Fraternity and the Modern Age," 5; and Margaret Archer, "No Man Is an Island," *The Tablet* 263 (July 18, 2009), 10–11.

39. The "Economy of Communion in Freedom," as it is officially called, refers to a network of some 754 companies worldwide associated with the Focolare Movement launched in 1991 by Chiara Lubich in Brazil. These companies dedicate some of their profit to building up the common good through direct aid and educational programs. Italian economist Stefano Zamagni is closely associated with the movement and with the economic idea. See several articles on this topic in the *Houston Catholic Worker* 29 (September–October 2009); and *www.edc-online.org*.

40. Longley, "Fraternity and the Modern Age," 5.

41. On globalization and Catholic social thought see John A. Coleman and William F. Ryan, eds., *Globalization and Catholic Social Thought: Present Crisis, Future Hope* (Maryknoll, N.Y.: Orbis Books, 2005); and Daniel G. Groody, *Globalization, Spirituality, and Justice: Navigating the Path to Peace* (Maryknoll, N.Y.: Orbis Books, 2007).

42. Besides the articles already referred to, see George Weigel, "*Caritas in Veritate* in Gold and Red," *National Review Online, article.nationalreview.com,* July 7, 2009; and Daniel Finn, "Economics of Charity: Pope Benedict's *Caritas in Veritate*," *Commonweal* 136 (August 14, 2009): 8–10.

43. Peter Steinfels, "From the Vatican, a Tough Read," *New York Times* (July 18, 2009), A12. See also J. Milburn Thompson, "If Only the Pope Had Paid Attention to This Memo," *American Catholic* (October 2009): 4.

44. On this point see Charles E. Curran, Kenneth R. Himes, and Thomas Shannon, "Commentary on *Sollicitudo rei socialis* (*On Social Concern*)" in *Modern Catholic Social Teaching,* ed. Kenneth R. Himes (Washington, D.C.: Georgetown University Press, 2005), 415–35, at 424.

45. The issues addressed in the encyclical are complex and Vatican documents are notorious for dense prose, but I think *Charity in Truth* is in a league of its own. Admittedly this is partially a matter of taste. The two pastoral letters of the U.S. Conference of Catholic Bishops, *The Challenge of Peace* (1983) and *Economic Justice for All* (1986), demonstrate that social documents can be informed, substantive, and accessible.

46. See Tracy Kidder, *Mountains beyond Mountains: The Quest of Dr. Paul Farmer, a Man Who Would Cure the World* (New York: Random House, 2003).

47. *Time* magazine named Bono and Bill and Melinda Gates "Persons of the Year" for 2005. This portrait of Bono is based on two articles in *Time* (December 29, 2005–January 2, 2006): Josh Tyrangiel, "The Constant Charmer," 46–62; and Nancy Gibbs, "Persons of the Year," 44–45.

48. See Jeffery Sachs, *The End of Poverty: Economic Possibilities for Our Time* (New York: Penguin Press, 2005); and *Common Wealth: Economics for a Crowded Planet* (New York: Penguin Press, 2008).

49. There are at least two books on the faith and spirituality of Bono and U2: Greg Garrett, *We Get to Carry Each Other: The Gospel according to U2* (Louisville: Westminster John Knox Press, 2009); and Steve Stockman, *Walk On: The Spiritual Journey of U2,* rev. ed. (Orlando: Relevant Books, 2005).

Chapter 4: War and Peace

1. *The Pastoral Constitution on the Church in the Modern World* (*Gaudium et Spes*), in *Catholic Social Thought: The Documentary Heritage,* ed. David J. O'Brien and Thomas A. Shannon, (Maryknoll, N.Y.: Orbis Books, 1992), #80.

2. See Walter C. Clemens and J. David Singer, "The Human Cost of War: Modern Warfare Kills More Civilians Than Soldiers," *Scientific American* 282 (June 2000): 56–57; and Ronald Waldman, "Public Health in War: Pursuing the Impossible," *Harvard International Review* 27 (Spring 2005): 60. Accurate statistics on war casualties are difficult to establish. For example, some say there were about 70 million war deaths in World War II.

It is interesting to note that the most devastating domestic attack experienced by the United States was on September 11, 2001, when 2,973 people, all but 125 civilians, were killed. In comparison, the German Blitz against Britain, from September 1941 to May 1942, killed 40,000 civilians. The greatest loss of American life in war was during the Civil War. In World War II, Russia lost nearly 10 percent of its population.

3. Helpful surveys of the Catholic tradition on war and peace include Roland H. Bainton, *Christian Attitudes toward War and Peace: A Historical Survey and Critical Re-Evaluation* (Nashville: Abingdon, 1960); Lisa Sowle Cahill, *Love Your Enemies: Discipleship, Pacifism, and Just War Theory* (Minneapolis: Fortress Press, 1994); Kenneth R. Himes, "War" in *The Dictionary of Catholic Social Thought,* ed. Judith A. Dwyer (Collegeville, Minn.: Liturgical Press, 1994); James Turner Johnson, *The Quest for Peace: Three Moral Traditions in Western Cultural History* (Princeton: Princeton University Press, 1987); and Ronald G. Musto, *The Catholic Peace Tradition* (Maryknoll, N.Y.: Orbis Books, 1986). Among the texts that explore the models that emerge in the Catholic tradition see Mark J. Allman, *Who Would Jesus Kill? War, Peace, and the Christian Tradition* (Winona, Minn.: Saint Mary's Press, 2008); Michael K. Duffey, *Peacemaking Christians: The Future of Just Wars, Pacifism, and Nonviolent Resistance* (Kansas City: Sheed & Ward, 1995); and Joseph J. Fahey, *War and the Christian Conscience: Where Do You Stand?* (Maryknoll, N.Y.: Orbis Books, 2005).

4. There are a variety of interpretations of the pacifism of the early church. In general pacifist authors interpret Constantine and the emergence of the just war position as a fall from grace. Just war theorists see this as a gradual accommodation to reality. See Bainton, *Christian Attitudes toward War and Peace,* chap. 5; C. John Cadoux, *The Early Christian Attitude to War: A Contribution to the History of Christian Ethics* (New York: Seabury Press, 1982); Cahill, *Love Your Enemies,* chap. 3; Eileen Egan, *Peace Be with You: Justified Warfare or the Way of Nonviolence* (Maryknoll, N.Y.: Orbis Books, 1999), chap. 2; John Helgeland, Robert J. Daly, and J. Patout Burns, *Christians and the Military: The Early Experience* (Philadelphia: Fortress Press, 1985); Johnson, *The Quest for Peace,* chap. 1.

5. Cahill, *Love Your Enemies,* chap. 4.

6. Ibid., chap. 5.

7. Allman, *Who Would Jesus Kill?* 159–95; Fahey, *War and the Christian Conscience,* 70–114, at 100–102; LeRoy B. Walters, "Five Classic Just-War Theories: A Study in the Thought of Thomas Aquinas, Vitoria, Suarez, Gentili, and Grotius" (Ph.D. diss., Yale University, 1971). See also Eileen P. Flynn, *How Just Is the War on*

Terror? A Question of Morality (New York: Paulist Press, 2007), 7–19, where she chronicles the "major benchmarks in the development of the just war tradition."

8. This pastoral letter can be found in *Catholic Social Thought*, ed. O'Brien and Shannon, 492–571. I will use the paragraph numbers to refer to *The Challenge of Peace*. For comparable contemporary statements of the just war theory see Allman, *Who Would Jesus Kill?* 195–206; Fahey, *War and Christian Conscience*, 72; and Flynn, *How Just Is the War on Terror?* 19–23.

9. Musto, *The Catholic Peace Tradition*; Fahey, *War and the Christian Conscience*, 29–69.

10. Fahey, *War and the Christian Conscience*, 121–29.

11. Bainton, *Christian Attitudes toward War and Peace*, 148.

12. Fahey, *War and the Christian Conscience*, 129–34, calls the Inquisition "Crusades at home."

13. Musto, *The Catholic Peace Tradition*, 170–71.

14. This section depends on Richard P. McBrien, *Lives of the Popes: The Pontiffs from St. Peter to John Paul II* (San Francisco: HarperSanFrancisco, 1997), 353–56; and Musto, *The Catholic Peace Tradition*, 171–73.

15. In the midst of this horrific barbarity and suffering, there is the true story of the Christmas truce of 1914, when the two sides celebrated Christmas together at various places along the trench lines. This is dramatized in the movie *Merry Christmas* (originally *Joyeux Noël*, 2005), directed by Christian Carion. Two films that convey something of the conditions in the trenches in World War I are *All Quiet on the Western Front* (1930), directed by Lewis Milestone; and *A Very Long Engagement* (French, 2004), directed by Jean Pierre Jeunet.

16. This section depends on McBrien, *Lives of the Popes*, 358–63; and Musto, *The Catholic Peace Tradition*, 173–75.

17. The film *Schindler's List* (1993), directed by Steven Spielberg, movingly depicts the concentration camps. See also Elie Wiesel, *Night*, rev. ed. (New York: Hill and Wang, 2006). The Holocaust is a clear demonstration of the depravity, inhumanity, and evil of the Nazi regime (which was sponsored by a largely Christian nation) but it was not a cause of World War II. The extent of this horror came to light only after the war.

18. Musto, *The Catholic Peace Tradition*, 176.

19. John P. Langan, "The Christmas Messages of Pius XII (1939–1945): Catholic Social Teaching in a Time of Extreme Crisis," in *Modern Catholic Social Teaching*, ed. Kenneth R. Himes (Washington, D.C.: Georgetown University Press, 2005), 175–90, at 188–89.

20. McBrien, *Lives of the Popes*, 366.

21. Kenneth R. Himes, "War" in *The Dictionary of Catholic Social Thought*, ed. Kenneth R. Himes (Washington, D.C.: Georgetown University Press, 2005), 978.

22. Ibid., 978–79; Joseph Bernardin, "*The Challenge of Peace* Revisited," in *One Hundred Years of Catholic Social Thought: Celebration and Challenge*, ed. John A. Coleman (Maryknoll, N.Y.: Orbis Books, 1991), 278; J. Bryan Hehir, "The Just-War Ethic and Catholic Theology: Dynamics of Change and Continuity," in *War or Peace? The Search for New Answers*, ed. Thomas A. Shannon (Maryknoll, N.Y.: Orbis Books, 1980); Musto, *The Catholic Peace Tradition*, 185–86. See Pius XII, *Christmas Message of 1956*.

23. There are several films that dramatize the reality of World War II: *Saving Private Ryan* (1998), directed by Steven Spielberg; *Patton* (1970), directed by Franklin

Shaffner; *Das Boot* (German, 1981), directed by Wolfgang Petersen; *Flags of our Fathers* (2006), directed by Clint Eastwood; and *Letters from Iwo Jima* (2007), directed by Clint Eastwood.

24. Musto, *The Catholic Peace Tradition*, 178–79.

25. Ibid., 179–81. On the captivity to nationalism of the American Catholic church, see Todd D. Whitmore, "The Reception of Catholic Approaches to Peace and War in the United States," in *Modern Catholic Social Teaching*, ed. Kenneth R. Himes (Washington, D.C.: Georgetown University Press, 2005), 495–500.

26. Charles E. Moore, "Introduction," in Andre Trocmé, *Jesus and the Non-violent Revolution*, ed. Charles E. Moore, rev. exp. ed. (Maryknoll, N.Y.: Orbis Books, 2003), ix–xiv. See also Philip P. Hallie, *Lest Innocent Blood Be Shed: The Story of Le Chambon and How Goodness Happened There* (New York: Harper & Row, 1979), although Moore says that this influential book, while inspiring and informative, is not historically or biographically (regarding Trocmé) accurate.

27. Musto, *The Catholic Peace Tradition*, 181–82.

28. Thomas Merton, "A Martyr for Peace and Unity: Father Max Josef Metzger (1887–1944)," in *The Nonviolent Alternative*, ed. Gordon C. Zahn, rev. ed. (New York: Farrar, Straus, Giroux, 1980), 139–43; Robert Ellsberg, *All Saints: Daily Reflections on Saints, Prophets, and Witnesses for Our Time* (New York: Crossroad, 2001), 171–72.

29. Musto, *The Catholic Peace Tradition*, 182.

30. There is a vast literature about Bonhoeffer. For a brief introduction to his story see Mary Craig, *Six Modern Martyrs* (New York: Crossroad, 1985), 11–55; and Melanie Morrison, "Dietrich Bonhoeffer: Faith and Conviction," in *Cloud of Witnesses*, ed. Jim Wallis and Joyce Hollyday, rev. ed. (Maryknoll, N.Y.: Orbis Books, 2005), 261–65. There is a theological controversy about whether it is proper to call Bonhoeffer a martyr.

31. Ellsberg, *All Saints*, 350–51; and Craig, *Six Modern Martyrs*, 97–130.

32. Gordon Zahn, *In Solitary Witness: The Life and Death of Franz Jägerstätter* (Collegeville, Minn.: Liturgical Press, 1964, reissued 1977); and Zahn, *Franz Jägerstätter: Martyr for Conscience*, Pax Christi USA Peacemakers Pamphlet Series (Erie, Pa.: Benet Press, n.d.). See also Erna Putz, ed., *Franz Jägerstätter: Letters and Writings from Prison* (Maryknoll, N.Y.: Orbis Books, 2009).

33. See Thomas Merton, "An Enemy of the State," in *The Nonviolent Alternative*, ed. Gordon C. Zahn, rev. ed. (New York: Farrar, Straus, Giroux, 1980), 134–38.

34. See Gordon Zahn, *Another Part of the War: The Camp Simon Story* (Amherst: University of Massachusetts Press, 1979).

35. Gordon Zahn, *German Catholics and Hitler's Wars: A Study in Social Control* (New York: Sheed & Ward, 1962).

36. Christa Pongratz-Lippitt, "Hard History to Face," *The Tablet* 261 (October 20, 2007), 10–11; and John Thavis, "Austrian Killed in 1943 Beatified as Martyr," *The Record* (November 1, 2007), 5.

37. There are several films related to events during the Cold War and the threat of nuclear weapons: *Fat Man and Little Boy* (1989), directed by Roland Jaffe; *The Hunt for Red October* (1990), directed by John McTiernan; *Thirteen Days* (2000), directed by Roger Donaldson; *Testament* (1983), directed by Lynne Littman; *The Day After* (1983), directed by Nicholas Meyer; and *Dr. Strangelove or: How I Learned to Stop Worrying and Love the Bomb* (1964), directed by Stanley Kubrick.

38. Musto, *The Catholic Peace Tradition*, 195–209. Musto also tells the stories of Danilo Dolci in Italy and Lanzo Del Vasto in France. Both were impressive peacemakers who were inspired by Christianity and Catholicism.

39. Ira Chernus, *American Nonviolence: The History of an Idea* (Maryknoll, N.Y.: Orbis Books, 2004), 145.

40. Whitmore, "The Reception of Catholic Approaches to War and Peace," 502. There is a significant literature on Dorothy Day and the Catholic Worker Movement. See Dorothy Day, *The Long Loneliness: The Autobiography of Dorothy Day* (New York: Harper & Row, 1952); Eileen Egan, *Dorothy Day and the Permanent Revolution*, Pax Christi USA Peacemakers Pamphlet Series (Erie, Pa., Benet Press, 1983); Egan, *Peace Be with You*, chaps. 16, 17; Robert Ellsberg, ed., *By Little and by Little: The Selected Writings of Dorothy Day* (New York: Alfred A Knopf, 1983); and William D. Miller, *Dorothy Day: A Biography* (San Francisco: Harper & Row, 1982).

41. On Peter Maurin see his *Easy Essays* (Chicago: Franciscan Herald, 1984); and Marc H. Ellis, *Peter Maurin: Prophet in the Twentieth Century* (New York: Paulist Press, 1981).

42. Whitmore, "The Reception of Catholic Approaches to Peace and War," 503; and Musto, *The Catholic Peace Tradition*, 243–45. Patricia McNeal, *Harder Than War: Catholic Peacemaking in Twentieth-Century America* (New Brunswick, N.J.: Rutgers University Press, 1992), 47, says the circulation of the *Catholic Worker* dropped from 130,000 in 1939 to 50,500 by 1944.

43. Quotes taken from the *Hartford Catholic Worker* 17, no. 1 (Lent 2009), 9.

44. McNeal, *Harder Than War*, 46.

45. On conscientious objection, see Allman, *Who Would Jesus Kill?* 67–69. For the Catholic Church's position see Vatican II, *The Church in the Modern World*, #78–79; USCCB, "Declaration on Conscientious Objection and Selective Conscientious Objection" (1971); and *The Challenge of Peace*, #231–33.

46. The book was finally published in 2004, well after Merton's death in 1968. The account here is based on the Foreword by Jim Forest (ix–xviii) and the Introduction by Patricia A. Burton (xxxiii–xlii), who also edited the book (Thomas Merton, *Peace in the Post-Christian Era* [Maryknoll, N.Y.: Orbis Books, 2004]). See also James H. Forest, *Thomas Merton's Struggle with Peacemaking*, Pax Christi USA Peacemakers Pamphlet Series (Erie, Pa.: Benet Press, n.d.). Merton's essays related to peace were first published in *Faith and Violence: Christian Teaching and Christian Practice* (Notre Dame, Ind.: University of Notre Dame Press, 1968). Gordon Zahn included those essays in a collection of Merton's writings on peace titled *The Nonviolent Alternative*.

47. Jim Forest, a Catholic worker in close touch with Merton, says that Merton sent a mimeographed copy to Cardinal Montini, who became Pope Paul VI, and that it may have influenced Cardinal Ottaviani, who worked on the drafts for *The Pastoral Constitution of the Church in the Modern World*. Merton also corresponded with Pope John XXIII, but apparently not directly about the peace issue (Forest, Foreword, xiv–xviii).

48. McNeal, *Harder Than War*, chap. 5, offers this insightful interpretation of Merton's thought on war and peace.

49. In October 1962, the United States and the Soviet Union came to the brink of nuclear war over the deployment of Soviet missiles in Cuba. Pope John helped U.S.

President Kennedy and Soviet Premier Khrushchev step back from war and resolve the crisis.

50. Drew Christiansen, "Commentary on *Pacem in Terris (Peace on Earth)*," in *Modern Catholic Social Teaching*, ed. Kenneth R. Himes (Washington, D.C.: Georgetown University Press, 2005), 217, 223.

51. This section depends on Christiansen, "Commentary on *Pacem in Terris*," 227–32; and Musto, *The Catholic Peace Tradition*, 188. The relevant paragraphs in *Peace on Earth* are noted in parentheses after each point.

52. Christiansen, "Commentary on *Pacem in Terris*," 233.

53. Musto, *The Catholic Peace Tradition*, 252–53; Merton, "Christian Ethics and Nuclear War," *The Nonviolent Alternative*, 82–87.

54. Egan, *Peace Be with You*, chap. 10; Egan, *Dorothy Day and the Permanent Revolution*, 14–15; McNeal, *Harder Than War*, 96–104; and Miller, *Dorothy Day*, 480–81.

55. See John C. Ford, "The Morality of Obliteration Bombing," *Theological Studies* 5 (1944): 261–309, reprinted in *War in the Twentieth Century*, ed. Richard B. Miller (Louisville: Westminster John Knox Press, 1992). This issue is discussed by Whitmore, "The Reception of Catholic Approaches to War and Peace," 496–97.

56. See David Hollenbach, "Commentary on *Gaudium et Spes (Pastoral Constitution on the Church in the Modern World)*," in *Modern Catholic Social Teaching*, ed. Kenneth R. Himes (Washington, D.C.: Georgetown University Press, 2005), 280–84; and Musto, *The Catholic Peace Tradition*, 191–93.

57. Musto, *The Catholic Peace Tradition*, 193–95. John Paul II reiterates Paul VI's concern about violent revolution and his point about integral development as the basis for peace in his encyclical *On Social Concern*, #10, issued in 1987, the twentieth anniversary of *On the Development of Peoples*.

58. Dom Helder Camara, *The Desert Is Fertile*, trans. Dinah Livingstone (Maryknoll, N.Y.: Orbis Books, 1974), 41–42.

59. Helder Camara, *Spiral of Violence* (London: Sheed & Ward, 1971). See also Daniel M. Bell Jr., "A Question of Dominion: Religion, Violence, and the Latin American Liberationists," in *Conflict and Conciliation: Faith and Politics in an Age of Global Dissonance*, ed. Jason W. Daverth (Dublin: Columba Press, 2007), 205–26; and Thomas J. Gumbleton, "Peacemaking as a Way of Life" in *One Hundred Years of Catholic Social Thought: Celebration and Challenge*, ed. John A Coleman (Maryknoll, N.Y.: Orbis Books, 1991), 311–12.

60. Vickie Kemper and Larry Engel, "Dom Helder Camara: Hope against Hope," in *Cloud of Witnesses*, ed. Jim Wallis and Joyce Hollyday, rev. ed. (Maryknoll, N.Y.: Orbis Books, 2005), 207–15; Marjorie Hope and James Young, *The Struggle for Humanity: Agents of Nonviolent Change in a Violent World* (Maryknoll, N.Y.: Orbis Books, 1977), chap. 4; and Musto, *The Catholic Peace Tradition*, 224–28.

61. Musto, *The Catholic Peace Tradition*, chap. 14. Nelson Mandela received the Nobel Peace Prize jointly with Fredrik Willem De Klerk, then president of South Africa.

62. See J. Milburn Thompson, *Martin Luther King Jr. and the Dream of a Just Community*, rev. ed., Pax Christi USA Peacemakers Pamphlet Series (Erie, Pa.: Pax Christi USA, 2007).

63. Martin Luther King Jr., *Where Do We Go from Here: Chaos or Community?* (Boston: Beacon Press, 1967), 62–63.

64. Musto, *The Catholic Peace Tradition,* 253–59; see also McNeal, *Harder Than War,* chap. 7, on the Berrigans.

65. Musto, *The Catholic Peace Tradition,* 255–57. The draft law allowed for conscientious objection, but was never modified to allow for selective conscientious objection. By 1969, there were 2,494 Catholic COs among the 34,255 so classified, the largest percentage of all American religious groups (254). See also McNeal, *Harder Than War,* chap. 6.

66. Among many books see Stanley Karnow, *Vietnam: A History* (New York: Penguin Books, 1991). See also the PBS documentary *Vietnam: A Television History* (1983, 1997). Films related to Vietnam include: *Platoon* (1980), directed by Oliver Stone; *Good Morning Vietnam* (1987), directed by Barry Levison; and *Born on the Fourth of July* (1989), directed by Oliver Stone.

67. Musto, *The Catholic Peace Tradition,* 259.

68. This pastoral letter can be found in *Catholic Social Thought: The Documentary Heritage,* ed. O'Brien and Shannon, 492–571. I will use the paragraph numbers to refer to *The Challenge of Peace.*

69. McNeal, *Harder Than War,* 246–58, at 250. See also Jim Castelli, *The Bishops and the Bomb: Waging Peace in a Nuclear Age* (Garden City, N.Y.: Image Books, 1983), which tells the story of the development of the pastoral letter in detail.

70. The bishops themselves included an eight-page summary in the publication of the document distributed by the United States Catholic Conference (Washington, D.C.) in 1983. See also Joseph Bernardin, *"The Challenge of Peace Revisited,"* in *One Hundred Years of Catholic Social Thought: Celebration and Challenge,* ed. John A. Coleman (Maryknoll, N.Y.: Orbis Books, 1991), 279–82; Michael Hornsby-Smith, *An Introduction to Catholic Social Thought* (New York: Cambridge University Press, 2006), 293–98; Whitmore, "The Reception of Catholic Approaches to War and Peace," 506–18. For commentaries on and analysis of *The Challenge of Peace,* see *Catholics and Nuclear War: A Commentary on "The Challenge of Peace,"* ed. Philip J. Murnion (New York: Crossroad, 1983); and *Biblical and Theological Reflections on "The Challenge of Peace,"* ed. John T. Pawlikowski and Donald Senior (Wilmington, Del.: Michael Glazier, 1984). Both include the document.

71. See Donald Senior, "Jesus' Most Scandalous Teaching," in *Biblical and Theological Reflections,* ed. John T. Palikowski and Donald Senior *on "The Challenge of Peace,"* ed. John T. Pawlikowski and Donald Senior (Wilmington, Del.: Michael Glazier, 1984), 67.

72. Whitmore, "The Reception of Catholic Approaches to War and Peace," 509–10; and Sandra M. Schneiders, "New Testament Reflections on Peace and Nuclear Arms," in *Catholics and Nuclear War: A Commentary on "The Challenge of Peace,"* ed. Philip J. Murnion (New York: Crossroad, 1983), 91. From a Christian pacifist perspective the bishops have found a way *around* the Sermon on the Mount, and pacifists think Christians should go *through* the Sermon on the Mount. Contrast the bishops' approach to scripture with that of American Baptist theologian Glen Stassen in chaps. 2 and 3 of his *Just Peacemaking: Transforming Initiatives for Justice and Peace* (Louisville: Westminster John Knox Press, 1992). As the charts on pp. 44–45, 56–57 demonstrate, Stassen, who is not a pacifist, finds specific directions and strategies for peacemaking in scripture.

73. Kenneth R. Himes, "Pacifism and the Just War Tradition in Roman Catholic Social Teaching," in *One Hundred Years of Catholic Social Thought: Celebration and Challenge,* ed. John A. Coleman (Maryknoll, N.Y.: Orbis Books, 1991), 338.

Himes begins his analysis by properly noting the pluralism of both pacifist and just war positions. Catholic social teaching affirms active nonviolent resistance, not nonresistance.

74. This is not new in Christian tradition. One of the ways that nonviolence was kept alive in the Christian community after Constantine was by including it in the vocation of clerics and religious. See Fahey, *War and Christian Conscience,* 45–47. Here it is a vocational possibility for clergy and laity alike.

75. Himes, "Pacifism and the Just War Tradition," 339–42.

76. Bernardin, "*The Challenge of Peace* Revisited," 280; and David Hollenbach, "*The Challenge of Peace* in the Context of Recent Church Teachings," in *Catholics and Nuclear War,* ed. Philip J. Murnion (New York: Crossroad, 1983), 11–12.

77. Bruce M. Russett, "The Doctrine of Deterrence," in *Catholics and Nuclear War,* ed. Philip J. Murnion (New York: Crossroad, 1983), 164. Russett, a political scientist at Yale, was a consultant to the bishops committee that produced *The Challenge of Peace.*

78. See Richard McCormick's suggested prudential wording for the bishops in his "Nuclear Deterrence and the Problem of Intention: A Review of the Positions," in *Catholics and Nuclear War,* ed. Philip J. Murnion (New York: Crossroad, 1983), 179–80. See also David Hollenbach, *Nuclear Ethics: A Christian Moral Argument* (New York: Paulist Press, 1983), chap. 6, esp. 83–85, for a similar prudential argument.

79. Available at the website of the United States Conference of Catholic Bishops, *www.usccb.org.* Also reprinted in *Origins* 23, no. 26 (December 9, 1993): 449–64.

80. This section on John Paul II and the U.S. bishops relies on Whitmore, "The Reception of Catholic Approaches to Peace and War," 513–18.

81. All of the World Day of Peace messages (1968–present) and most of the less formal statements of the popes are available on the website for the Holy See, *www.vatican.va.*

82. John Paul II, "Address to the Diplomatic Corps, January 13, 2003" (Vatican website). Also in *Origins* 32, no. 33 (January 30, 2003): 543–45, at 544.

83. See the section "Restraining Nationalism and Eliminating Religious Violence," in *The Harvest of Justice Is Sown In Peace.*

84. Whitmore, "The Reception of Catholic Approaches to Peace and War," 515.

85. Three theologians suggest something similar. They compare John Paul II's position on the death penalty — that it is forbidden in practice — to his position on war. See Drew Christiansen, "Whither the Just War?" *America* 188 (March 24, 2003): 7–11, at 11; Niall O'Brien, "War — *The* Moral Issue," *The Furrow* 54 (2003): 529–33, at 533; and John Sniegocki, "Catholic Teaching on War, Peace, and Nonviolence since Vatican II," in *Vatican II: Forty Years Later,* ed. William Madges, *College Theology Society Annual Volume* 51 (2005) (Maryknoll, N.Y.: Orbis Books, 2006), 224–44, at 237.

86. Eileen P. Flynn, *How Just Is the War on Terror?* includes a list of suspected Al Qaeda terrorist bombings on 105–6.

87. Patrick T. McCormick, "Violence: Religion, Terror, War," *Theological Studies* 67 (March 2006): 150–57.

88. Edward LeRoy Long, *Facing Terrorism: Responding as Christians* (Louisville: Westminster John Knox Press, 2004), 19–26, 41–42, 50–60; and J. Milburn

Thompson, "Just Peacemaking and the Bush Doctrine: A Moral Analysis of Preemptive War," in *Conflict and Conciliation: Faith and Politics in an Age of Global Dissonance,* ed. Jason W. Daverth (Dublin: Columba Press, 2007), 77–80.

89. James Burtchaell, "A Moral Response to Terrorism," in his *The Giving and Taking of Life: Essays Ethical* (Notre Dame, Ind.: University of Notre Dame Press, 1989), 213–28; J. Milburn Thompson, *Justice and Peace: A Christian Primer,* rev. ed. (Maryknoll, N.Y.: Orbis Books, 2003), 143–46.

90. The president of the USCCB at the time, Bishop Wilton D. Gregory, wrote President Bush a letter on behalf of the USCCB on September 13, 2002, and again on February 26, 2003. The USCCB as a whole made a similar statement on November 13, 2002, at its annual fall meeting. The bishops concluded that a preemptive, unilateral use of force was difficult to justify on the basis of the conditions for a just war. The USCCB has continued to address this issue. See, for example, the statement of Bishop William S. Skylstad on November 13, 2007. These statements are available on the website of the USCCB. The Vatican even sent Cardinal Pio Laghi, an old friend of the Bush family, to try to personally dissuade President Bush from his plan to invade Iraq, to no effect.

91. Kenneth R. Himes, "Intervention, Just War, and U.S. National Security," *Theological Studies* 65 (March 2004): 150–52; McCormick, "Violence," 159–60; and David P. Gushee, "Just War Divide: One Tradition, Two Views," *Christian Century* 119 (August 14–22, 2002): 26–28.

92. For example, Richard B. Miller argues that there is a presumption against war in Aquinas in "Aquinas and the Presumption against Killing and War," *Journal of Religion* 82 (2002): 173–204. Indeed the question Aquinas addresses is "Is it always a sin to wage war?" Gregory M. Reichberg argues the opposite in "Is There a 'Presumption against War' in Aquinas' Ethics?" *Thomist* 66, no. 3 (2002): 337–67. See McCormick, "Violence," 159. Gushee, "Just War Divide," 28, states that there is no presumption against war in classic just war theory, but does not provide any evidence.

93. *The National Security Strategy of the United States* (2002) is available at *www.whitehouse.gov/nsc/nss* or *www.globalsecurity.org.* The policy on preemption is in section V.

94. See George W. Bush, "Speech to the Nation on the Invasion of Iraq, March 17, 2003," *New York Times* (March 18, 2003), A10.

95. Himes, "Intervention," 144–50; Jeffrey Record, "The Bush Doctrine and the War with Iraq," *Parameters* 33 (2003): 4–22; J. Milburn Thompson, "Just Peacemaking and the Bush Doctrine," in *Conflict and Conciliation: Faith and Politics in an Age of Global Dissonance,* ed. Jason W. Daverth (Dublin: Columba Press, 2007), 76–93.

96. Hanigan, *War and the Christian Conscience,* 101. See also p. 72.

97. Michael Schuck, "When the Shooting Stops: Missing Elements in Just War Theory," *Christian Century* 101 (October 26, 1994): 982–84.

98. See, for example, Brian Orend, "Justice after War," *Ethics and International Affairs* 16 (2002): 43–56; Himes, "Intervention," 154–56; and Mark J. Allman, "Postwar Justice," *America* 193 (October 17, 2005): 9–13. Kenneth Himes gave a paper on "Renewing a Tradition: The Development of *Jus Post Bellum,*" at the 2007 Annual Convention of the Catholic Theological Society of America, which is summarized by Brian Berry in the *CTSA Proceedings* 62, ed. Jonathan Y. Tan (2007): 125. Mark Allman and Tobias Winright, "*Jus Post Bellum:* Extending the Just War

Theory," in *Faith in Public Life*, ed. William Collinge, *College Theology Society Annual Volume* 53 (2007), 241–64. Allman also addressed *jus post bellum* criteria in *Who Would Jesus Kill?* 233–39, and he and Tobias Winright are writing a book on the topic forthcoming from Orbis Books.

99. Maureen O'Connell, "*Jus Ante Bellum*: Faith-Based Diplomacy as an Emergent Trajectory of the Just War Tradition," presented at the 2007 Annual Convention of the CTSA, summarized by Brian Berry in the *CTSA Proceedings* 62 (2007): 124.

100. Glen H. Stassen, *Just Peacemaking: Transforming Initiatives for Justice and Peace* (Louisville: Westminster John Knox Press, 1992).

101. Glen Stassen, ed., *Just Peacemaking: Ten Practices for Abolishing War*, rev. ed. (Cleveland: Pilgrim Press, 2004, 2008). The group of twenty-three included Christian ethicists, biblical and moral theologians, international relations scholars, peace activists, and conflict resolution practitioners. At least three of them are Catholic: peace activist Patricia McCullough, political scientist Bruce Russett (a consultant for *The Challenge of Peace*), and Jesuit moral theologian John Langan. Stassen later explained that the subtitle of the book was chosen by the publisher, not the group, which is under no illusion that these ten practices will abolish war. See Glen H. Stassen, "The Unity, Realism, and Obligatoriness of Just Peacemaking Theory," *Journal of the Society of Christian Ethics* 23, no. 1 (Spring–Summer 2003): 171–94, at 180. Indeed the subtitle of the 2008 revision of *Just Peacemaking* is *The New Paradigm for the Ethics of Peace and War*. For further references to just peacemaking see Theodore J. Koontz and Michael L. Westmoreland-White, "A Just Peacemaking Bibliography," in ibid., 269–84.

102. Stassen, "The Unity, Realism, and Obligatoriness," and Duane Friesen, John Langan, and Glen Stassen, "Introduction: Just Peacemaking as a New Ethic," in *Just Peacemaking: Ten Practices for Abolishing War* (Cleveland: Pilgrim Press, 2004), 1–30.

103. Lisa Sowle Cahill, "Just Peacemaking: Theory, Practice, and Prospects," *Journal of the Society of Christian Ethics* 23, no. 1 (Spring–Summer 2003): 195–212.

104. Martin L. Cook, "Just Peacemaking: Challenges of Humanitarian Intervention," *Journal of the Society of Christian Ethics* 23, no. 1 (Spring–Summer 2003): 240–53; and Ronald H. Stone, "Realist Criticism of Just Peacemaking Theory," ibid., 255–67.

105. Tobias Winright, "What Might a Policing Approach Contribute to the Pacifist/Just-War Debate on Dealing with Terrorism?" in *Conflict and Conciliation: Faith and Politics in an Age of Global Dissonance*, ed. Jason W. Daverth (Dublin: Columba Press, 2007), 39–69; Gerald Schlabach, "Just Policing, Not War," *America* 189 (July 7–14, 2003): 19–21; and Gerald W. Schlabach, ed., *Just Policing, Not War* (Collegeville, Minn.: Liturgical Press, 2007), which has three articles by Schlabach, one by Winright, and one by Glen Stassen, among others, and a substantial bibliography.

Chapter 5: A Consistent Ethic of Life and Care for the Earth

1. This section about John Timothy Leary is based on Gordon C. Zahn et al., *John Timothy Leary: A Different Sort of Hero*, Pax Christi USA Peacemakers Pamphlet Series (Erie, Pa.: Pax Christi USA, 983).

2. This portrait of Cardinal Bernardin is based on John P. Langan, "Introduction," in Joseph Cardinal Bernardin, *A Moral Vision for America,* ed. John P. Langan (Washington, D.C.: Georgetown University Press, 1998), 2–3.

3. Thomas A. Nairn briefly tells the story of the birth of the consistent ethic of life framework at the Gannon Lecture in his "Introduction" to *The Consistent Ethic of Life: Assessing Its Reception and Relevance* (Maryknoll, N.Y.: Orbis Books, 2008), xi–xiii. Cardinal Bernardin worked with Fr. J. Bryan Hehir on the Gannon Lecture, and later with Frs. Alphonse Spilly and Michael Place in developing his thought on the consistent ethic of life. *The Consistent Ethic of Life* is a collection of ten essays on the topic collaboratively produced by ten top scholars over a three-year period and edited by Nairn.

There are three collections of Cardinal Joseph Bernardin's presentations related to a consistent ethic of life. The first, *The Consistent Ethic of Life,* ed. Thomas G. Fuechtmann (Kansas City: Sheed & Ward, 1988) is based on a symposium on the topic at Loyola University in Chicago. It includes ten of Bernardin's talks to that point in time, four major academic presentations by Richard A. McCormick, John C. Finnis, James M. Gustafson, and J. Bryan Hehir, with briefer responses to each by Franz Jozef van Beeck, James J. Walter, Lisa Sowle Cahill, and Sidney Callahan. There is a response to the conference by Cardinal Bernardin. The second collection *A Moral Vision for America* is edited and introduced by John P. Langan. The fifteen addresses assembled by Langan span the whole of Bernardin's ministry. The most recent and most complete is Joseph L. Bernardin, *The Seamless Garment: Writings on the Consistent Ethic of Life,* ed. Thomas A. Nairn (Maryknoll, N.Y.: Orbis Books, 2008), with an Introduction by Thomas A. Shannon. There are, however, a few pieces in the Langan collection that are not included in the thirty-five presented by Nairn. Fr. Alphonse Spilly has edited a broader collection of Cardinal Bernardin's works, *Selected Works of Joseph Cardinal Bernardin,* 2 vols. (Collegeville, Minn.: Liturgical Press, 2000).

4. Bernardin, *The Seamless Garment: Assessing Its Reception and Relevance* (Maryknoll, N.Y.: Orbis Books, 2008), 296. Emphasis in the original.

5. Ibid. "A Consistent Ethic of Life," December 6, 1983, 13.

6. See Bernardin, "Faithful and Hopeful: The Catholic Common Ground Project," in *A Moral Vision for America,* ed. John P. Langan (Washington, D.C.: Georgetown University Press, 1998), 158–68; and Catholic Common Ground Project, "Called to Be Catholic: Church in Time of Peril," *Origins* 26 (August 29, 1996): 165–70.

7. This section depends on Marvin L. Krier Mich, *Catholic Social Teaching and Movements* (Mystic, Conn.: Twenty-Third Publications, 2000), 210–18.

8. For an obituary of Eileen Egan, see Patrick Jordan, "Go in Peace: Remembering Eileen Egan," *Commonweal* 127 (November 17, 2000): 6–7. Egan was also a writer. She recounts her experiences of working with refugees in *For Whom There Is No Room: Scenes from the Refugee World* (New York: Paulist Press, 1995). Her biography of Mother Teresa is titled *Such a Vision of the Street* (Garden City, N.Y.: Doubleday, 1985). Her case for Christian nonviolence is presented in *Peace Be with You: Justified Warfare or the Way of Nonviolence* (Maryknoll, N.Y.: Orbis Books, 1999).

9. The story is recounted by Mich, *Catholic Social Teaching and Movements,* 210–11, citing Margaret O'Brien Steinfels, "Consider the Seamless Garment," in

Abortion and Catholicism: The American Debate, ed. Patricia Jung and Thomas Shannon (New York: Crossroad, 1988), 268.

10. Mich, *Catholic Social Teaching and Movements,* 212, citing Humberto Medeiros, "A Call to a Consistent Ethic of Life and the Law," *Pilot* (July 10, 1971): 7. Nairn points out that Fr. J. Bryan Hehir collaborated with Archbishop Medeiros on his essay and with Cardinal Bernardin on his Gannon Lecture. See Nairn, Introduction to *A Consistent Ethic of Life: Assessing Its Reception and Relevance* (Maryknoll, N.Y.: Orbis Books, 2008), xii.

11. Sidney Callahan, "Abortion and the Sexual Agenda: A Case for Pro-Life Feminism," *Commonweal* 123 (April 25, 1986): 232–38.

12. See *www.feministsforlife.org.* As far as I am aware, Cardinal Bernardin did not make women's rights the focus of any of his three dozen addresses on the consistent ethic.

13. See *www.consistent-life.org.*

14. See Gordon C. Zahn, "A Religious Pacifist Looks at Abortion," *Commonweal* (May 28, 1971): 279–82.

15. Cardinal Joseph Bernardin recognized that the substance of the consistent ethic was consistent with Christian tradition and contemporary Catholic teaching. See, for example, his "The Consistent Ethic of Life (February 23, 1995)," in *The Seamless Garment,* 259–60. Mich develops this point in *Catholic Social Teaching and Movements,* chap. 8.

16. See Timothy A. Byrnes, "How Seamless a Garment? The Catholic Bishops and the Politics of Abortion," *Journal of Church and State* 33 (Winter 1991): 17–36, for a discussion of the consistent ethic of life in the political responsibility statements of the U.S. bishops and in U.S. presidential politics.

17. Unfortunately this document is no longer available on the USCCB website. It is discussed by Mich, *Catholic Social Teaching and Movements,* 235–37.

18. Ibid., 443, n. 49.

19. This report of the press conference is taken from the blog of John L. Allen, senior correspondent for the *National Catholic Reporter* and biographer of Pope Benedict XVI. See also John L. Allen, "Deft Timing for *Caritas in Veritate,*" *National Catholic Reporter* 45 (July 24, 2009): 6–7, on the link between pro-life and peace and justice issues in the encyclical.

20. Indeed, this position is currently so deeply entrenched in the teaching of the church that it seems to function as a litmus test for a man to be appointed a bishop. Thus it becomes self-perpetuating.

21. Margaret Farley argues that the church suffers from a credibility gap on the issue of abortion and that placing it at the center of its political agenda is counterproductive in "The Church in the Public Forum: Scandal or Prophetic Witness," in *The Catholic Church, Morality and Politics: Readings in Moral Theology No. 12,* ed. Charles E. Curran and Leslie Griffin (New York: Paulist Press, 2001), 205–23.

22. Bernardin, "Post Webster Reflections on the Consistent Ethic of Life," in *The Seamless Garment,* 187; John Paul II, *The Gospel of Life,* #58–59.

23. Patricia Beattie Jung, "Constructing a Consistent Ethic of Life," in *The Consistent Ethic of Life: Assessing Its Reception and Relevance,* ed. Thomas A. Nairn (Maryknoll, N.Y.: Orbis Books, 2008), 61–78.

24. See ibid.; Christine Gudorf, "To Make a Seamless Garment, Use a Single Piece of Cloth," *Cross Currents* 34 (Winter, 1984): 473–91; Rosemary Radford Ruether,

"Consistent Life Ethic Is Inconsistent," *National Catholic Reporter* 43 (November 17, 2006): 13–16; Patricia Beattie Jung, "Constructing a Consistent Ethic of Life: Feminist Contributions to Its Foundation," in *The Consistent Ethic of Life: Assessing Its Reception and Relevance,* ed. Thomas A. Nairn (Maryknoll, N.Y.: Orbis Books, 2008), 61–78; and the articles by McCormick and Walters in *Consistent Ethic of Life,* ed. Thomas G. Fuechtmann (Kansas City: Sheed & Ward, 1988), who argue for a proportionalist ethical method, and by Finnis, who defends moral absolutes. Bernardin points out that the church has not accepted proportionalism. Indeed, John Paul II also argues for moral absolutes, not only in *The Gospel of Life,* but also in *The Splendor of Truth (Veritatis Splendor),* 1993, chap. 2, esp. #76–83.

25. See Michael Pakaluk, "A Cardinal Error: Does the Seamless Garment Make Sense?" *The Catholic Church, Morality, and Politics,* ed. Charles E. Curran and Leslie Griffin (New York: Paulist Press, 2001), 196–204.

26. J. Bryan Hehir, "The Consistent Ethic of Life: Public Policy Implications," in *Consistent Ethic of Life,* ed. Thomas G. Fuechtmann (Kansas City: Sheed & Ward, 1988), 228. Cardinal Bernardin himself says, "In recent decades, however, the presumptions against taking human life have been strengthened and the exceptions made ever more restrictive." in *The Seamless Garment: Assessing Its Reception and Relevance,* ed. Thomas A. Nairn (Maryknoll, N.Y.: Orbis Books, 2008), 261.

27. John C. Finnis, "The Consistent Ethic: A Philosophical Critique," in *Consistent Ethic of Life,* ed. Thomas G. Fuechtmann (Kansas City: Sheed & Ward, 1988), 157–67.

28. The USCCB explicitly acknowledges this difference between principles and policies in *The Challenge of Peace* (#8–12) and *Economic Justice for All* (#20). I am not aware of this distinction being made in statements on abortion and related matters.

29. Hehir, "The Consistent Ethic of Life," 227–31.

30. Mich, *Catholic Social Teaching and Movements,* 233–34.

31. Farley, "The Church in the Public Forum," 205–23, at 209–10; Cathleen Kaveny, "The 'New' Feminism? John Paul II and the 1912 Encyclopedia," *Commonweal* (March 28, 2008), 8; and Richard A. McCormick, "The Consistent Ethic of Life: Is There an Historical Soft Underbelly?" in *Consistent Ethic of Life,* ed. Thomas G. Fuechtmann (Kansas City: Sheed & Ward, 1988), 104–5.

32. Bernardin, *The Seamless Garment,* 261.

33. Bernardin, "The Consistent Ethic of Life: Stage Two," *Consistent Ethic of Life,* ed. Thomas G. Fuechtmann (Kansas City: Sheed & Ward, 1988), 250. See James M. Gustafson, "The Consistent Ethic of Life: A Protestant Response," in ibid., 204–5.

34. Farley, "The Church in the Public Forum," 215–18; and Sidney Callahan, "Response to J. Bryan Hehir," in *Consistent Ethic of Life,* ed. Thomas G. Fuechtmann (Kansas City: Sheed & Ward, 1988), 243.

35. Hehir, "The Consistent Ethic of Life," 224–26.

36. Franz Jozef van Beeck, "Weaknesses in the Consistent Ethic of Life? Some Systematic Theological Observations," in *Consistent Ethic of Life,* 131–34, makes this point. This is also an emphasis of those who bring a commitment to nonviolence as the basis of a consistent ethic, such as John Timothy Leary, Dorothy Day, Gordon Zahn, Eileen Egan, and the Protestant theologian Stanley Hauerwas.

37. There is a certain logic to the connection Benedict XVI makes among life issues, environmental responsibility, and integral development and between human ecology and environmental ecology, yet it is not self-evident.

38. There are two biographies of Dorothy Stang: Binka Le Breton, *The Greatest Gift: The Courageous Life and Martyrdom of Sister Dorothy Stang* (New York: Doubleday, 2008) and Roseanne Murphy, *Martyr of the Amazon: The Life of Sister Dorothy Stang* (Maryknoll, N.Y.: Orbis Books, 2007). This account relies on these two books.

39. "The Americas: A Martyr for the Amazon: Dorothy Stang," *The Economist* 374 (February 19, 2005): 56.

40. J. Milburn Thompson, *Justice and Peace: A Christian Primer* (Maryknoll, N.Y.: Orbis Books, 2003), 73–74.

41. Murphy, *Martyr of the Amazon,* 95–97; Le Breton, *The Greatest Gift,* 127–36.

42. Murphy, *Martyr of the Amazon,* 100–101; Marvin L. Krier Mich, *The Challenge and Spirituality of Catholic Social Teaching* (Louisville: JustFaith, Inc., 2005), 35–36.

43. On Dorothy's stubbornness and obstinancy regarding justice for the poor and care for the earth see Le Breton, *The Greatest Gift,* 108, 168, 187–88.

44. Murphy, *Martyr of the Amazon,* 122; Le Breton, *The Greatest Gift,* 189. The two gunmen, the intermediary, and one of the ranchers who ordered Dorothy murdered are serving long jail terms. The other rancher was brought to trial in 2009.

45. Le Breton, *The Greatest Gift,* 111.

46. Perhaps the first serious environmental statement from the Vatican is in *Justice in the World* (Synod of Bishops, 1971), par. 11. In *Redeemer of Man* (*Redemptor Hominis,* 1979) Pope John Paul II summarized his humanism, which becomes the foundation of the church's environmental ethic, and expressed his fear of human regression, including environmental degradation (#15–16). John Paul II addressed the environment in a fairly serious way in *On Social Concern* (1987), #34. His World Day of Peace message in 1990, *The Ecological Crisis: A Common Responsibility* (also referred to as *Peace with God the Creator, Peace with All of Creation*) is the most substantial papal statement on ecology. In 2002, John Paul II issued a brief *Common Declaration on the Environment* with Bartholomew I, the patriarch of Constantinople. The *Compendium of the Social Doctrine of the Church* by the Pontifical Council for Justice and Peace (2004) addressed "Safeguarding the Environment" in chap. 10, #197–208. Pope Benedict XVI addressed the environment in *Charity in Truth* (2009), #48–51, and the Vatican announced that Benedict's World Day of Peace Message for 2010 will focus on the environment. All of these documents are available on the Vatican website, *www.vatican.va.*

For a discussion of the development of this teaching see Marvin L. Krier Mich, *Catholic Social Teaching and Movements* (Mystic, Conn.: Twenty-third Publications, 1998), 385–95; Pamela Smith, *What Are They Saying about Environmental Ethics* (New York: Paulist Press, 1997), 79–84; and Michael Hornsby-Smith, *An Introduction to Catholic Social Thought* (Cambridge: Cambridge University Press, 2006), 249–52. On Benedict XVI see Woodeene Koenig-Bricker, *Ten Commandments for the Environment: Pope Benedict XVI Speaks Out for Creation and Justice* (Notre Dame, Ind.: Ave Maria Press, 2009).

The Catholic bishops of the Philippines published a significant statement on the environment in *What Is Happening to Our Beautiful Land* in 1988. The United

States Conference of Catholic Bishops (USCCB) published *Renewing the Earth* in 1991. These documents, and statements by the Catholic Bishops of Australia, Dominican Republic, Guatemala, and northern Italy are reprinted in *And God Saw That It Was Good: Catholic Theology and the Environment,* ed. Drew Christiansen and Walter Grazer (Washington, D.C.: United States Catholic Conference, 1996). This volume also includes John Paul II's *The Ecological Crisis* (1990). The USCCB has also published *Global Climate Change: A Plea for Dialogue, Prudence, and the Common Good* (2001). Twelve U.S. and Canadian bishops in the northwest area of North America published a pastoral letter titled *The Columbia River Watershed: Caring for Creation and the Common Good* in early 2001. It can be found in *Origins* 30 (March 8, 2001): 609–19. On the importance of responding to environmental issues on both a bioregional and a planetary level, see Drew Christiansen, "Catholic Environmentalism," in *We Hold These Truths: Catholicism and American Public Life,* ed. Richard W. Miller (St. Louis: Liguori Publications, 2008), 94–97.

47. See Koenig-Bricker, *Ten Commandments for the Environment,* 6, 33–37, passim; and Sean McDonagh, *To Care for the Earth: A Call to a New Theology* (Santa Fe, N.Mex.: Bear & Company, 1986), 119, 125–28. Scripture references that indicate the redemption of all of creation include Colossians 1:20, 3:11, Ephesians 1:8–12, and Romans 8:18–23.

48. The USCCB's *Renewing the Earth* explicitly refers to the principles of Catholic social teaching, and John Paul II implicitly does so in *The Ecological Crisis.*

49. See the *Compendium of the Social Doctrine of the Church,* #171–84.

50. John Paul II, *The Ecological Crisis,* #9.

51. Drew Christiansen, "Ecology and the Common Good: Catholic Social Teaching and Environmental Responsibility," in *And God Saw That It Was Good,* ed. Drew Christiansen and Walter Grazer (Washington, D.C.: United States Catholic Conference, 1996), 183–95, at 191.

52. John Paul II, *The Ecological Crisis,* #6.

53. As I write this, Bellarmine University, where I teach, is implementing a project to use geo-thermal wells to heat and cool several buildings, and Bellarmine is establishing an Environmental Studies program. My parish, St. Francis of Assisi in Louisville, has an active environmental committee.

54. Lynn White, "The Historical Roots of Our Ecological Crisis," *Science* 155, no. 3767 (March 10, 1967): 1203–7.

55. See, for example, Anne M. Clifford, "Foundations for a Catholic Ecological Theology of God," in *And God Saw That It Was Good,* ed. Drew Christiansen and Walter Grazer (Washington, D.C.: USCCB, 1996), 19–46, at 24–28.

56. Michael J. Himes and Kenneth R. Himes, *Fullness of Faith: the Public Significance of Theology* (New York: Paulist Press, 1993), 104–24, at 108–10. On mutuality see Dawn M. Nothwehr, "From Ontology, Ecology, and Normativity to Mutuality: The Attitude and Principle Grounding the Ethic of Life," in *The Consistent Ethic of Life: Assessing Its Reception and Relevance,* ed. Thomas A. Nairn (Maryknoll, N.Y.: Orbis Books, 2008), 132–51.

57. Martin Buber, *I and Thou,* trans. Walter Kaufman (New York: Charles' Scribner's Sons, 1970).

58. Thomas Aquinas seems to be another source for this relational environmental ethic. See Christine Firer Hinze, "Catholic Social Teaching and Ecological Ethics," in *And God Saw That It Was Good,* ed. Drew Christiansen and Walter Grazer (Washington, D.C.: USCCB, 1996), 172–73.

59. See Koenig-Bricker, *Ten Commandments for the Environment,* 139–40.
60. Hinze, "Catholic Social Teaching and Ecological Ethics," 169.
61. Himes and Himes, *Fullness of Faith,* 124.
62. Thompson, *Justice and Peace,* 63, 68, 88–90.
63. Himes and Himes, *Fullness of Faith,* 119–22.

Chapter 6: Conclusion

1. See Donal Dorr, *Option for the Poor: A Hundred Years of Vatican Social Teaching,* rev. ed. (Maryknoll, N.Y.: Orbis Books, 1992), chap. 14, for a similar project.

2. For other examples of development in Catholic social teaching, see Charles E. Curran, *Catholic Social Teaching, 1891–Present: A Historical, Theological, and Ethical Analysis* (Washington, D.C.: Georgetown University Press, 2002), chap. 6.

3. Michael P. Hornsby-Smith, *An Introduction to Catholic Social Thought* (New York: Cambridge University Press, 2006), 183–84, passim.

4. The downside to this moderation in Catholic social teaching is that it is difficult for the church to take prophetic stands when called for.

Selected Bibliography
on Catholic Social Thought

Abbott, Walter M., ed. *The Documents of Vatican II*. New York: America Press, 1966.

Allen, John L. "Deft Timing for *Caritas in Veritate*." *National Catholic Reporter* 45 (July 24, 2009), 6–7.

Allman, Mark J. "Postwar Justice." *America* 193 (October 17, 2005): 9–13.

Allman, Mark J. *Who Would Jesus Kill? War, Peace, and the Christian Tradition*. Winona, Minn.: Saint Mary's Press, 2008.

Au, William A. *The Cross, the Flag, and the Bomb: American Catholics Debate War and Peace, 1960–1983*. Westport, Conn.: Greenwood Press, 1985.

Aubert, Jean Marie. "Human Rights: Challenges to the Churches." *Theology Digest* 33, no. 1 (1986): 139–42.

Aubert, Roger. *Catholic Social Teaching: An Historical Perspective*, rev. ed. Milwaukee, Wis.: Marquette University Press, 2005.

Bainton, Roland H. *Christian Attitudes toward War and Peace: A Historical Survey and Critical Re-Evaluation*. Nashville: Abingdon, 1960.

Baum, Gregory. *Compassion and Solidarity: The Church for Others*. 1987 Massey Lectures. New York: Paulist Press, 1990.

Beigel, Gerard. *Faith and Social Justice in the Teaching of Pope John Paul II*. New York: Peter Lang Publishing, Inc., 2000.

Bernardin, Joseph L. *A Moral Vision for America*, ed. John P. Langan. Washington, D.C.: Georgetown University Press, 1998.

———. *The Seamless Garment: Writings on the Consistent Ethic of Life*, ed. Thomas A. Nairn. Maryknoll, N.Y.: Orbis Books, 2008.

Berryman, Phillip. *Our Unfinished Business: The U.S. Catholic Bishops' Letters on Peace and the Economy*. New York: Pantheon Books, 1989.

Bilgrien, Marie Vianney. *Solidarity: A Principle, an Attitude, a Duty? Or the Virtue for an Independent World?* New York: Peter Lang Publishing, Inc., 1999.

Boff, Leonardo. *Saint Francis: A Model for Human Liberation*. New York: Crossroad, 1982.

Boff, Leonardo and Clodovis Boff, *Introducing Liberation Theology*. Maryknoll, N.Y.: Orbis Books, 1986, 1987.

Boswell, J. S., F. P. McHugh, and J. Verstraeten, eds. *Catholic Social Thought: Twilight or Renaissance?* Leuven: Leuven University Press, 2000.

Brackley, Dean. *Divine Revolution: Salvation and Liberation in Catholic Thought*. Maryknoll, N.Y.: Orbis Books, 1996.

Brady, Bernard V., *Essential Catholic Social Thought*. Maryknoll, N.Y.: Orbis Books, 2008.

Brubaker, Pamela K., Rebecca Todd Peters, and Laura A. Stivers, eds. *Justice in a Global Economy: Strategies for Home, Community, and Work*. Louisville: Westminster John Knox Press, 2006.

Burtchaell, James. *The Giving and Taking of Life: Essays Ethical*. Notre Dame, Ind.: University of Notre Dame Press, 1989.

Byrnes, Timothy A. "How Seamless a Garment?" *Journal of Church and State* 33 (Winter 1991): 17–36.

Cadoux, C. John. *The Early Christian Attitude to War: A Contribution to the History of Christian Ethics*. New York: Seabury Press, 1982.

Cahill, Lisa Sowle. "Feminist Ethics and the Challenge of Culture." *Proceedings of the Catholic Theological Society of America* 48 (1993): 65–83.

Cahill, Lisa Sowle. "Just Peacemaking: Theory, Practice, and Prospects." *Journal of the Society of Christian Ethics* 23, no. 1 (Spring–Summer 2003): 195–212.

———. *Love Your Enemies: Discipleship, Pacifism, and Just War Theory*. Minneapolis, Minn.: Fortress Press, 1994.

Callahan, Sidney. "Abortion and the Sexual Agenda: A Case for Pro-Life Feminism." *Commonweal* 123 (April 25, 1986): 232–38.

Camara, Helder. *The Desert Is Fertile*. Trans. Dinah Livingstone. Maryknoll, N.Y.: Orbis Books, 1974.

———. *Spiral of Violence*. London: Sheed & Ward, 1971.

Catechism of the Catholic Church, ed. Pope John Paul II and United States Catholic Conference, 2nd ed. Washington, D.C.: United States Catholic Conference, 2000.

Cavanaugh, William T. *Being Consumed: Economics and Christian Desire*. Grand Rapids, Mich.: William B. Eerdmans, 2008.

Charles, Roger. *Christian Social Witness and Teaching: The Catholic Tradition from Genesis to Centesimus Annus*. Vol. 1: *From Biblical Times to the Late Nineteenth Century*; Vol. 2: *The Modern Social Teaching: Contexts, Summaries, Analysis*. Leominster: Gracewing, 1998.

Charles, Roger. *An Introduction to Catholic Social Teaching*. San Francisco: Ignatius Press, 2000.

Chernus, Ira. *American Nonviolence: The History of an Idea*. Maryknoll, N.Y.: Orbis Books, 2004.

Christiansen, Drew. "Whither the Just War?" *America* 188 (March 24, 2003): 7–11.

Christiansen, Drew, and Walter Grazer, eds. *And God Saw That It Was Good: Catholic Theology and the Environment*. Washington, D.C.: United States Catholic Conference, 1996.

Cochran, Clarke E. and David Carroll Cochran. *Catholics, Politics, and Public Policy: Beyond Left and Right*. Maryknoll, N.Y.: Orbis Books, 2003.

———. *The Catholic Vote: A Guide for the Perplexed*. Maryknoll, N.Y.: Orbis Books, 2008.

Coffey, Joan L. *Leon Harmel: Entrepreneur as Catholic Social Reformer*. Notre Dame, Ind.: University of Notre Dame Press, 2003.

Coleman, John A., and William F. Ryan, eds. *Globalization and Catholic Social Thought: Present Crisis, Future Hope*. Maryknoll, N.Y.: Orbis Books, 2005.

Coleman, John A., S.J., ed. *One Hundred Years of Catholic Social Thought: Celebration and Challenge*. Maryknoll, N.Y.: Orbis Books, 1991.

————. "Vision and Praxis in American Theology: Orestes Brownson, John A. Ryan, and John Courtney Murray," *Theological Studies* 37 (March 1976).

Collinge, William J. " 'Doing Well a Thing That Is Well Worth Doing': Teaching Dorothy L. Sayers on Work." *Horizons* 33 (Spring 2006): 101–10.

————, ed. *Faith in Public Life: Annual Volume of the College Theology Society 53* (2007). Maryknoll, N.Y.: Orbis Books, 2008.

Collins, Chuck, and Mary Wright. *The Moral Measure of the Economy.* Maryknoll, N.Y.: Orbis Books, 2007.

Compendium of the Social Doctrine of the Church. Pontifical Council for Justice and Peace. Washington, D.C.: United States Conference of Catholic Bishops, 2004.

Cook, Martin L. "Just Peacemaking: Challenges of Humanitarian Intervention." *Journal of the Society of Christian Ethics* 23, no. 1 (Spring–Summer 2003): 240–53.

Cowdin, Daniel M. "John Paul II and Environmental Concern: Problems and Possibilities." *Living Light* 28 (1991): 44–52.

Craig, Mary. *Six Modern Martyrs.* New York: Crossroad, 1985.

Crosthwaite, Mia. *Go and Do Likewise: Catholic Social Teaching in Action.* New London, Conn.: Twenty-Third Publications, 2006.

Curran, Charles E. *American Catholic Social Ethics: Twentieth-Century Approaches.* Notre Dame, Ind.: University of Notre Dame Press, 1984.

————. *Catholic Social Teaching, 1891–Present: A Historical, Theological, and Ethical Analysis.* Washington, D.C.: Georgetown University Press, 2002.

————. *The Church and Morality: An Ecumenical and Catholic Approach.* Minneapolis: Fortress Press, 1993.

————. *Directions in Catholic Social Ethics.* Notre Dame, Ind.: University of Notre Dame Press, 1985.

————. "The Global Ethic." *Ecumenist* 37 (Spring 2000): 6–10.

Curran, Charles E., and Leslie Griffin, eds. *The Catholic Church, Morality, and Politics: Readings in Moral Theology No. 12.* New York: Paulist Press, 2001.

Curran, Charles E., and Richard A. McCormick, eds. *John Paul II and Moral Theology: Readings in Moral Theology No. 10.* New York: Paulist Press, 1998.

————. *Official Catholic Social Teaching: Readings in Moral Theology No. 5.* New York: Paulist Press, 1986.

Czerby, Michael. "University and Globalization: Yes, But." *The Santa Clara Lectures* 9 (November 7, 2002), 1–24.

Dalton, Frederick John. *The Moral Vision of Cesar Chavez.* Maryknoll N.Y.: Orbis Books, 2003.

Daly, Herman E., and John B. Cobb. *For the Common Good: Redirecting the Economy toward Community, the Environment, and a Sustainable Future.* Boston: Beacon Press, 1989.

Daverth, Jason W., ed. *Conflict and Conciliation: Faith and Politics in an Age of Global Dissonance.* Dublin: Columba Press, 2007.

Day, Dorothy. *The Long Loneliness: The Autobiography of Dorothy Day.* New York: Harper & Row, 1952.

DeBerri, Edward P., and James E. Hug, with Peter J. Henriot and Michael Schultheis. *Catholic Social Teaching: Our Best Kept Secret,* 4th rev. ed. Maryknoll, N.Y.: Orbis Books, 2003.

Derr, Thomas Sieger. *Barriers to Ecumenism: The Holy See and the World Council of Churches on Social Questions.* Maryknoll, N.Y.: Orbis Books, 1983.

Doak, Mary. "Resisting the Eclipse of *Dignitatis Humanae*," *Horizons* 33 (Spring 2006): 33–52.

Donahue, James, and M. Theresa Moser, eds. *Religion, Ethics, and the Common Good: The Annual of the College Theology Society*. Vol. 41. Mystic, Conn.: Twenty-Third Publications, 1996.

Donnelly, Jack. *International Human Rights*. Boulder, Colo.: Westview Press, 1993.

Dorr, Donal. *Integral Spirituality: Resources for Community, Peace, Justice, and the Earth*. Maryknoll, N.Y.: Orbis Books, 1990.

———. *Option for the Poor: A Hundred Years of Catholic Social Teaching*. Rev. ed. Maryknoll, N.Y.: Orbis Books, 1992.

Douglass, R. Bruce and David Hollenbach, eds. *Catholicism and Liberalism: Contributions to American Public Philosophy*. Cambridge and New York: Cambridge University Press, 1994.

Duffey, Michael. *Peacemaking Christians: The Future of Just Wars, Pacifism, and Nonviolent Resistance*. Kansas City, Mo.: Sheed & Ward, 1995.

———. *Sowing Justice, Reaping Peace: Case Studies of Racial, Religious and Ethnic Healing around the World*. Lanham, Md.: Sheed & Ward, 2001.

Dwyer, Judith A., ed. *The New Dictionary of Catholic Social Thought*. Collegeville, Minn.: Liturgical Press, 1994.

Egan, Eileen. *Dorothy Day and the Permanent Revolution*. Pax Christi USA Peacemakers Pamphlet Series. Erie, Pa.: Benet Press, 1983.

———. *Peace Be with You: Justified Warfare or the Way of Nonviolence*. Maryknoll, N.Y.: Orbis Books, 1999.

Elizondo, Virgilio. "Collaborative Theology: Latin American Bishops, the Pope and the Poor." *Commonweal* 135 (January 31, 2008): 8–9.

Ellacuría, Ignacio, and Jon Sobrino, eds. *Mysterium Liberationis: Fundamental Concepts of Liberation Theology*. Maryknoll, N.Y.: Orbis Books, 1993.

Ellis, Marc H. *Peter Maurin: Prophet in the Twentieth Century*. New York: Paulist Press, 1981.

Ellsberg, Robert. *All Saints: Daily Reflections on Saints, Prophets, and Witnesses for Our Time*. New York: Crossroad, 1997.

Ellsberg, Robert, ed. *By Little and By Little: The Selected Writings of Dorothy Day*. New York: Alfred A. Knopf, 1983.

Elsbernd, Mary. "Social Ethics." *Theological Studies* 66 (March, 2005): 137–59.

———. "What Ever Happened to *Octogesima Adveniens?*" *Theological Studies* 56 (1995): 39–60.

Engel, Lawrence J. "The Influence of Saul Alinsky on the Campaign for Human Development." *Theological Studies* 59 (1998): 636–61.

Evans, Bernard F. *Lazarus at the Table: Catholics and Social Justice*. Collegeville, Minn.: Liturgical Press, 2006.

Fahey, Joseph J. *War and Christian Conscience: Where Do You Stand?* Maryknoll, N.Y.: Orbis Books, 2005.

Ferguson, Thomas P. *Catholic and American: The Political Theology of John Courtney Murray*. Kansas City, Mo.: Sheed & Ward, 1993.

Finn, Daniel. "Economics of Charity: Pope Benedict's *Caritas in Veritate*," *Commonweal* 136 (August 14, 2009): 8–10.

Flynn, Eileen P. *How Just Is the War on Terror? A Question of Morality*. New York: Paulist Press, 2007.

Forest, James H. *Thomas Merton's Struggle with Peacemaking.* Pax Christi USA Peacemakers Pamphlet Series. Erie, Pa.: Benet Press, n.d.

Fuechtmann, Thomas G., ed. *The Consistent Ethic of Life.* Kansas City, Mo.: Sheed & Ward, 1988.

Gallagher, Vincent A. *The True Cost of Low Prices: The Violence of Globalization.* Maryknoll, N.Y.: Orbis Books, 2006.

Gascoigne, Robert. *The Public Forum and Christian Ethics.* Cambridge and New York: Cambridge University Press, 2001.

Gower, Joseph F. *Religion and Economic Ethics: The Annual of the College Theology Society.* Vol. 31 (1985). Lanham, Md.: University Press of America, 1990.

Grassi, Joseph. *Broken Bread and Broken Bodies.* Maryknoll, N.Y.: Orbis Books, 2004.

Grasso, Kenneth L., Gerard V. Bradley, and Robert P. Hunt, eds. *Catholicism, Liberalism, and Communitarianism: The Catholic Intellectual Tradition and the Moral Foundations of Democracy.* Lanham, Md.: Rowman & Littlefield, 1995.

Gregg, Samuel. *Challenging the Modern World: Karol Wojtyla/John Paul II and the Development of Catholic Social Teaching.* Lanham, Md.: Lexington Books, 1999.

Gremillion, Joseph, ed. *The Gospel of Peace and Justice: Catholic Social Teaching since Pope John.* Maryknoll, N.Y.: Orbis Books, 1976.

Groody, Daniel G. *Globalization, Spirituality, and Justice: Navigating the Path to Peace.* Maryknoll, N.Y.: Orbis Books, 2007.

Gudorf, Christine E. "Encountering the Other: The Modern Papacy on Women." *Social Compass* 36 (1989): 295–310.

———. "To Make a Seamless Garment, Use a Single Piece of Cloth." *Cross Currents* 34 (Winter 1984): 473–91.

Gushee, David P. "Against Torture: An Evangelical Perspective." *Theology Today* 63 (2006): 252–60.

———. "Just War Divide: One Tradition, Two Views." *Christian Century* 119 (August 14–27, 2002): 26–28.

Gutiérrez, Gustavo. *A Theology of Liberation: History, Politics, and Salvation,* rev. ed. Maryknoll, N.Y.: Orbis Books, 1988.

Haight, Roger, and John Langan. "Recent Catholic Ethical and Social Teaching in Light of the Social Gospel." *Journal of Religious Ethics* 18 (Spring 1990): 103–29.

Hallie, Philip P. *Lest Innocent Blood Be Shed: The Story of Le Chambon and How Goodness Happened There.* New York: Harper & Row, 1979.

Haughey, John C. *The Faith That Does Justice: Examining the Christian Sources for Social Change.* New York: Paulist Press, 1977.

Hebblethwaite, Peter. *Paul VI: The First Modern Pope.* New York: Paulist Press, 1993.

———. *Pope John XXIII: Shepherd of the Modern World.* Garden City, N.Y.: Double Day, 1984.

Helgeland, John, Robert J. Daly, and J. Patout Burns. *Christians and the Military: The Early Experience.* Philadelphia: Fortress Press, 1985.

Hennelly, Alfred T., ed. *Liberation Theologies: The Global Pursuit of Justice.* Mystic, Conn.: Twenty-Third Publications, 1995.

———. *Liberation Theology: A Documentary History.* Maryknoll, N.Y.: Orbis Books, 1990.

Henriot, Peter J. *Opting for the Poor: A Challenge for North Americans.* Washington, D.C.: Center for Concern, 2004.

Hehir, J. Bryan. "Church-State and Church-World: The Ecclesiological Implications." *Catholic Theological Society of America Proceedings* 41 (1986): 54–74.

Heyer, Kristin E. *Prophetic and Public: The Social Witness of U.S. Catholicism.* Washington, D.C.: Georgetown University Press, 2006.

Himes, Kenneth R. "Intervention, Just War, and U.S. National Security." *Theological Studies* 65 (March 2004): 141–58.

Himes, Kenneth R. et al., eds. *Modern Catholic Social Teaching: Commentaries and Interpretations.* Washington, D.C.: Georgetown University Press, 2005.

Himes, Kenneth R. *Responses to 101 Questions on Catholic Social Teaching.* New York: Paulist Press, 2001.

———. "Social Sin and the Role of the Individual." *Annual of the Society of Christian Ethics* (1986): 183–218.

Himes, Michael J., and Kenneth R. Himes. *Fullness of Faith: The Public Significance of Theology.* New York: Paulist Press, 1993.

Hobgood, Mary E. *Catholic Social Teaching and Economic Theory: Paradigms in Conflict.* Philadelphia: Temple University Press, 1991.

Holl, Adolph. *The Last Christian: A Biography of Francis of Assisi,* trans. Peter Heinegg. Garden City, N.Y.: Doubleday, 1980.

Holland, Joe. *Modern Catholic Social Teaching: The Popes Confront the Industrial Age, 1740–1958.* New York: Paulist Press, 2003.

Holland, Joe, and Peter J. Henriot. *Social Analysis: Linking Faith and Justice.* Rev. ed. Maryknoll, N.Y.: Orbis Books, 1983.

Hollenbach, David. *Claims in Conflict: Retrieving and Renewing the Catholic Human Rights Tradition.* New York: Paulist Press, 1979.

———. *The Common Good and Christian Ethics.* Cambridge and New York: Cambridge University Press, 2002.

———. "The Common Good Revisited." *Theological Studies* 50 (1989): 70–94.

———. *The Global Face of Public Faith: Politics, Human Rights, and Christian Ethics.* Washington, D.C.: Georgetown University Press, 2003.

———. "Joy and Hope, Grief and Anguish." *America* 193 (December 5, 2005).

———. *Justice, Peace, and Human Rights: American Catholic Social Ethics in a Pluralistic World.* New York: Crossroad, 1988.

———. *Nuclear Ethics: A Christian Moral Argument.* New York: Paulist Press, 1983.

———. "The Pope and Capitalism." *America* 164 (June 1, 1991): 590–91.

———. "Social Ethics under the Sign of the Cross." *The Annual of the Society of Christian Ethics* (1996): 3–20.

Hope, Marjorie, and James Young, eds. *The Struggle for Humanity: Agents of Nonviolent Change in a Violent World.* Maryknoll, N.Y.: Orbis Books, 1977.

Hornsby-Smith, Michael P. *An Introduction to Catholic Social Thought.* Cambridge and New York: Cambridge University Press, 2006.

Jegen, Mary Evelyn. "Catholic Social Teaching on Peace: Development within a Tradition." *Listening: Journal of Religion and Culture* 37 (Winter 2002): 65–75.

Jesuit Centre for Faith and Justice, ed. *Catholic Social Teaching in Action.* Blackrock, CO/Dublin: Columba Press, 2005.

Johnson, James Turner. *The Quest for Peace: Three Moral Traditions in Western Cultural History.* Princeton, N.J.: Princeton University Press, 1987.

Jordan, Mary, and Kevin Sullivan. *The Prison Angel: Mother Antonia's Life of Service in a Mexican Jail.* New York: Penguin Press, 2006.

Kammer, Fred, S.J. *Doing Faithjustice: An Introduction to Catholic Social Thought.* New York/Mahwah, N.J.: Paulist Press, 1991.

Kavanaugh, John F. *Following Christ in a Consumer Society: The Spirituality of Cultural Resistance.* 2nd rev. ed. Maryknoll, N.Y.: Orbis Books, 2006.

Keenan, James. *The Works of Mercy: The Heart of Catholicism.* 2nd ed. Lanham, Md.: Sheed & Ward, 2008.

Kidder, Tracy. *Mountains beyond Mountains: The Quest of Dr. Paul Farmer, a Man Who Would Cure the World.* New York: Random House, 2003.

Koenig-Bricker, Woodeene. *Ten Commandments for the Environment: Pope Benedict XVI Speaks Out for Creation and Justice.* Notre Dame, Ind.: Ave Maria Press, 2009.

Land, Philip S. and James Hug. *Catholic Social Teaching: As I Have Lived, Loathed and Loved It.* Chicago: Loyola Press, 1995.

Le Breton, Binka. *The Greatest Gift: The Courageous Life and Martyrdom of Sister Dorothy Stang.* New York: Doubleday, 2008.

Linden, Ian. *Back to Basics: Revisiting Catholic Social Teaching.* London: Catholic Institute for International Relations, 1994.

Long, Edward LeRoy. *Facing Terrorism: Responding as Christians.* Louisville: Westminster John Knox Press, 2004.

Madges, William, ed. *Vatican II Forty Years Later: The Annual of the College Theology Society,* vol. 51 (2005). Maryknoll, N.Y.: Orbis Books, 2006.

Maguire, Daniel. "The Abnormality of War: Dissecting the 'Just War' Euphemisms and Building an Ethics of Peace." *Horizons* 33 (Spring 2006): 111–26.

Martin, James. *My Life with the Saints.* Chicago: Loyola Press, 2006.

Massaro, Thomas. *Catholic Social Teaching and United States Welfare Reform.* Collegeville, Minn.: Liturgical Press, 1998.

Massaro, Thomas J. *Living Justice: Catholic Social Teaching in Action.* Rev. ed. New York: Rowan and Littlefield, 2008.

Massaro, Thomas J., and Thomas A. Shannon, eds. *American Catholic Social Teaching.* Collegeville, Minn.: Liturgical Press, 2002.

Maurin, Peter. *Easy Essays.* Chicago: Franciscan Herald, 1984.

Mayer, Jane. *The Dark Side: The Inside Story of How the War on Terror Turned into a War on American Ideals.* Garden City, N.Y.: Doubleday/Anchor Books, 2009.

McBrien, Richard P. *Lives of the Popes: The Pontiffs from St. Peter to John Paul II.* San Francisco: HarperSanFrancisco, 1997.

McCarthy, David Matzko, ed. *The Heart of Catholic Social Teaching: Its Origins and Contemporary Significance.* Grand Rapids, Mich.: Brazos Press, 2009.

McCormick, Patrick. "The Changing Voice of Catholic Social Teachings: The Evolution of a Conversation." *Journal of Justice and Peace Studies* 4, no. 2 (1992): 97–116.

———. "Violence: Religion, Terror, War." *Theological Studies* 67 (March 2006): 143–62.

McDonagh, Sean. *Passion for the Earth.* Maryknoll, N.Y.: Orbis Books, 1994.

————. *To Care for the Earth: A Call to a New Theology.* Santa Fe, N.Mex.: Bear & Co., 1986.

McElroy, Robert W. *The Search for an American Public Theology: The Contribution of John Courtney Murray.* New York: Paulist Press, 1989.

McKenna, Kevin E. *A Concise Guide to Catholic Social Thought.* Notre Dame, Ind.: Ave Maria Press, 2002.

McNeal, Patricia. *Harder Than War: Catholic Peacemaking in Twentieth-Century America.* New Brunswick, N.J.: Rutgers University Press, 1992.

Merkle, Judith A. *From the Heart of the Church: The Catholic Social Tradition.* Collegeville, Minn.: Liturgical Press, 2004.

Merton, Thomas. *The Nonviolent Alternative.* Ed. Gordon C. Zahn. Rev. ed. New York: Farrar, Straus, Giroux, 1980.

————. *Peace in the Post-Christian Era.* Maryknoll, N.Y.: Orbis Books, 2004.

Mich, Marvin L. Krier. *Catholic Social Teaching and Movements.* Mystic, Conn.: Twenty-Third Publications, 2000.

Mich, Marvin L. Krier. *The Challenge and Spirituality of Catholic Social Teaching.* Louisville: JustFaith, Inc., 2005.

Miller, Richard B. "Aquinas and the Presumption against Killing and War." *Journal of Religion* 82 (2002): 173–204.

Miller, Richard W., ed. *We Hold These Truths: Catholicism and American Public Life.* St. Louis: Liguori Publications, 2008.

Miller, William D. *Dorothy Day: A Biography.* San Francisco: Harper & Row, 1982.

Miller, Vincent. "Encyclical Signals Church Not Pulling Out of Politics." *National Catholic Reporter* 45 (July 24, 2009): 8.

Misner, Paul. *Social Catholicism in Europe: From the Onset of Industrialization to the First World War.* New York: Crossroad, 1991.

Mitchell, John J. "Embracing a Socialist Vision: The Evolution of Catholic Social Thought, Leo XIII–John Paul II." *Journal of Church and State* 27 (Autumn 1985): 465–81.

Modras, Ronald. "The Moral Philosophy of John Paul II." *Theological Studies* 41 (1980): 683–97.

Muldoon, Tim. *Catholic Identity and the Laity: The Annual of the College Theology Society.* Vol. 54 (2008). Maryknoll, N.Y.: Orbis Books, 2009.

Murnion, Philip J., ed. *Catholics and Nuclear War: A Commentary on "The Challenge of Peace."* New York: Crossroad, 1983.

Murphy, Charles M. "Charity, Not Justice, as Constitutive of the Church's Mission." *Theological Studies* 68 (June 2007): 274–86.

Murphy, Roseanne. *Martyr of the Amazon: The Life of Sister Dorothy Stang.* Maryknoll, N.Y.: Orbis Books, 2007.

Murray, John Courtney. *The Problem of Religious Freedom.* Westminster, Md.: Newman Press, 1965.

————. *We Hold These Truths: Catholic Reflections on the American Proposition.* New York: Sheed & Ward, 1960.

Musto, Ronald G. *The Catholic Peace Tradition.* Maryknoll, N.Y.: Orbis Books, 1986.

Nairn, Thomas A., ed. *The Consistent Ethic of Life: Assessing Its Reception and Relevance.* Maryknoll, N.Y.: Orbis Books, 2008.

Nouwen, Henri J. M., Donald P. McNeill, and Douglas A. Morrison. *Compassion: A Reflection on the Christian Life.* New York: Doubleday, 1982.

O'Brien, David J., and Thomas A. Shannon, eds. *Catholic Social Thought: The Documentary Heritage*. Maryknoll, N.Y.: Orbis Books, 1999.

O'Brien, David J. and Thomas A. Shannon, eds. *Renewing the Earth: Catholic Documents on Peace, Justice, and Liberation*. Garden City, N.Y.: Image Books, 1977.

O'Brien, John J. *George C. Higgins and the Quest for Worker Justice: The Evolution of Catholic Social Thought in America*. Lanham, Md.: Sheed & Ward, 2004.

O'Brien, Niall. "War — the Moral Issue." *The Furrow* 54 (2003): 529–33.

O'Neill, William R. "No Amnesty for Sorrow: The Privilege of the Poor in Christian Social Ethics." *Theological Studies* 55 (1994): 638–56.

Orend, Brian. "Justice after War." *Ethics and International Affairs* 16 (2002): 43–56.

Pawlikowski, John T. "Human Rights in the Roman Catholic Tradition: Some Theological Reflections." *The American Society of Christian Ethics, Selected Papers* (1979): 145–65.

Pawlikowski, John T., and Donald Senior. *Biblical and Theological Reflections on "The Challenge of Peace."* Wilmington, Del.: Michael Glazier, 1984.

Pelotte, Donald E. *John Courtney Murray: Theologian in Conflict*. New York: Paulist Press, 1975.

Pennock, Michael. *Catholic Social Teaching: Living and Learning Justice*. Notre Dame, Ind.: Ave Maria Press, Inc., 2000.

Perry, John. *Torture: Religious Ethics and National Security*. Maryknoll, N.Y.: Orbis Books, 2005.

Peters, Rebecca Todd, and Elizabeth Hinson-Hasty, eds.. *To Do Justice: A Guide for Progressive Christians*. Louisville: Westminster John Knox Press, 2008.

Phan, Peter C. *Social Thought: Message of the Fathers of the Church*. Wilmington, Del.: Michael Glazer, 1984.

Pope, Stephen J. "Christian Love for the Poor: Almsgiving and the 'Preferential Option.'" *Horizons* 21 (1994): 303–8.

———. "Proper and Improper Partiality and the Preferential Option for the Poor." *Theological Studies* 54 (1993): 242–71.

Prejean, Helen. *Dead Man Walking: An Eyewitness Account of the Death Penalty in the United States*. New York: Vintage Books, Random House, 1993.

Preston, Ronald H. *Confusions in Christian Social Ethics: Problems for Geneva and Rome*. Grand Rapids, Mich.: William B. Eerdmans, 1994.

Prevallet, Elaine. *Toward a Spirituality for Global Justice: A Call to Kinship*. Louisville: JustFaith, Inc., 2005.

Prevoznik Heins, Peggy. *Becoming a Community of Salt and Light*. Notre Dame, Ind.: Ave Marie Press, 2003.

Putz, Erna, ed. *Franz Jägerstätter: Letters and Writings from Prison*. Maryknoll, N.Y.: Orbis Books, 2009.

Record, Jeffrey, "The Bush Doctrine and the War with Iraq." *Parameters* 33 (2003): 4–22.

Reed-Bouley, Jennifer. "Service and Justice: Understanding the Relationship through Community Service-Learning." *Listening: Journal of Religion and Culture* 37 (Winter 2002): 54–64.

Reichberg, Gregory M. "Is There a 'Presumption against War' in Aquinas's Ethics?" *Thomist* 66, no. 3 (2002):337–67.

Roman, Jose Maria. *St. Vincent de Paul: A Biography*. London: Melisende, 1999.

Ruether, Rosemary Radford. "Consistent Life Ethic Is Inconsistent." *National Catholic Reporter* 43 (November 17, 2006): 13–16.

Sachs, Jeffrey. *Common Wealth: Economics for a Crowded Planet.* New York: Penguin Press, 2008.

———. *The End of Poverty: Economic Possibilities for Our Time.* New York: Penguin Press, 2005.

Schlabach, Gerald W., ed. *Just Policing, Not War.* Collegeville, Minn.: Liturgical Press, 2007.

Schuck, Michael J. *That They Be One: The Social Teachings of the Papal Encyclicals, 1740–1989.* Washington, D.C.: Georgetown University Press, 1991.

———. "When the Shooting Stops: Missing Elements in Just War Theory." *Christian Century* 101 (October 26, 1994): 982–84.

Shannon, Thomas A., ed. *War or Peace? The Search for New Answers.* Maryknoll, N.Y.: Orbis Books, 1980.

Sider, Ronald. *Rich Christians in an Age of Hunger: Moving from Affluence to Generosity.* Rev. ed. Dallas: Word Publishing, 1997.

Simon, Arthur. *Christian Faith and Public Policy: No Grounds for Divorce.* Grand Rapids, Mich.: William B. Eerdmans, 1987.

Smith, Pamela. *What Are They Saying about Environmental Ethics?* New York: Paulist Press, 1997.

Sniegocki, John. "The Social Ethics of Pope John Paul II: A Critique of Neoconservative Interpretations." *Horizons* 33 (Spring 2006): 7–32.

Spilly, Alphonse, ed. *Selected Works of Joseph Cardinal Bernardin.* 2 vols. Collegeville, Minn.: Liturgical Press, 2000.

Sobrino, Jon. "The Kingdom of God and the Theological Dimension of the Poor." In *Who Do You Say That I Am? Confessing the Mystery of Christ,* ed. John C. Cavidini and Laura Holt, 109–45. Notre Dame, Ind.: University of Notre Dame Press, 2004.

Stassen, Glen H. *Just Peacemaking: Transforming Initiatives for Justice and Peace.* Louisville: Westminster John Knox Press, 1992.

———. *Just Peacemaking: Ten Practices for Abolishing War.* Rev. ed. Cleveland: Pilgrim Press, 1998, 2004, and 2008.

———. "The Unity, Realism, and Obligatoriness of Just Peacemaking Theory." *Journal of the Society of Christian Ethics* 23, no. 1 (Spring–Summer 2003): 171–94.

Stone, Ronald H. "Realist Criticism of Just Peacemaking Theory." *Journal of the Society of Christian Ethics* 23, no. 1 (Spring–Summer 2003): 255–67.

Stone, Ronald H., and Robert L. Stivers, eds. *Resistance and Theological Ethics.* Lanham, Md.: Rowman & Littlefield, 2004.

Sullivan, Joe. "Social Justice for Dummies." *U.S. Catholic* (July 1997).

Thompson, J. Milburn, "Catholic Social Teaching and the Ethics of Torture." *Journal of Peace and Justice Studies* 17, no. 2 (Autumn 2008): 22–42.

———. *Justice and Peace: A Christian Primer.* Rev. ed. Maryknoll, N.Y.: Orbis Books, 2003.

———. *Martin Luther King Jr. and the Dream of a Just Community.* Rev. ed. Pax Christi USA Peacemakers Pamphlet Series. Erie, Pa.: Pax Christi USA, 2007.

Trocmé, André. *Jesus and the Nonviolent Revolution.* Ed. Charles E. Moore. Rev. ed. Maryknoll, N.Y.: Orbis Books, 2003.

Tropman, John E. *The Catholic Ethic in American Society*. San Francisco: Jossey Bass, 1995.

True, Michael. *Justice Seekers, Peace Makers: 32 Portraits in Courage*. Mystic, Conn.: Twenty-Third Publications, 1985.

———. *To Construct Peace: 30 More Justice Seekers, Peace Makers*. Mystic, Conn.: Twenty-Third Publications, 1992.

Twomey, Gerald S. *The "Preferential Option for the Poor" in Catholic Social Thought from John XXIII to John Paul II*. Lewiston, N.Y.: Edwin Mellen Press, 2005.

Ulrich, Tom. *Parish Social Ministry: Strategies for Success*. Notre Dame, Ind.: Ave Maria Press, 2001.

Vallely, Paul, ed. *The New Politics: Catholic Social Teaching for the Twenty-First Century*. London: SCM Press, 1998.

Wallis, Jim, and Joyce Hollyday, eds. *Cloud of Witnesses*. Rev. ed. Maryknoll, N.Y.: Orbis Books, 2005.

Walsh, Michael, and Brian Davies, eds. *Proclaiming Justice and Peace: Papal Documents from Rerum Novarum through Centesimus Annus*. Mystic, Conn.: Twenty-Third Publications, 1991.

Weigel, George, and Robert Royal, eds. *Building the Free Society: Democracy, Capitalism, and Catholic Social Teaching*. Grand Rapids, Mich.: William B. Eerdmans, 1993.

Weigert, Kathleen Maas, and Alexia K. Kelley, eds. *Living the Catholic Social Tradition: Cases and Commentary*. Lanham, Md.: Rowman & Littlefield, Sheed & Ward, 2005.

Weigert, Kathleen Maas. "Transforming the World: Shaping a Compassionate and Just Society." *Listening: Journal of Religion and Culture* 37 (Winter 2002): 26–40.

White, Lynn. "The Historical Roots of Our Ecological Crisis." *Science* 155 no. 3767 (March 10, 1967): 1203–7.

Windley-Daoust, Jerry. *Living Justice and Peace: Catholic Social Teaching in Practice*. Winona, Minn.: St. Mary's Press, 2002.

Zahn, Gordon C. *Franz Jägerstätter: Martyr for Conscience*. Pax Christi USA Peacemakers Pamphlet Series. Erie, Pa.: Benet Press, n.d.

———. "A Religious Pacifist Looks at Abortion." *Commonweal* (May 28, 1971): 279–82.

———. *In Solitary Witness: The Life and Death of Franz Jägerstätter*. Collegeville, Minn.: Liturgical Press, 1964, reissued 1977.

Zahn, Gordon C., et al. *John Timothy Leary: A Different Sort of Hero*. Pax Christi USA Peacemakers Pamphlet Series. Erie, Pa.: Pax Christi USA, 1983.

Index